Virginia Woolf and the Ethics of Intimacy

Virginia Woolf and the Ethics of Intimacy

Elsa Högberg

BLOOMSBURY ACADEMIC
LONDON • NEW YORK • OXFORD • NEW DELHI • SYDNEY

BLOOMSBURY ACADEMIC
Bloomsbury Publishing Plc
50 Bedford Square, London, WC1B 3DP, UK
1385 Broadway, New York, NY 10018, USA
29 Earlsfort Terrace, Dublin 2, Ireland

BLOOMSBURY, BLOOMSBURY ACADEMIC and the Diana logo
are trademarks of Bloomsbury Publishing Plc

First published in Great Britain 2020
This paperback edition published in 2021

Copyright © Elsa Högberg, 2020

Elsa Högberg has asserted her right under the Copyright, Designs and
Patents Act, 1988, to be identified as Author of this work.

Cover design: Anna Berzovan
Cover image © Science Source

All rights reserved. No part of this publication may be reproduced or
transmitted in any form or by any means, electronic or mechanical,
including photocopying, recording, or any information storage or retrieval
system, without prior permission in writing from the publishers.

Bloomsbury Publishing Plc does not have any control over, or responsibility for,
any third-party websites referred to or in this book. All internet addresses given
in this book were correct at the time of going to press. The author and publisher regret
any inconvenience caused if addresses have changed or sites have ceased to exist,
but can accept no responsibility for any such changes.

A catalogue record for this book is available from the British Library.

Library of Congress Cataloging-in-Publication Data
Names: Högberg, Elsa, 1983- author.
Title: Virginia Woolf and the ethics of intimacy / Elsa Högberg.
Description: New York: Bloomsbury Academic, 2020. | Includes bibliographical
references and index. |
Identifiers: LCCN 2019043973 (print) | LCCN 2019043974 (ebook) |
ISBN 9781350022737 (hardback) | ISBN 9781350022720 (epub) |
ISBN 9781350022737 (ebook)
Subjects: LCSH: Woolf, Virginia, 1882-1941–Criticism and interpretation. |
Woolf, Virginia, 1882-1941–Political and social views. | Intimacy (Psychology) in literature. |
Violence in literature. | Literature and society–History–20th century.
Classification: LCC PR6045.O72 Z6977 2020 (print) | LCC PR6045.O72 (ebook) |
DDC 823/.912–dc23
LC record available at https://lccn.loc.gov/2019043973
LC ebook record available at https://lccn.loc.gov/2019043974

ISBN: HB: 978-1-3500-2271-3
PB: 978-1-3502-3743-8
ePDF: 978-1-3500-2273-7
eBook: 978-1-3500-2272-0

Typeset by Deanta Global Publishing Services, Chennai, India

To find out more about our authors and books visit www.bloomsbury.com and
sign up for our newsletters.

For David and William
In memory of my father, Peter Högberg (1954–2007)

Contents

Acknowledgements	viii
Abbreviations	x
Note on Sources	xii
Introduction: Towards an Ethics of Intimacy	1
1 *Jacob's Room*: Modernist Melancholia and the Eclipse of Primal Intimacy	31
2 "An Inner Meaning Almost Expressed": Introspection as Revolt in *Mrs Dalloway*	75
3 Post-Impressionist Intimacy and the Visual Ethics of *To the Lighthouse*	115
4 Chalk Marks: Violence and Vulnerability in *The Waves*	151
Notes	187
Bibliography	216
Index	228

Acknowledgements

This book would not have come about without the warm support, generous guidance and delightful company of two particular colleagues and friends: Ashleigh Harris, who supervised the doctoral research on which it is based, and Jane Goldman, whose field-defining scholarship and ground-breaking methods for pleasurable, intimate reading continue to be an unparalleled source of inspiration. For their insightful feedback at the early stages of this project, and for their support and encouragement, I am grateful to Robert Appelbaum, Randi Koppen, Christina Kullberg and Stuart Robertson. Many thanks to AnnKatrin Jonsson for her helpful commentary on an early draft of the manuscript, and to my colleagues at the Department of English, Uppsala University, for reading and engaging with my work.

I am immensely grateful to my colleagues and friends at the University of Glasgow's School of Critical Studies, where I spent two wonderful years as a postdoctoral researcher. Apart from Jane Goldman, I want to thank, in particular, Amy Bromley, Vassiliki Kolocotroni, Bryony Randall and Mia Spiro for making my time in Glasgow so rewarding and enjoyable. Warm thanks also to the international community of Virginia Woolf scholars for many inspirational conferences, collaborations and happy moments. Among my fellow Woolfians, I am especially grateful to Judith Allen, Todd Avery, Sanja Bahun, Suzanne Bellamy, Claire Davison, Benjamin Hagen, Derek Ryan and Angeliki Spiropoulou.

An international postdoctoral fellowship from the Swedish Research Council made the completion of this project possible, while a second postdoctoral grant from Åke Wibergs Stiftelse funded the very last stage. I am tremendously grateful to these foundations for their generous support and to Riksbankens Jubileumsfond for funding the symposium "Intimate Modernism," which I organised in Uppsala in 2015. I want to thank the participants at this intellectually vibrant event, which significantly shaped the direction of the present book.

The anonymous readers for Bloomsbury offered welcome and substantial feedback, and it has been a pleasure to work with Bloomsbury's editorial and production team. Thanks also to Nick Sergeant for his careful work formatting the final book manuscript and for his assistance in compiling the index. Earlier versions of material from the Introduction, Chapter 2 and Chapter 4 appeared in two journal articles: "Voices against Violence: Virginia Woolf and Judith Butler." *Le Tour critique*, no. 2, 2013, pp. 425–47, and "Virginia Woolf's Poetics of Revolt." *Études britanniques contemporaines*, no. 46, June 2014. I am much obliged to Richard Pedot and Jean-Michel Ganteau respectively for granting the permission to reprint.

Last but not least, I dedicate my deepest thanks to my family for their love and encouragement, and for many good times. I am grateful to my mother, Lena Högberg, to my siblings, Oscar and Agnes Högberg, and to my beloved grandmother, Barbro Högberg. I owe more than I can say to my late father, Peter Högberg, whose crystalline intelligence, warm generosity and steady conviction that every difficulty can be overcome have been a lighthouse for me all these years. How I wish that we could sit together once more, laugh and talk about life and books, including this one. Finally, to David Watson, my love, partner, most valued colleague and best friend: thank you for staying the course with me throughout the exacting process of bringing this book into being, for cooking way too many dinners while I was still at work, for your immeasurable intellectual input into this and other projects, and for our intimacy. This book was supposed to have seen the light of day before William Peter, my joy. But he came first, our beautiful, wise little boy, and always will.

Abbreviations

Judith Butler

FW	*Frames of War: When Is Life Grievable?* Verso, 2010.
GAO	*Giving an Account of Oneself.* Fordham UP, 2005.
PL	*Precarious Life: The Powers of Mourning and Violence.* Verso, 2004.

Roger Fry

T	*Transformations: Critical and Speculative Essays on Art.* Chatto & Windus, 1926.
VD	*Vision and Design.* 1920. Edited by J. B. Bullen, Dover, 1998.

Luce Irigaray

SW	*Sharing the World.* Continuum, 2008.
WL	*The Way of Love.* Translated by Heidi Bostic and Stephen Pluháček, Continuum, 2002.

Julia Kristeva

BS	*Black Sun: Depression and Melancholia.* 1987. Translated by Leon S. Roudiez, Columbia UP, 1989.
IR	*Intimate Revolt.* 1997. Translated by Jeanine Herman, Columbia UP, 2002.

RPL	*Revolution in Poetic Language*. 1974. Translated by Margaret Waller, Columbia UP, 1984.
SNR	*The Sense and Non-Sense of Revolt*. 1996. Translated by Jeanine Herman, Columbia UP, 2000.

Virginia Woolf

AROO	*A Room of One's Own*. 1929. A Room of One's Own *and* Three Guineas, edited and introduction by Morag Shiach, Oxford UP, 2008.
CSF	*The Complete Shorter Fiction of Virginia Woolf*. Edited by Susan Dick, Harcourt, 1989.
D	*The Diary of Virginia Woolf*. Edited by Anne Olivier Bell and Andrew McNeillie, Penguin, 1979–85. 5 vols.
E	*The Essays of Virginia Woolf*. Edited by Andrew McNeillie (vols. 1–4) and Stuart N. Clarke (vols. 5–6), Hogarth, 1986–2011. 6 vols.
JR	*Jacob's Room*. 1922. Edited and introduction by Sue Roe, Penguin, 1992.
L	*The Letters of Virginia Woolf*. Edited by Nigel Nicolson and Joanne Trautmann, Hogarth, 1975–80. 6 vols.
MD	*Mrs Dalloway*. 1925. Edited and introduction by David Bradshaw, Oxford UP, 2009.
O	*Orlando: A Biography*. 1928. Edited by Brenda Lyons, introduction and notes by Sandra M. Gilbert, Penguin, 1993.
RF	*Roger Fry: A Biography*. 1940. Introduction by Frances Spalding, Hogarth, 1991.
TG	*Three Guineas*. 1938. A Room of One's Own *and* Three Guineas, edited and introduction by Morag Shiach, Oxford UP, 2008.
TL	*To the Lighthouse*. 1927. Edited by Stella McNichol, introduction and notes by Hermione Lee, Penguin, 1992.
W	*The Waves*. 1931. Edited and introduction by Kate Flint, Penguin, 2006.

Note on Sources

All italics in quotes are in the original unless otherwise indicated.

Introduction: Towards an Ethics of Intimacy

Sitting on the floor with her arms round Mrs. Ramsay's knees, close as she could get, smiling to think that Mrs. Ramsay would never know the reason of that pressure, she imagined how in the chambers of the mind and heart of the woman who was, physically, touching her, were stood, like the treasures in the tombs of kings, tablets bearing sacred inscriptions, which if one could spell them out would teach one everything, but they would never be offered openly, never made public. What art was there, known to love or cunning, by which one pressed through into those secret chambers? What device for becoming, like waters poured into one jar, inextricably the same, one with the object one adored? Could the body achieve it, or the mind, subtly mingling in the intricate passages of the brain? or the heart? Could loving, as people called it, make her and Mrs. Ramsay one? for it was not knowledge but unity that she desired, not inscriptions on tablets, nothing that could be written in any language known to men, but intimacy itself, which is knowledge, she had thought, leaning her head on Mrs. Ramsay's knee. (*TL* 57)

This is a scene which comes back to Lily Briscoe as she paints the portrait of Mrs Ramsay. Remembering the intimate moment when the two were physically touching, Lily now asks herself, paintbrush in hand: can her model be represented not merely as the object of her painting, but as a psychologically complex individual whose inner life must remain inscrutable? Recalling her arms embracing Mrs Ramsay's legs, her head on Mrs Ramsay's knee, Lily is acutely aware of the contrast between their bodily closeness and the unbridgeable distance separating the other woman's "mind and heart" from her own. Seeking, at first, to know Mrs Ramsay's interiority as if it were a text to be deciphered by her own mind, she eventually visualises this text as a set of opaque inscriptions defying interpretation. Lily realises that Mrs Ramsay's inner life resists depiction in the moment her quest for knowledge, the deciphering of "sacred inscriptions," gives way to her desire for intimacy, which she defines as a bodily and spiritual unity in which two individuals cease to perceive themselves as distinct from one another: "What device for becoming, like waters poured into one jar, inextricably the same, one with the object one adored?" Lily's awareness of Mrs

Ramsay's unknowability is coextensive with her desire for intimacy as a sharing of interiority, a state in which her model ceases to be an adored or idealised object because the separate perspectives of painter and model merge into one.

Lily's introspective reflections parallel Woolf's own queries as a novelist: the writing of intimacy and interiority is configured as an aesthetic, but also ethical, process in her major modernist texts from *Jacob's Room* (1922) to *The Waves* (1931). Her famous claim, in "Modern Fiction" (1925), that her generation of experimental writers must explore "the dark places of psychology" (*E* 4: 162) emerges in her inter-war novels as a question of intimacy in the sense of "Pertaining to the inmost thoughts or feelings; proceeding from, concerning or affecting one's inmost self" ("intimate, *adj.* and *n.*," def. A.2). That is, she casts artistic introspection as bound up with the writer's desire to represent the inner life of another, a desire prompted by the unsettling experience of having one's thinking and feeling self affected by this other. The problem of Woolf's "Character in Fiction" (1924) – how can another's interiority, the cognitive, affective and spiritual life of the mind, be adequately conveyed? – is addressed in *Jacob's Room* through the narrator's effort and ultimate failure to know the protagonist. Overcome by the presence of the one whose story she sets out to narrate, she continuously interrogates her position as a storyteller with access to his inner life. Her relationship to Jacob resembles that of one character to another, and her introspective narration becomes the telling of her encounter with another individual. *Jacob's Room* emerged out of the short story "An Unwritten Novel" (1921), in which the narrator is located in a railway carriage, sitting face-to-face with Minnie Marsh, the character whose interiority she seeks to decipher and describe. However, like the author-narrator of "Character in Fiction," who finds herself opposite the enigmatic Mrs Brown in another railway carriage, the narrator of the earlier short story fails to see beyond the "Marks of reticence" on her fellow traveller's face (*CSF* 112). The novel about Minnie Marsh will remain unwritten, just as Mrs Brown's interiority continues to elude her observer.

Woolf's interrogation of narrative omniscience in her essays of the 1920s amounts to a questioning of the relationship between narrator and character, observer and observed, in the realist novel – a hierarchical vertical relationship which is turned, in Woolf's own writing, into a one-to-one horizontal encounter between two individuals. What she finds ethically as well as politically problematic about the focus on external rather than psychological detail in the novels of Arnold Bennett and H. G. Wells is these writers' claim to master the art of writing fictional character without considering the difficulties involved in the representation of interiority. In "Character in Fiction," she suggests that the novelist's creation of "real, true, and convincing" characters (*E* 3: 421) is an ethically fraught task: while the inner life of those we meet resists knowledge and description, it nonetheless needs to be conveyed in an intimate transaction reminiscent of Lily Briscoe's effort. Indeed, Woolf imagines her own encounter with Mrs Brown, a stranger, as overpoweringly intimate. A "seductive and charming" whisper in the ear – "Come and catch me if you can" (420) – is followed by a physical awareness of the other woman's suffering: "The impression she made was overwhelming. It came pouring out like a draught, like a smell of burning" (425). This strange, unsettling intimacy impinges on the novelist-observer's self and spurs her claim that a character, like its flesh-and-blood model, will only appear "real" if it compels the reader to see the world "through its eyes" (426). By contrast, the omniscient, realist perspective emerges as unethical because it performs an individual's elimination of another's being and worldview. Arnold Bennett's imagined observation of Mrs Brown's physical appearance amounts to not seeing her at all, just as the female protagonist's voice in his 1911 novel *Hilda Lessways* is drowned by "Mr Bennett's voice telling us facts about rents and freeholds" (430; see 428–30).¹ It is difficult not to recall the "self-assertive virility" (134) pervading the fictional writer Mr A's prose in *A Room of One's Own* (1929):

> But after reading a chapter or two a shadow seemed to lie across the page. It was a straight dark bar, a shadow shaped something like the letter "I." One began dodging this way and that to get a glimpse of the landscape behind it. . . . Is that a tree? No, it is a woman. But . . . [ellipsis in original] she has not a bone in her body, I thought, watching Phoebe, for that was her name, coming across the beach. Then Alan got up and the shadow of Alan once obliterated Phoebe. For Alan had views and Phoebe was quenched in the flood of his views. (130)

Woolf is denouncing here the aggressive, "unmitigated masculinity" of her contemporaries from the British novelist who, like Mr A, writes in protest against the suffrage movement and other political gains by women in the public sphere, to the fascist poet (134; see 131–34). The complicity of this 'I' with a patriarchal, militaristic and imperialist civilisation sustained by "the instinct for possession, the rage for acquisition which drives [the patriarchs] to desire other people's fields and goods perpetually; to make frontiers and flags; battleships and poison gas" (*AROO* 49–50) – a destructive and self-destructive civilisation constituted by violence and perpetual war – was to be more fully analysed in *Three Guineas* (1938).

Against such assertions of the hyper-masculine 'I,' whose aggression is political as well as ethical, Woolf posits the hesitancy compelling the modernist writer and artist. Much attention has been given to the ways in which her argument with contemporary male novelists is played out in her fictional texts on the level of form and style, notably through her innovative play with focalisation and point of view, which unsettles textual devices such as narrative coherence and omniscience.[2] It is no coincidence that she has Lily Briscoe ask whether Mrs Ramsay's inner life can be known and depicted. As a modernist, Post-Impressionist painter, Lily sees art as a question of form rather than mimetic representation, and her aesthetic experiments enter the realm of ethics insofar as they convey her model's unknowability. Instead of painting "Mother and child... objects of universal veneration" (*TL* 59), she portrays Mrs Ramsay reading to James as an abstract triangular shape. Lily's portrait defamiliarises her model because it is motivated by the questions which make her pause before painting the individual before her: how can the inner life of another be represented, when it must remain unknown to the artist? What would be the implications for artistic creation if the artist could share that person's interiority, if the two could become "like waters poured into one jar, inextricably the same, one"? In addition to Lily's questions, Woolf's own writing prompts us to ask the following: what if a related but more unsettling mode of intimacy, in which another's physical presence affects the knowing and observing self to the point of dissolving its boundaries, emerges most forcefully not in relations with family, friends and loved ones, but in unwilled, fleeting encounters with strangers? If "intimacy itself... is knowledge," as Lily concludes in the epigraph above – and the adjective "intimate" does indeed refer to close familiarity with persons and things[3] – can the modernist artist disrupt the frequently aggressive, even violent ways in which we tend to figure others as objects of our knowledge and imagination, so that we are literally compelled to see the world through another's eyes? And is there not a form of violence inherent in the common association of intimacy with familiarity and emotional attachment, in how Lily's physical pressure against a loved one's body risks stimulating an art "known to love or cunning, by which one presse[s] through into th[e] secret chambers" of another's interiority (*TL* 57)?

This book begins with the observation that Woolf expands the realm of intimacy far beyond the comfortable zone of knowledge, familiarity, affection and love, and that she thereby places intimacy at the centre of public and political as well as private relations. By focusing on intimacy as pertaining to the unfamiliar and unknown, an idea central to Woolf's most radically experimental novels as well as to recent developments in contemporary theory, *Virginia Woolf and the Ethics of Intimacy* claims that Woolf's aesthetic configuration of interiority was a way of expressing ethical and political commitments. In this sense, the book contributes to a growing body of Woolf scholarship considering the many ways in which ethical intersubjective relations and the politics of power and public institutions are brought together in the writing of this pioneering modernist, whose novels were once thought to have little to say about what Alex Zwerdling calls "the real world" of society and politics.[4] However, while most scholars today read Woolf's aesthetic practice as a vehicle for ethico-political engagement, there remains a tendency to distinguish between, on the one hand, her interest in the external world of facts and events and, on the other, her concern with the thinking, perceiving and feeling mind.[5] By engaging late twentieth- and early twenty-first-century theories of ethics, politics and introspection by Judith Butler, Luce Irigaray and Julia Kristeva, I argue that Woolf develops an ethics of intimacy in which the suspension of the self as an autonomous entity, distinct from the other and outside, inspires recognition of each individual's opacity and inviolable irreducibility. Lily Briscoe's idea of intimacy as becoming "one" with another exemplifies the mode of intimacy explored in this study: the momentary suspension of subjective autonomy in one-to-one encounters. I shall trace this notion of intimacy – which both deepens and unsettles the common definitions relating to knowledge, closeness and interiority – as Woolf develops it in her novels *Jacob's Room*, *Mrs Dalloway* (1925), *To the Lighthouse* (1927) and *The Waves*, where it accumulates expressions particular to each text. I will examine the close connections between Woolf's modernist aesthetic and her affirmation of intimacy as a sustainable alternative to realist omniscience and, as we shall see in Chapter 1, a representational economy of exchangeability and substitution particular to modernity, both of which she deems politically and ethically problematic because of their complicity with an inherently violent logic of objectification. On the level of form and style, her novels raise thought-provoking questions of intimacy and recognition in dyadic encounters, thereby revealing the substantial capacity of inward-looking modernist fiction to both conceptualise and foster ethical relations.

Woolf's inter-war reflections on the ethical and political implications of intimacy are highly relevant to contemporary critical and theoretical debates around intimacy. Since the beginning of this century, intimacy has become the focus of increasing attention in fields as different as psychology, sociology and literary studies. The emergence of affect studies in particular has prompted a redefinition of intimacy as commonly understood: relations of familiarity and closeness that, whether between lovers, friends or family, constitute an exclusively private sphere of physical, sexual and emotional contact. Alongside edited volumes by Julie Seymour and Paul Bagguley (1999), Lauren Berlant (2000) and Tam Sanger and Yvette Taylor (2013), Eva Illouz's *Cold Intimacies: The Making of Emotional Capitalism* (2007) and Leo Bersani and Adam Phillips's *Intimacies* (2008) are among the many works to consider intimacy in subject-to-subject relationships as inextricable from power relations in the realm of politics. A central term in the academic discourse of our century, intimacy has proved to be particularly crucial in accounts of contemporary affective, political and ethical relations. If intimacy is seen today as the very nexus in which private and public converge, the following aspects remain to be fully explored: that many of these intersections can be traced back to the first decades of the twentieth century, and that Woolf's writing offers a deep engagement with the historically new forms of intimacy emerging in the modernist period. Taking as its starting point Jessica Berman's important claim that Woolf's depiction of intimate relations creates multiple "connections among ethics/politics/aesthetics" ("Ethical Folds" 170), this book argues that Woolf's aesthetic concern with interiority is immediately related to her incisive analysis of the psychological motivations of violence and war. It enters from there into a dialogue with works from the past two decades by prominent critics such as Karen L. Levenback, Vincent Sherry, Christine Froula, Rebecca Walkowitz, Andrew John Miller and Sarah Cole, all of whom have offered compelling, historically grounded accounts of Woolf's pacifist and/or feminist response to the legacy of the First World War and the hostile international relations which would make a second war inevitable. The insight that Woolf's engagement with violence between nations begins on the level of the psychological and private underpins their projects as well as my own.[6] I am also indebted to the crucial observation by poststructuralist and feminist critics that Woolf subverts the persistent cultural figure of the masculine 'I,' which continues to sustain patriarchal militarism and imperialist wars in our own time.

The recent upsurge of studies focusing on Woolf's non-violent textual politics would not have come about without the ground-breaking work by feminist scholars from Jane Marcus, who was among the first to consider Woolf's pacifism as a political stance which remains intellectually and ethically radical,[7] to a generation of poststructuralist critics inspired by Toril Moi's well-known response to Elaine Showalter in *Sexual/Textual Politics: Feminist Literary Theory* (1985).[8] Against Showalter's argument that the textual play of *A Room of One's Own* undermines its feminist agenda, Moi claims that "remaining detached from the narrative strategies of *Room* is equivalent to not reading it at all" (3). While

Showalter criticises Woolf's experimental writing for not delivering political statements grounded in a distinct subject position, Moi argues that the feminist politics of *A Room of One's Own* proceeds by unsettling the realist notion of "unified, integrated self-identity" on which Showalter relies (7).[9] In the wake of *Sexual/Textual Politics*, a range of critics employed deconstructive feminist theories of the 1970s and '80s to trace political positions on the level of Woolf's modernist aesthetic practice. Rachel Blau DuPlessis, Susan Stanford Friedman and William Handley, for instance, all observe that Woolf depicts militarism and nationalism as patriarchal discourses sustained through the act of composing coherent, realist narratives. Handley notes, further, that the omniscient narrator's mastery over an unbroken narrative is linked in *Jacob's Room* to the epic ideal of individual autonomy embodied by the protagonist, an ideal which enabled the patriotic celebration of militarism in Britain during the First World War. In this, Handley articulates an assumption which is now widely accepted: that Woolf's critique of British war-time politics is bound up with questions of aesthetics and subjectivity. Along similar lines, Makiko Minow-Pinkney follows Moi in her field-defining *Virginia Woolf and the Problem of the Subject* (1987), arguing for the value of continental feminist theory as a means for understanding the politically charged implications of Woolf's metaphor, in *A Room of One's Own*, of the writer casting the shadow of his 'I' like "a straight dark bar" across the pages of his novels (*AROO* 115).

However, as valuable as poststructuralist readings have been for pointing out Woolf's association of subjective autonomy with aggressive masculinity, understanding her textual politics primarily as subversive in a postmodern sense obscures her fictional accounts of ethical writing practices capable of promoting non-violent relations between individuals as well as between nations.[10] And while the postmodern lens rightly highlights a modernist critique of the masculine 'I' – the solipsistic consciousness reducing the external world to objects of thought – this once dominant theoretical tradition tends to depict interiority and introspection as sustaining the fiction of the self-centred individual. This book contests and revises the poststructuralist notion of an inevitable relationship between introspection and a fantasy of self-possessed individualism, showing that the ethical premises of Woolf's work incite such a revision. During the past fifteen years, the ethical turn in literary studies has brought thought-provoking readings of Woolf through Emmanuel Levinas's philosophy, which highlight an ethical dimension in her unsettling of autonomous subjectivity. AnnKatrin Jonsson, Rachel Hollander, David Sherman and Tamlyn Monson all observe a Levinasian concern, in Woolf's writing, with the individual's unwilled closeness to unknowable and therefore irreducible others, a closeness which dislocates the perspective of the aggressive 'I'.[11] The relevance of Levinas's non-violent ethics for Woolf's inter-war writing has been noted by Hollander, who aligns the Levinasian scene in which the face of the other compels respect for the commandment "you shall not commit murder" (45) with Woolf's reflection, in August 1918, that

> the existence of life in another human being is as difficult to realise as a play of Shakespeare when the book is shut. This occurred to me when I saw Adrian talking to the tall German prisoner. By rights they should have been killing each other. The reason why it is easy to kill another person must be that one's imagination is too sluggish to conceive what his life means to him–the infinite possibilities of a succession of days which are furled in him, & have already been spent. (*D* 1: 186)

Woolf's insight was triggered by her brother's encounter with a German prisoner of war, and as Hollander observes (43–45), it informs her fictional preoccupation with the ethical necessity to imagine the inaccessible interiority of others. *Virginia Woolf and the Ethics of Intimacy* takes these Levinasian readings of Woolf further, arguing that her modernist texts depict two possible outcomes of the unsettling experience of having one's worldview undermined by another: violence or, alternatively, a non-violent recognition of intimacy as a primary and persistent condition of *all* relations – close and friendly as well as strange and hostile.

From this perspective, Woolf's representation of self-other encounters emerges as integral to her resistance to violence and war, and this dimension of her work is arguably best understood in light of post-Levinasian theories of intimacy. Her idea of the suspended first-person point of view as a form of intimacy, apparent in her major manifestos and novels of the 1920s, resonates strongly with the more recent theoretical concerns of Kristeva, Butler and Irigaray. In works such as Butler's *Precarious Life: The Powers of Mourning and Violence* (2004), *Giving an Account of Oneself* (2005) and *Frames of War: When is Life Grievable?* (2010); Kristeva's two-volume series *The Powers and Limits of Psychoanalysis* (2000–02); as well as Irigaray's *The Way of Love* (2002) and *Sharing the World* (2008), the three theorists develop what I propose to call an ethics of intimacy. Butler's and Irigaray's theories are explicitly grounded in Levinas, while more than one reader of Kristeva has pointed out affinities between her work and Levinas's ethical philosophy.[12] Like Levinas, all three consider the assertion of absolute subjective autonomy to be ethically problematic. However, Butler and Kristeva in particular go beyond Levinas in their respective approaches to intimacy as a precondition for any non-violent resistance to nationalism and conformist thinking. And as Jessica Berman observes, Levinas's philosophy does not offer a sufficient framework for elucidating modernist configurations of intimacy. Engaging Irigaray's ethical theory, Berman interrogates Levinas's notion of ethics as separate from the intimate, personal and private, showing that Woolf's texts combine intimacy with a Levinasian respect for the unknowability of the other ("Ethical Folds"; *Modernist Commitments* 39–62). My own project begins with this crucial insight. Following the path opened up by Berman's inspiring work, I bring Irigaray, Kristeva and Butler together in my reading of Woolf because, their differences notwithstanding, they all develop notions of individuality in which moments of return to the fluidity of pre-subjective relations – moments without subject-object distinctions, where the self is no longer perceived as separate from other selves – enable a non-violent way of being with others. *Virginia Woolf and the Ethics of Intimacy* illuminates the ethical and political potential accorded to such intimate moments in Woolf's inter-war fiction.[13]

Insofar as the forms of intimacy explored in this book are bound up with Woolf's modernist aesthetic practice, this exploration builds on the three theorists' respective accounts of certain modes of experimental representation as a way of unsettling autonomous subjectivity. In this, my reading of Woolf is indebted to Irigaray's, Kristeva's and Butler's earlier works on subjectivity, writing and gender, too, even as it interrogates aspects of these theories. Kristeva's notion of poetic language, Butler's argument for the subversion of identities and Irigaray's theory of intimacy and ethics have inspired debates within Woolf criticism which impact on this project. In what follows, I position my study in relation to these debates, thereby indicating the ways in which Woolf configures the aesthetic as the primary site for intimate and non-violent relations.

Significantly with regard to Woolf's critique of violence, her concern with the aggressive 'I' has been read in terms of Irigaray's and Kristeva's respective dismantling of the masculine 'I' claimed by Western philosophy as a universal model for the individual subject. Minow-Pinkney, for one, maintains that Woolf's writing delivers a critique of this 'I' and, with it, the very structure of her society as a Lacanian symbolic order (*Virginia Woolf and the Problem of the Subject* 14). For Minow-Pinkney and Bonnie Kime Scott, both of whom rely on Kristeva, Woolf's writing functions like Kristeva's poetic language in that it reclaims the maternal and female body, repressed in Western philosophy, for representation. Scott conveys this sense in a chapter she entitles "Woolf's Rapture with Language" describing a writing style which combines the expression of female bodily experiences with radical aesthetic innovation. According to such postmodern, Kristevan readings, Woolf's opposition to the masculine values sustaining nationalism, imperialism and warfare proceeds through her writing as a woman. The emphasis here is on Woolf's idea, which dominates *A Room of One's Own* as well as *Three Guineas*, that women, and women writers, must remain the outsiders of a patriarchal civilisation and language. Taking as their starting point Kristeva's statement that "In women's writing, language seems to be seen from a foreign land . . . from the point of view of an asymbolic, spasmodic body" ("Oscillation" 166), Scott and Minow-Pinkney both argue that Woolf's fiction exemplifies the mode of writing she attributes to women in *A Room of One's Own*.[14] In an often-quoted passage, Woolf writes: "if one is a woman one is often surprised by a sudden splitting off of consciousness, say in walking down Whitehall, when from being the natural inheritor of that civilization, she becomes, on the contrary, outside of it, alien and critical" (*AROO* 127).[15] This dissatisfaction with a civilisation built by "generations of learned men" (*JR* 36) is also a discontent with a patriarchal literary tradition, and, as Woolf's narrator reflects, a novel expressive of a woman's mind and body would have poetic qualities: "No doubt we shall find [the female writer] knocking [the novel form] into shape for herself when she has the free use of her limbs and providing some new vehicle, not necessarily in verse, for the poetry in her. For it is the poetry that is still denied outlet" (*AROO* 100–01). In these strikingly physical metaphors, the "poetry" which has been denied release suggests repressed bodily experience, and the very act of writing poetic prose is done with "the limbs." Elsewhere, the narrator speaks of poetic writing as a "fountain of creative energy" blocked by the 'I' dominating Mr A's novels (131). Woolf's description of an orgasmic, creative fountain suggests Kristeva's notion of *jouissance* through writing, in which semiotic processes disrupt symbolic literary features. It is easy, then, to understand the appeal of Kristeva's theory of poetic language to Woolf scholars.

Kristeva's idea of a literary, poetic "semiotization of the symbolic" (*RPL* 79), or semiotic interruption of autonomous subjectivity, is central also to my own project; throughout Woolf's work, the intimate suspension of subjective boundaries is enabled by a Kristevan mode of writing which Woolf herself called poetic. However, to emphasise Woolf's association of the poetic with women's writing of their bodies as society's outsiders is to risk overlooking the ethical possibilities she ascribed to poetic expression from a position firmly within her socio-political context. In this respect, it is useful to consider the limitations of Kristeva's early work as a theoretical approach to Woolf. Indeed, Kristeva's connection of the maternal and female body with the semiotic before and beyond of cultural and social formations has met with opposition from other feminist thinkers. Judith Butler, for one, has questioned the political potential of Kristeva's poetic language: "If the semiotic promotes the possibility of the subversion, displacement, or disruption of the paternal law, what meanings can those terms have if the symbolic always reasserts its hegemony?" ("The Body Politics of Julia Kristeva" 165). Butler's critique of Kristeva follows her argument, in *Gender Trouble: Feminism and the Subversion of Identity* (1990), that "the subject of 'women'" claimed by feminist critics as a common, pre-cultural identity ultimately reinforces the "masculinist signifying economy" critiqued by, among others, Kristeva and Irigaray (*Gender Trouble* 6, 13). With this observation, Butler calls for a re-evaluation of the role of the body in feminist theories of representation, where sex and gender are not to be viewed as *a priori* biological categories, since both are established through "the repeated stylization of the body" (33). Butler, then, advocates the performative displacement of embodied subject positions rather than the disruption of the masculine 'I' through a specifically female or feminine writing.

Butler's notion of "troubled" identities has spurred debates around Woolf's ambivalence, in *A Room of One's Own*, between a call for a corporeal, poetic mode of writing specific to women and the claim that "it is fatal for anyone who writes to think of their sex" (*AROO* 136). Asking "whether there are two sexes in the mind corresponding to the two sexes in the body," the narrator goes on to state that "Perhaps a mind that is purely masculine cannot create, any more than a mind that is purely feminine" (128). Woolf's famous theory of androgyny – of the ideal artist's mind as "woman-manly" or "man-womanly" (128) – has motivated Butlerian accounts of her fictional connections between intimacy, aesthetics and politics, readings which illuminate her interrogation of binary sex and gender categories. Such focus has been given, in particular, to *Orlando: A Biography* (1928), which began to receive large-scale attention with the emergence of LGBTQ studies, and whose androgynous protagonist has erotic relations with individuals across the LGBTQ spectrum. A politically radical text in a time when fictional representations of same-sex love were subject to censorship and legal condemnation, *Orlando* allowed Woolf to probe questions around erotic intimacy in relations which defy heteronormative definitions of sexuality and gender. Writing in the 1990s, critics like Adam Parkes and Nancy Cervetti claimed that the novel's queering of intimacy proceeds through Butlerian stylistic means such as parody, satire and irony, rather than the communication of embodied affect favoured by an earlier generation of feminist critics.[16] The composition of *Orlando*, which inspired an intensely sensual correspondence between Woolf and Vita Sackville-West (the model for Orlando), may well have enabled Woolf to express what her friend and lover once called her "suppressed randiness" (Parkes 447; see 446–47).[17] But as scholars from Patricia Morgne Cramer to Madelyn Detloff have shown, Woolf's writing also remains politically significant for twenty-first-century debates within gender studies and queer theory. In two recent essays, Cramer and Detloff speak for two distinct approaches to Woolf, both of which illuminate her political configurations of non-heteronormative intimacies: lesbian readings, which advocate a focus on Woolf's "exploration of the emotional, political, and aesthetic possibilities of female same-sex love" (Cramer 132), and readings drawing on the work of Butler and other queer theorists.[18]

While critics embracing or disputing Butler's theory, and queer theory more generally, have highlighted the political implications of affectionate and erotic relations in Woolf's fiction, intimacy for Woolf is also a question of ethics, as Berman demonstrates. Following Irigaray's *An Ethics of Sexual Difference* (1993), Berman argues that Woolf's aesthetic practice cultivates a feminist "ethics of care (or eros)" ("Ethical Folds" 151). Unlike Butler's ethical theory, Irigaray's is based on "the difference of identity" in which "the other who is forever unknowable is the one who differs from me sexually" (*An Ethics* 18, 13). For Irigaray, intimate relations are ethical insofar as they bring about a recognition of male and female subjectivities as irrevocably different. Whereas "the subject has always been written in the masculine form, as *man*," thus failing "to leave [the woman-mother] a subjective life" (6, 10), the loving caress or embrace enables the creation of two distinct forms of subjectivity. Thus, in Berman's account, Woolf's writing combines a Levinasian ethics of alterity with "The intimate scene of a lover's embrace" characterising "women's private ethical experience" – a corporeal, affective experiential sphere "excluded by Levinas from the realm of ethics" ("Ethical Folds" 152).[19] In Berman's reading of Lily's touching Mrs Ramsay in the scene with which we began, "Lily's recognition of Mrs. Ramsay's alterity emerges directly out of Lily's intimacy with and desire to love Mrs. Ramsay" (*Modernist Commitments* 57).

Although I remain indebted to Berman's field-defining work, this book argues that Woolf defamiliarises and even dislocates habitual connections of intimacy with love, erotic desire or sexual intercourse in relations between lovers, family members or friends. In this, it departs from the focus of Jesse Wolfe's *Bloomsbury, Modernism, and the Reinvention of Intimacy* (2011), which traces the Bloomsbury group's engagement with the historically new forms of love, friendship and family constellations shaping the early twentieth century. That is to say, it follows Woolf's concern with face-to-face encounters between two individuals who may or may not be emotionally attached to one another, encounters in which the overwhelming presence of another, irreducible subject unsettles the perspective of the autonomous 'I.' Ranging from Lily Briscoe's desire to become "one" with a loved person to the author-narrator's disturbing experience of being affected by and made to see with a stranger in "Character in Fiction," such encounters are radically intimate because they dislodge the boundary separating subject and object, and subject and subject. And such intimacy emerges in the realm of aesthetics, in the modernist writer's communication of interiority or the life of the mind, which includes cognitive as well as affective experience. While Woolf's fiction unsettles the perspective of the knowing narrator and artist, it stages simultaneously the fluidity of the boundaries separating individuals. In *Mrs Dalloway*, for instance, where the narrator's voice merges with the voices of the novel's characters, or in *To the Lighthouse*, where the characters' separate points of view fuse momentarily into one, individual perspectives emerge as at once sharply distinct and on the verge of dissolution. This vertiginous state, into which the reader is drawn, forms a particularly compelling site for Woolf's ethics of intimacy.

By problematising dyadic encounters, Woolf's novels explore the intimacy of physical proximity, but the modes of intimacy she foregrounds do not express themselves primarily through bodily contact. Her actual descriptions of intimate moments in which two bodies touch – Lily's head on Mrs Ramsay's knee, or the furtive kiss between Clarissa Dalloway and Sally Seton – remain notably sparse and brief. Drawing on the post-Levinasian theories of Irigaray, Kristeva and Butler, this study ventures that Woolf extends the meaning of intimacy beyond the realm of eros and the loving touch.[20] These thinkers' earlier work has been central in preparing the ground for their respective ethics of intimacy and recognition; my project draws inspiration, in particular, from the poetic modes of writing affective experience theorised by Kristeva and Irigaray, and from Butler's politicising of intimacy as a dislocation of subject positions. Their more recent works, however, can make us see how Woolf, in making intimacy and recognition questions of aesthetics, develops an ethics relevant to a broader range of relations than those between friends and lovers: personal as well as impersonal and political relations in which the perspective of the autonomous 'I' is suspended in the presence of a 'you.' And, paradoxically though it may seem, such an ethics begins with the modernist writer's act of introspection. Through artist figures like Lily in *To the Lighthouse* and the poet Bernard in *The*

Waves, Woolf portrays the experimental painter and writer who question their capacity to depict interiority in the moment of facing the inscrutable presence of another. This questioning is configured as an act of self-reflection: by critically reviewing the self as an 'I' who claims to know another, Woolf's modern artists must confront and interrogate the social and cultural values which brought this 'I' into being in the first place.

Indeed, bringing Woolf into a dialogue with Butler, Irigaray and Kristeva highlights that they all conceive of both ethical positioning and social critique as operating through self-reflection. For the three theorists, the introspective act of taking one's self as an object of thought unsettles the autonomous, knowing 'I' and, thereby, the historically specific norms and values shaping this 'I.' This assumption informs Butler's concern, in her book from 2005, that the subject "give an account" of itself, Kristeva's notion of intimate revolt as a way of "going in quest of oneself" (*IR* 6), and Irigaray's repeated use of the term "dwelling" for the subject's worldview as only one among many. Unlike their earlier writings, their respective notions of ethical relations do not focus on the subversion of the (Lacanian symbolic) 'I.'[21] Instead, they seek to reconfigure the split subject of poststructuralist theory, a subject whose capacity for social critique is compromised by the values through which the autonomous 'I' is formed.[22] Self-reflection, they all argue, does not necessarily achieve a solipsistic protection of the normative horizon of which the transcendental ego is a product. It operates, rather, as a critical capacity to suspend the first-person point of view. This procedure is immediately relevant to Woolf's inter-war fiction and her artist figures' acts of self-reflection. By having the novelists narrating in "Character in Fiction" and *Jacob's Room* question themselves as all-knowing and autonomous subjects, Woolf suggests that modern fiction must be more than a channel for unproblematic communication of a writer's values and worldview to the reader. And crucially, as we have seen, she configures the process of introspection not only as a dislocation of the self but also as a form of intimacy. This dimension of her writing, too, becomes apparent if we read it via the theoretical terms of Kristeva, Butler and Irigaray, all of whom speak of the decentring of the subject as a return to a pre-subjective mode of being.

This focus on the pre-subjective raises the question of Irigaray's and Butler's selective use of psychoanalysis in works such as *Sharing the World* and *Giving an Account of Oneself*. In contrast to their respective reservations against fundamental psychoanalytic tenets in earlier works, their writings from this century turn to psychoanalysis, implicitly (Irigaray) and explicitly (Butler), in order to consider the ethical possibilities raised by the notion of a return, through spoken and written representation, to a pre-subjective way of relating to the world.[23] Ethical relations, they both suggest, emerge when two individuals acknowledge the primary absence of subject-object distinctions which precedes their formation as separate and autonomous. In *Giving an Account of Oneself*, Butler relies on a psychoanalytic notion of performative representation to argue that the narrative process of reflecting on the self enables the subject to relive momentarily the primary state in which any distinction between 'I' and 'you' is yet to be established. Such moments, she holds, enable an ethical way of being with others because they suspend the first-person perspective, the perspective of the 'I' prone to aggression and violence. Irigaray, on her part, theorises a coming together of self and other in an intimate union which recalls Lily Briscoe's "unity," a state in which intersubjective boundaries momentarily blur. For Irigaray, the recognition of another's irreducible subjectivity emerges out of two individuals' desire to "retur[n] to this natural site where they were in communion with one another through the same air, the same breath, the same energy" (*SW* 70).

If the three theorists develop psychoanalytically informed notions of the intimate as a site for ethics, this site is also political, and such correlations between intimacy, ethics and politics are equally deep in Woolf's writing. Thus Kristeva's series *The Powers and Limits of Psychoanalysis* offers a compelling idea of poetic writing as a form of "intimate revolt," that is, a "reuniting with affect" through *jouissance* (*IR* 26) which brings about a momentary return to a state preceding gender formation and subject-object relations. The intimate as defined by Kristeva operates differently from the all-encompassing protest against a patriarchal civilisation which Kristevan critics have ascribed to Woolf: it is, rather, the very process by which a subject becomes capable of non-conformist thought, of what Woolf herself called "thinking against the current, not with it" (*E* 6: 243). In this line from her 1940 essay "Thoughts on Peace in an Air Raid," Woolf dwells on William Blake's dictum "I will not cease from mental fight" as she urges her contemporaries as well as future readers to resist the "current" of patriotic sentiment and think of peace – of the psychological, social and political conditions which make peace possible – in the midst of war (242–43). "Unless we can think peace into existence," she writes, "we – not this one body in this one bed but millions of bodies yet to be born – will lie in the same darkness and hear the same death rattle overhead" (242). This claim is intrinsic to the pacifist stance outlined in *Three Guineas*, and in Chapter 4, I examine *The Waves* as a pacifist text whose politics proceeds as a Kristevan act of intimate revolt: the momentary surrender of individual autonomy through the self-reflective communication of interiority, an introspective process vital to the subject's capacity to question the nationalist and proto-fascist ideals shaping its formation.

Woolf's Kristevan, non-violent politics also resonates with Butler's. In *Giving an Account of Oneself*, which builds on Levinas's ethical theory, Butler speaks of "a certain ethical violence, which demands that we manifest and maintain self-identity at all times and require that others do the same" (42). In her recent work on ethics and politics, Butler takes issue with a psychological ideal of absolute subjective autonomy which, she argues, is indissociably related to an aggressive defence of state sovereignty. Published a few years after 9/11, *Precarious Life* casts the assertion of the autonomous 'I' as an ethically violent act which causes private as well as public forms of violence. Directing a sharp critique against the increasingly militaristic and imperialist foreign policy adopted by the US government after the attacks, Butler asks: how can the vicious circle of violence and counter-violence be broken, and is there a more sustainable way of relating to others?[24] Woolf's fiction of the 1920s and '30s poses similar questions in response to the rise of extreme nationalisms and the increasingly hostile international relations which would bring about a second world war. Since Alex Zwerdling wrote *Virginia Woolf and the Real World* (1986) and Mark Hussey's 1991 volume *Virginia Woolf and War: Fiction, Reality, and Myth* drew attention to the fact that "*all* Woolf's work is deeply concerned with war" in how it exposes "the connections between private and public violence . . . between male supremacy and the absence of peace, and between ethics and aesthetics" (Hussey, Introduction 3), critics have examined the ways in which the pacifist convictions expressed in texts such as *Three Guineas* fundamentally shaped her modernist novels. In relation to Butler's conception of psychological insight as a vehicle for explaining and resisting nationalism and ethico-political violence, a foundational assumption in *Three Guineas*, that "The psychology of private life" justifies the pacifist belief that women's abstention from patriotic practices "would help materially to prevent war," is particularly resonant (*TG* 314).

Butler's notion of ethical violence is central to my claim that Woolf's inter-war fiction depicts the representational violence of objectification as inseparable from the systematic modes of violence she critiques in her political essays, and from the ways in which these perpetuate the violence of war. More specifically, this book argues that the introspective features of her novels from *Jacob's Room* to *The Waves* convey an ethical and political stance against the systemic violence structuring British pre-war and inter-war life. According to Butler, an individual whose subjective perspective is suspended in the encounter with an irreducible other cannot commit acts of violence. Introspection is central to Butler's ethics;

the act of looking within, of reflecting on the self and its formation, is capable of achieving not only the assertion of the subject of Western philosophy vis-à-vis a world of objects, but also a Levinasian dislocation of the first-person point of view in the recognition of the psychologically complex subjects whose worldviews might conflict with, and thereby undermine, that 'I.' Analogically, as Butler puts it in *Precarious Life*, "If national sovereignty is challenged, that does not mean it must be shored up at all costs" (xii). She argues thereby for the ethico-political necessity of acknowledging the primary, fluid relations to others which never cease to destabilise the autonomous entities of self and nation. Woolf anticipates Butler's thought in emphasising the capacity of intimacy and introspection to produce a notion of, on the one hand, the individual subject and, on the other, the nation-state, as not strictly autonomous. Considered alongside Kristeva's and Irigaray's work, Butler's theory enables a new insight about Woolf: that her modernist focus on interiority and psychological complexity does not suggest the detachment of her most radically experimental fiction from socio-political concerns, as has often been claimed. It is, on the contrary, central to the ethical and political comment delivered by her inter-war novels. Kristeva's idea of revolt through poetic language as a means for resisting conformist and authoritarian social structures, Irigaray's notion of "sharing the world" through acknowledging worldviews and perspectives irreducible to one's own, and Butler's equation of US militarism with a defensive drawing of boundaries around the self, all illuminate key questions around intimacy and violence with which Woolf was grappling in the first decades of the twentieth century. Through their nuanced depiction of interiority and intimate relations, her novels of the period 1922–31 respond to the complicity of Britain in the rise of aggressive nationalisms following the Treaty of Versailles,[25] a widespread anxiety regarding a perceived crisis of national sovereignty after the First World War, the beginnings of the decline of the British Empire, and the rise of fascism in Europe.[26]

Butler, Irigaray and Kristeva all base their theories of public and political relations in the psychological and the intersubjective, as did many of Woolf's contemporaries. In the 1920s and '30s, a time when the autonomy of the self as well as the sovereignty of the nation were perceived to be in a state of crisis (Miller), intellectuals all over Europe considered the socio-political implications of aggression and repression, sensitivity and rationality, as well as emotional effusion and restraint. The question whether the instincts and affects threatening to disintegrate the weak ego were a direct cause of the precarious state of European civilisation was widely discussed, and most famously, perhaps, by psychoanalysts like Freud and Melanie Klein. Needless to say, these debates around individuality, interiority and affect shaped the aesthetic expressions of literary modernism. In view of these discussions, Butler's and Irigaray's hesitant recourse to psychoanalysis is suggestive considering Woolf's frequent use of psychoanalytic concepts despite her famously critical attitude to them. As Elizabeth Abel has shown, her scepticism towards psychoanalysis throughout the 1920s is directed specifically at Freud. Despite the enthusiastic reception of Freud's ideas by many members of the Bloomsbury circle, and despite the Woolfs' Hogarth Press publishing his works in English at the time Virginia Woolf wrote her inter-war novels, she remained notoriously critical of the psychoanalytic terms she could not avoid becoming familiar with, and claimed not to have read Freud properly until 1939.[27] In a review entitled "Freudian Fiction" (1920), Woolf expresses her suspicion of what she takes to be a reductive scientific and medical outlook which turns individuals into cases, or objects of study (*E* 3: 195–98). Abel detects a disciplinary rivalry in Woolf's critique of Freud. While Freudian psychoanalysis in Britain was widely considered to be close to the humanities, and to literature in particular, Woolf aligns it with the medical establishment she denounces in *Mrs Dalloway*, claiming for fiction the representation of psychic complexity.[28] Abel suggests, further, that her critique of psychoanalysis is aimed particularly at the centrality of the Oedipus complex to Freud's works of the 1920s: in the years Woolf was composing *Mrs Dalloway*, Freud theorised his narrative of acculturation in which the male 'I' emerges as the inheritor of the laws of culture and society.[29] If we follow Abel, then, Woolf's inter-war fiction does not only expose the aggression of which this subject is capable. It targets simultaneously the figure of the doctor, Freud the psychoanalyst and Bradshaw, the psychiatrist in *Mrs Dalloway*, both representatives of the establishment she criticises in *A Room of One's Own* for advocating a mode of individuality predicated on the autonomous 'I.'

What Woolf might not have considered until she engaged with his work in 1939 is that Freud himself saw the ego, the 'I' making culture and civilisation possible, as a frail construct prone to aggression, violence and destruction. When she eventually read works such as "Thoughts for the Times on War and Death" (1915) and *Civilization and Its Discontents* (1930), she was both fascinated and troubled: "Freud is upsetting: reducing one to whirlpool; & I daresay truly. If we're all instinct, the unconscious, whats (sic) all this about civilisation, the whole man, freedom &c?" (*D* 5: 250). As this diary entry indicates, Woolf finds her own, earlier analyses of aggression at odds with Freud's claim that war is inevitable since the human instinct for violence will always threaten to destroy civilisation. After all, as Froula points out in *Virginia Woolf and the*

Bloomsbury Avant-Garde (2004), Woolf shared the belief, held by members of the Bloomsbury circle such as Leonard Woolf, John Maynard Keynes and Roger Fry, in the freethinking individual's capacity to overcome aggression and build a civilisation, extending across national borders, on the foundations of democracy and peace. This is not to say that Keynes's and Leonard Woolf's political work for peaceful international relations or Woolf's pacifism was not influenced by psychoanalytic accounts of aggression.[30] On the contrary, among the British modernists, the writers and thinkers of Bloomsbury engaged most committedly the theories of Freud and Klein.[31] In her excellent book on modernism and psychoanalysis, Lyndsey Stonebridge observes that "Bloomsbury not only popularized psychoanalysis for the British intelligentsia, but also domesticated it by incorporating psychoanalysis within its over-arching liberal ethos of the 'free and civilized individual'" (10). Klein's work on primary aggression, which embraced Freud's theory of the death drive in *Beyond the Pleasure Principle* (1920), was widely adopted in Britain as offering an explanation of "the intractable complicity between the destructive element within and cultural and social violence without" (Stonebridge 16). In a chapter on the aesthetic theories of Bloomsbury, Stonebridge traces Klein's thought, in which the infant's aggressive impulses cannot be clearly distinguished from violence in the realm of politics, across the writings of Woolf and Roger Fry (46–78). Given the many parallels which can be drawn between Woolf's, Klein's and Freud's work of the inter-war years, as Stonebridge and Abel both show, Woolf's lack of interest in psychoanalysis when writing her most experimental modernist novels remains intriguing.

This study proposes that Woolf's reserved attitude to psychoanalysis lies at least partly in her unwillingness to embrace the psychoanalytic notion of the individual as barely capable of suppressing its destructive instincts. Her writing prompts us to ask: what if the aggressive instinct is not so much "the original nature of man" (Freud, *Civilization* 303) as the product of a particularly violent civilisation? In this respect, Butler's, Kristeva's and Irigaray's more recent works are central to my reading of Woolf because they all combine psychoanalysis and ethics in order to delineate an understanding of individuality as something other than autonomous subjectivity. While Woolf's novels frequently dramatise aggression, they also explore the psychology of non-violent encounters. They do so by raising the question which is the starting point of *Three Guineas*, and which Einstein and Freud debated in 1932: "Is there any way of delivering mankind from the menace of war?" (*Why War?* 345). However, Woolf's answers to this question differ remarkably from Freud's. For Freud, violence can be resisted only at the cost of repressing the aggressive impulses an individual instinctively feels when encountering another, impulses which make the ethical and aesthetic ideals of civilisation virtually impossible to sustain. For Woolf, who may not have conceived of the individual as inherently aggressive in the period covered here, a non-violent ethics cannot emerge from repression. Her writing can be better understood, I suggest, in the light of later developments in psychoanalytic thought, in which the psychological and social norm of absolute subjective autonomy is considered a primal cause of violence. Whereas Freud and Klein theorised the regressive, destructive instinct threatening to dissolve the 'I,' Woolf's fiction configures the momentary dislocation of the coherent self as a form of intimacy by which the individual becomes self-reflective and capable of calling violent social ideals into question. Also and crucially, this interrogation is both depicted and performed in Woolf's work as the act of writing interiority. In her capacity as a modernist writer, she pursued questions touched on by Freud, who only hinted at the potential of "identification" (*Group Psychology* 134–40) and "oceanic feeling" (*Civilization* 251–55, 291) to counter aggression: both designate primary relational modes which precede erotic object-ties, and to which an individual can return by sharing the feelings of another. Freud was far more emphatic in his view of the phenomenon that Woolf called intimacy as "emotional contagion," a form of regression hampering the intellect and thereby ethical and political thought (*Group Psychology* 112; see 101–05, 112–16, 154–55).

It was only in the late twentieth and early twenty-first centuries that the correlation between politics, ethics and intimacy would be substantially theorised as central to the realm of aesthetics, and so the contemporary thinkers represented here allow us to see Woolf's introspective writing in a new light. Their accounts of intimacy present a clear divergence from Freud's influential theory of ethics and violence in works such as *Group Psychology and the Analysis of the Ego* (1921) and *Civilization and Its Discontents*. While Freud claimed that communities are constructed through ethical prescriptions and affectionate or erotic ties between individuals, he also maintained that a primary aggressive instinct makes it impossible to fulfil the commandment "Love thy neighbour as thyself" (*Civilization* 337; see 299–305), and that a community united by affectionate bonds can only be sustained at the cost of aggression towards non-members (*Group Psychology* 130–31; *Civilization* 305). If primal violence gave rise to the earliest ethical commandment – "Thou shalt not kill" ("Thoughts for the Times" 84; see 81–86) – violence, in Freud's account, continues to alternatively sustain and destroy two foundations of a frail civilisation: high moral standards and intimacy, conceived as affective ties where the libidinal impulse is inhibited. This is so because the renunciation of instinct required to uphold civilisation runs counter to a "primary mutual hostility of human beings" (*Civilization* 302).[32] By contrast, the perspectives offered by Woolf, Butler, Kristeva and Irigaray provide a more viable model for non-violent relations: one that affirms those ethical duties towards strangers which, as Freud notes, break down in a situation of war ("Thoughts for the Times" 84). A notion of intimacy which is not limited to love and kinship might also form a way out of the eternal struggle between libidinal and destructive instincts, eros and death, which, according to Freud, makes the most intimate relations the breeding ground for violence and war as a constant threat to the most civilised of societies.[33] In this, Woolf's foregrounding of intimacy as the basis for an ethical recognition of each individual's inviolability is as valid for the twentieth as for the twenty-first century.

Crucial to the many parallels drawn in this book between Woolf's thought and that of Kristeva, Irigaray and Butler is the question of aesthetic form and style. While Kristeva is the only one among the three who extensively theorises modernist writing, they all privilege representational modes which share key features of the modernist poetics developed by Woolf in her novels from *Jacob's Room* to *The Waves*. All three promote forms of expression which challenge mimetic depictions of reality, and Irigaray and Kristeva argue for the capacity of intensely sensory, poetic expression to dislocate the autonomous 'I.' Kristeva's poetic language, Irigaray's "unique," poetic saying, and Butler's broken narrative exposing the limits of representability, all exemplify an investment in a defamiliarising language capable of unsettling habitual thinking. Unlike Levinas, for whom all representation is inherently violent, Butler, Irigaray and Kristeva theorise ethical representational practices of a kind that Woolf creates. By showing that her sensual, poetic and introspective writing both denounces ethical violence and conceptualises non-violent relations, this book claims a central position for Woolf's work in the ongoing critical discussions about the ways in which contemporary theory and modernist aesthetic practices continue to speak to one another.

While theory may well have been marginalised with this century's return to archival and historicist methodologies in modernist studies, as Stephen Ross claims, this marginalisation does indeed "verge on modernist absurdity" given the unique relationship between modernism and theory: "Modernist writing thinks theoretically and theory writes modernistically; they are . . . mutually sustaining aspects of the same project" (1, 1–2). Ross's call for a revitalisation of theoretical approaches to modernism has been articulated with particular force by leading Woolf scholars.[34] As events such as the 2012 symposium "Virginia Woolf among the Philosophers" indicate, Woolf studies today is far from an a-theoretical field. On the contrary, there has been a noteworthy philosophical turn in recent years, with the publication of numerous field-defining books offering compelling readings of Woolf alongside a wide range of philosophical traditions – traditions predating and contemporaneous with Woolf as well as developments in late twentieth- and early twenty-first-century philosophy.[35] Monographs by Ann Banfield (2000), Judith Allen (2010), Angeliki Spiropoulou (2010) and Derek Ryan (2013), to name a few, explore the tensions and resonances between the philosophical, aesthetic and ethico-political aspects of her writing. While Woolf's fiction can perhaps not be said to actually theorise ethics, violence or intimacy, much contemporary scholarship investigates both the philosophical dimension of her aesthetic practice and the aesthetic dimension of her essays and political texts. As I situate my study in this expanding field of enquiry, my intention is not to say that Woolf invented, or simply anticipated, post-Levinasian theory: rather, I explore a deep historical genealogy of thought, in which contemporary theories of intimacy are very much a legacy of modernist configurations of intimacy. This is not only true of Kristeva, whose political theory is explicitly grounded in modernist aesthetics, but of post-Levinasian thought more generally. And Woolf's legacy is, I propose, central to this genealogy.

One aim of this project, then, is to demonstrate the continuing value of poststructuralist theory – or, rather, its afterlife – for twenty-first-century approaches to affect and intimacy in literary modernism and Woolf's writing. While Derek Ryan's *Virginia Woolf and the Materiality of Theory: Sex, Animal, Life* follows a (partial) deviation, in much present-day literary criticism, from the language- and subject-oriented focus of poststructuralism, *Virginia Woolf and the Ethics of Intimacy* explores some of the rich intersections between subjectivity, ethics, aesthetics, affect and politics in Woolf's major novels – intersections which might not have become visible without the ground-breaking work of poststructuralist critics and theorists. In particular, my alignment of present-day theories of intimacy with Woolf's writing of interiority contributes to the burgeoning field of affect studies, an area which is gaining ground in modernist scholarship, as Jean-Michel Rabaté's *The Pathos of Distance: Affects of the Moderns* (2016) and Julie Taylor's essay collection *Modernism and Affect* (2015) attest. Taylor's volume partakes in a significant shift from a long-held notion of modernism as detached from affective and emotional expression, to a growing interest in the centrality of affect to modernist writing. As Taylor notes, recent accounts of the affective life of modernism tend to conceptualise affect as a mode of "feeling beyond the subject" (6). Justus Nieland's *Feeling Modern: The Eccentricities of Public Life* (2008) is a prominent example of such studies: modernist affect, Nieland argues, is socio-politically embedded by virtue of being publicly mediated, rather than originating in the feeling individual. For Nieland, modernism should not be understood as divided between romantic and anti-sentimental traditions, where, we could add, the former cultivates and the latter rejects intimacy in the sense of "Pertaining to the inmost thoughts or feelings; proceeding from . . . one's inmost self" ("intimate, *adj.* and *n.*," def. A.2). Instead, he suggests that we should think of modernist emotion as eccentric, "worrying the boundaries of the self's most intimate interiors" (19), and in affect studies more generally, affect is seen as undermining the self-contained subject.

Such notions of affect both can and cannot illuminate the affective dimension of Woolf's novels. In one sense, the affects she explores are eccentric: in Chapters 1 and 2, I examine melancholia and *jouissance* as relational affective states which shape the non-violent ethics of *Jacob's Room* and *Mrs Dalloway* respectively, states in which the self is affected by, or acted upon, by another. At the same time, her writing belongs to an introspective modernist tradition committed to intimacy as defined above, a line of writers resisting the familiar modernist discourse exemplified by T. S. Eliot's paradigmatic notion, in "Tradition and the Individual Talent" (1919), of poetic writing as "an escape from emotion" (2559). While several recent theories distinguish emotion from affect, viewing the latter as extra-linguistic and primarily corporeal, Woolf's idea of the poetic resonates with traditional conceptions of emotion as cognitive and, as Taylor puts it, "the property of an expressive subject" (8). Indeed, her ethics of intimacy begins with the conscious, cognitive and creative act of introspection – the thinking and feeling self reflecting on itself – which brings about eccentric affects and the momentary suspension of subject positions. While affect theory's conception of affect in terms of bodily materiality often departs from poststructuralism's focus on language and discourse, I believe that there is much to be gained for the field of Woolf studies by exploring the theoretical legacy and afterlife of those poststructuralist approaches which have made us see her formidable contribution to ethico-political debates around intimacy and violence as linguistic-poetic and discursive phenomena.[36]

This leads me to another reason to explore Woolf's configurations of intimacy as a more ethically and politically productive category than affect *per se*: her scepticism, particularly in her work of the 1930s and early '40s, towards the deep-rooted idea that affective, empathetic identification with others will prompt ethical action in contexts of war. In *Three Guineas*, Woolf's narrator-correspondent famously maintains that looking at the same photographs of dead bodies from the Spanish Civil War will create the same feelings of outrage, of "horror and disgust," in her and her addressee, an affective "fusion" which will spur their joint efforts to prevent war (*TG* 165). However, as Madelyn Detloff (*Persistence* 119–30) and Meghan Marie Hammond (161) both observe, the text ultimately resists such connections between affective and ethico-political responses. Addressing Susan Sontag's critique, in *Regarding the Pain of Others* (2003), of Woolf's alleged naiveté in assuming that such shared feelings of outrage will lead to ethically and politically responsible measures, Detloff argues persuasively that Woolf's insistence on the impossibility of empathetic identification with the war victims highlights that "affect in itself cannot be the endpoint of ethics" (*Persistence* 122; see 128–29). Hammond, whose 2014 book traces the development of empathy as an affective structure specific to the inward-looking strand of literary modernism, also claims that Woolf's political texts and later novels from *The Waves* onwards expose the ethico-political limits of the empathetic attempt at "feeling with" or "feeling into" another (149; see 148–75)[37] – an effort central, as we have seen, to Woolf's writing of the 1920s. While Hammond offers a compelling account of modernist empathy as distinct from the "feeling for" of sympathy, in which the boundary between self and other stays intact, she does not consider psychoanalytic approaches to empathy, but calls for further research that might illuminate such connections (18). What Hammond calls empathic forms of representation "that strive to provide an immediate sense of another's thoughts and feelings" (4), I see as the starting point of Woolf's ethics of intimacy, but by no means its end. In Woolf's creative hands, intimacy as a psychoanalytically informed, linguistic-poetic and discursive concept becomes a far more forceful vehicle for resisting violence than the primarily affective realm of empathy, and "fellow feeling" more generally.

Even *Three Guineas* – the most prosaic of Woolf's texts if *The Waves* is the most poetic – ends with the reflection that if poetic writing may not have the power to spur socio-political measures aimed at preventing another world war, it has a crucial role to play in shaping a vital "dream of peace":

> Even here, even now your letter tempts us ... to listen not to the bark of the guns and the bray of the gramophones but to the voices of the poets, answering each other, assuring us of a unity that rubs out divisions as if they were chalk marks only. (*TG* 365)

I show in Chapter 4 that Woolf imagines this "unity" in Butlerian and Kristevan terms, as a primary relational mode of intimacy whose persistent force can make us perceive the boundaries separating individuals as well as nations as discursive "chalk marks" which are at once violent (aggressively drawn) and frail (easily erased). And, as we shall see, this discursive and poetic form of intimacy inspires the non-violent ethics of her novels from *Jacob's Room* to *The Waves*. However, it also enables the pacifist "dream of peace" outlined in *Three Guineas*, and this act of dreaming through writing is everything but escapist: as late as in "Thoughts on Peace in an Air Raid," whose composition in September 1940 was followed closely by the Blitz, Woolf insists on the need to not only imagine peace, but "think peace into existence" even when bombs are falling (*E* 6: 242). Jean Mills is one among several Woolf scholars who have demonstrated the urgency, in Woolf's time and ours, of this political stance.[38] She makes a particularly convincing case for Woolf's relevance to a change of direction, in the field of Peace Studies at the end of the twentieth century, from a focus on negative peace, or the cessation of violence, to positive peace: the conditions necessary for sustaining peaceful relations (134–52). It is in this light, I suggest, that we should consider Woolf's introspective, inter-war exploration of intimacy and violence. While there is a clear shift, in her later work, in *how* she imagines the ethical and political relationships between art, affect and intimacy, we should not overlook the ways in which her earlier, poetic vision of non-violent relations was central in shaping her compelling ideal of sustainable peace. In tracing one, hopefully rewarding path towards such enquiry, this book reads Woolf as a writer and political thinker whose vital contribution to the modernist scene of inter-war Britain remains strikingly relevant to debates around intimacy, ethics and geopolitical power in our own time.

In Chapter 1, I trace a non-violent ethics running across Woolf's first distinctly modernist novel *Jacob's Room*, in which formal innovation evinces a pervasive textual melancholia. I take the novel's fragmented and arguably melancholic poetics to be not only symptomatic of but also a critical engagement with the crisis of literary intimacy and ethics shaping modernist writing after the First World War. While Woolf's post-war journalism often voices nostalgia for modernity's favoured modes of intimate storytelling, I see the melancholic aesthetic features of *Jacob's Room* – notably its libidinal and affective voiding of the literary medium – as betraying a loss of more archaic, extra-textual forms of intimacy and affective transmission. This reading has ethical as well as political consequences: departing from a critical consensus about Woolf's political break with realism and its complicity with the violence of global capitalism and militarisation, I detect in the novel's melancholic, formal fragmentation a radical, and primarily ethical, severing of bonds with modernity's literary legacy. In this endeavour, I engage Kristeva's figure of the black sun and Butler's theory of melancholic dispossession, both of which illuminate Woolf's attempt to recover pre-modern and pre-subjective modes of intimate attachment eclipsed by an ethically violent notion of the subject's autonomy – and the other's exchangeability – sustaining the affective-libidinal economy of modern letters. I argue that *Jacob's Room* both exposes a ubiquitous nexus of intimacy and letters as the very site of literary modernity's entanglement with the violence of political modernity and voices a yearning to extricate the post-war novel from this relationship in a quest for non-violent modes of textual intimacy. This chapter also explores the ethical implications of Woolf's vivid engagement with Roger Fry's aesthetic theory, considering *Jacob's Room* as a unique modernist experiment in which melancholic expression and a formalist aesthetic converge. While melancholia and Bloomsbury formalism both tend to be associated with a separation of art and aesthetics from ethical obligations, I propose that Woolf's joining of these radically different representational modes forms the primary ground for her creation of anti-war ideals.

In *Mrs Dalloway*, published three years after *Jacob's Room*, intimate moments in which the individual self cannot be comfortably distinguished from the other and outside emerge through the novel's exploration of individual psychic life. The narrator's voice floats into the "beautiful caves" (*D* 2: 263) of the characters' interiority, while Woolf seduces her reader into these glistening caves, creating a breathtakingly intimate experience whereby to read is to be held in a blissful suspension of autonomous and conflicting viewpoints. Like *Jacob's Room*, Woolf's subsequent novel reveals a quest for pre-subjective forms of intimacy in a thought-provoking challenge to the violence sanctioned by the ideal of absolute subjective autonomy. But if the dominant affect of *Jacob's Room* is the primal sadness of melancholia, what erupts in the intensely sensual aesthetic of *Mrs Dalloway* is exuberant joy, a manifestation of the orgasmic "fountain of creative energy" (*AROO* 131) by which the writer and reader of poetic text can be transported from intense pleasure into the momentary self-annihilation of bliss or *jouissance*. I argue, in Chapter 2, that writing *Mrs Dalloway* enabled Woolf to develop a Kristevan aesthetic practice of intimate revolt: a form of artistic creation in which systematic social, political and ethical violence – exemplified in the novel through the lethal healing practices of Septimus Smith's medical doctors – is resisted not primarily through the indignant exposure of such violence, but through the reparative practice of writing poetically and, more specifically, through the pleasure particular to poetic introspection. In my reparative reading of *Mrs Dalloway*, I draw on Kristeva's and Butler's respective theories of intimate opacity, accountability and revolt in the timeless to propose that in Woolf's hands, the lyrical probing of psychic depths, and the blissful "reuniting with affect" (*IR* 26) it entails, become a vehicle for non-violent resistance to a nationalistic social order sustained through a disciplinary imperative to suppress affective intensity.

While the introspective poetics of *Mrs Dalloway* elicits recognition of the opacity marking the integrity, and therefore inviolability, of individual psychic life, such recognition acquires philosophical as well as further aesthetic dimensions in *To the Lighthouse*. Taking as its starting point the scene in which Lily Briscoe's desire for intimacy with Mrs Ramsay alerts the artist to her model's irreducible presence, Chapter 3 explores an ethics of radical intimacy in Woolf's appropriation of key Post-Impressionist strategies described by Roger Fry. I argue that in translating Lily's painterly, Post-Impressionist experiments into writing, Woolf conceptualised a notion of ethical encounters based on a quest for intimacy as defined by Irigaray in her recent work: a desire to return to a primal mode of sharing the world, of "being-within and being-with" another (*SW* 70), in which intersubjective boundaries briefly dissolve and two individuals feel and perceive as one. However, while Irigaray notably excludes the visual from her ethically productive category of sensory perception, foregrounding instead the erotically charged touch, Woolf's sensual literary ethics emerged directly out of her adaptation of Fry's formalist tenets, and *To the Lighthouse* both validates and prompts interrogation of Irigaray's philosophy in favouring sight rather than touch as the primary medium of a non-possessive and non-objectifying mode of intimacy. Indeed, Woolf locates the ethical quest for intimacy mainly in the visual; the wish to apprehend an unknowable, irreducible other's worldview and share it, as if self and other were one, is bound up in the novel with painterly, formalist textual devices and the process of creating an experimental and distinctly Post-Impressionist artwork.

In Chapter 4, I examine how *The Waves*, Woolf's most abstract and poetic novel, develops central aspects of the pacifist position articulated in *Three Guineas*. While the novel's lyrical, introspective qualities have long been read as evidence of Woolf's detachment from socio-political realities, I propose that *The Waves* offers a forceful, non-violent response to the rise of extreme nationalisms in the time of its composition, a response which proceeds precisely through Woolf's poetic devices, and her reinvention of the soliloquy form in particular. As a lyrical engagement with intimacy and self-reflection on the one hand, and a dramatic performance of vocal utterance and the dynamics of the address on the other, Woolf's monologues become the locus of an anti-nationalist ethics. *Three Guineas* demonstrates Woolf's keen insight into the aggressive patriotism and celebration of violence defining fascism as inevitable outcomes of unreflected action by instinct, and underlines the transformative potential of lyrical introspection and contemplation as pacifist means of resistance. *The Waves*, I argue, should be understood as Woolf's jointly aesthetic and ethical realisation of this mode of resisting fascism, violence and war. I read the novel with Butler's theory of vulnerability as a transhistorically and transnationally shared predicament, showing that Woolf locates ethical relations in the recognition that the boundaries separating individuals as well as nations are contingent and frail. I also draw on Kristeva's theory of the constructive semiotic, Butler's notion of a primary, passive receptivity to sensory impressions, and Adriana Cavarero's philosophy of vocal expression to illuminate an ethics of sensitivity and exposure in Woolf's text. Throughout *The Waves*, heightened sensitivity brings about an intimate blurring of the boundaries separating 'I' and 'you.' By suggesting that we never cease to be formed through such fluid relations with others, the novel develops a non-static model of the subject in which the momentary disintegration of the autonomous 'I' in the presence of another creates a relational self capable of non-conformist, critical thought. In this sense, intimacy emerges in *The Waves* as a precondition for non-violent relations and sustainable peace.

It is high time that we politicise Woolf's modernist writing of interiority. Kristeva's notion of intimate revolt offers the terms for such a re-evaluation: the avant-garde aesthetic which interests Kristeva reconciles intimacy, the return to the pre-subjective through introspection, with the oppositional and political connotations of revolt. We could, then, approach Woolf's poetic writing as an act of revolt which operates not as political action, but as a return – a turning back on the self, exploring one's inner life. This definition of revolt interrogates a distinction between political commitment and the expression of interiority, a distinction which has informed Woolf scholarship for decades, but which her texts continuously undermine. If we consider the centrality of both intimacy and non-violent revolt to her aesthetic experiments, we can begin to see Woolf's privileging of the life of the mind over a realist focus on action and external detail from a new angle, as a political as well as an ethical statement. When Woolf observes the Edwardians' lack of interest in psychological complexity, or when she complains that to read a novel by Arnold Bennett or H. G. Wells one must "do something" – "join a society" or "write a cheque" – she does not dissociate the introspective impulse of formally experimental, early twentieth-century poetic prose from the socio-political realm (*E* 3: 427). What she offers in her own writing is a call for an alternative notion of fiction as a site of engagement. Later, on the brink of a second war, Woolf writes again about political action through joining societies and signing petitions that "some more active method" is needed for expressing the conviction that war "must be stopped at whatever cost" (*TG* 166, 165). *Virginia Woolf and the Ethics of Intimacy* shows that she developed such a method in her poetic exploration of individual psychic life. By unsettling familiar binaries such as active/passive, looking within/looking without, introspective/engaged and poetic/political, Woolf continues to challenge the way we read and make sense of modernist fiction. Her poetic depictions of interiority reveal an ethically and politically committed writer engaged in posing some of the most pressing questions of the inter-war years as well as the twenty-first century: questions around violence and vulnerability, thought and affect, loss and intimacy.

1

Jacob's Room: Modernist Melancholia and the Eclipse of Primal Intimacy

In "Character in Fiction," Woolf describes literary convention as a vehicle for interactive co-creation, "a common meeting-place," "a means of communication between writer and reader" (*E* 3: 431, 434). Towards the end of the essay, she addresses a collective readership: "May I . . . remind you of the duties and responsibilities that are yours as partners in this business of writing books, as companions in the railway carriage, as fellow travellers with Mrs Brown?" (435–36). The writing process, when framed by conventions, is defined as an ethical contract of sorts, a horizontal, democratic site held together by "duties and responsibilities" shared reciprocally by the writer and more than one reader, as if the novelist's text was a public space for communal storytelling. And this idea of a "common meeting-place" is what enables intimate relations even in the necessarily dyadic encounter between a novelist and a reader who will likely never meet:

> Both in life and in literature it is necessary to have some means of bridging the gulf between the hostess and her unknown guest on the one hand, the writer and his unknown reader on the other. . . . The writer must get into touch with his reader by putting before him something which he recognises, which therefore stimulates his imagination, and makes him willing to co-operate in the far more difficult business of intimacy. (431)

That is, a mutual recognition of fictional conventions is considered a precondition for socially binding relationships of which the defining characteristics are intimacy and responsibility.

Woolf's linking of intimacy and storytelling conventions intersects with the key concerns of Walter Benjamin's "The Storyteller: Reflections on the Works of Nikolai Leskov" (1936), an essay which looks back from a present located in the inter-war years to a past time in which storytelling remained an unbroken tradition. Benjamin's storyteller is "a man who has counsel" for his audience, and the capacity to tell is founded on "the ability to exchange experiences" (364, 362). The essay underscores the reciprocal dimension of storytelling: the act of telling is "for others," an exchange where social bonds are created and epistemological and moral certainties, shared by the storyteller, are received collectively. For Benjamin's contemporaries, however, "the communicability of experience is decreasing. In consequence we have no counsel either for ourselves or for others" (3). This decreasing communicability is described as a historical process coextensive with the rise of the modern novel, a process precipitated by the Great War, so that in the post-war years, the storyteller "has already become something remote from us and something that is getting even more distant" (364, 362). For Benjamin, the decline of storytelling brought about by political and literary modernity caused a breakdown of an intimate, communal space. The crisis of communicability described in the essay is held to coincide with a loss of shared truths and values, a loss which entailed a pervasive sense of alienation and isolation. In Benjamin's influential account, the modern novelist is a "solitary individual" who "has isolated himself" and, "himself uncounseled," "cannot counsel others" (364).

The idea of storytelling as a lost art figures also in Woolf's essays of the 1920s which set up a distinction between her post-war contemporaries and earlier generations of writers. In "How It Strikes a Contemporary" (1923), Woolf's phrasing evokes Benjamin's separation of the storyteller and the isolated, modern novelist. In contrast to "the power of [nineteenth-century writers'] belief – their conviction," corroborated by "their judgement of conduct," "our contemporaries afflict us because they have ceased to believe. The most sincere of them will only tell us what it is that happens to himself. . . . They cannot tell stories, because they do not believe that stories are true" (*E* 3: 358–59). And when she rejects Edwardian writing methods in "Character in Fiction," it is because "convention ceases to be a means of communication . . . and becomes instead an obstacle and an impediment." However, in the Georgian writer's optimistic determination to destroy this obstacle to communication and thereby intimacy, there is an insistent sense of something lost: "the sound of breaking and falling, crashing and destruction. It is the prevailing sound of the Georgian age – *rather a melancholy one*" (434, emphasis added).

Insofar as the crisis of intimacy and fictional representation described in these essays is also a crisis of storytelling, Woolf's formulations differ notably from Benjamin's in their arguably melancholic rhetoric of break and rupture. Unlike her late, unfinished essay "Anon" (composed 1940–41), which closely echoes Benjamin's idea of modernity as bringing about a historically gradual loss of pre-modern storytelling, the lost object imagined in her literary journalism of the 1920s is the entire tradition of literary modernity and those very conventions of modern literature through which, in Woolf's account, the intimate, social and moral bonds forged by storytelling remained intact. Her reliance on metaphors of destruction and radical separation is indeed "rather ... melancholy," suggesting, as it does, a conception of the Georgian age as irrevocably distanced from not only Edwardian realist conventions – "For us those conventions are ruin, those tools are death" (*E* 3: 430) – but, effectively, "the very foundations and rules of literary society" (434). "It is an age of fragments," Woolf observes in 1923 about the writing of her contemporaries: "We are sharply cut off from our predecessors" (355, 357).¹ A later essay, "The Leaning Tower" (1940), contrasts this slanting, precarious worldview with the straight, serene edifice structuring past writers' literary conventions: "their model, their vision of human life was not disturbed or agitated or changed by war. Nor were they themselves. It is easy to see why that was so. Wars were then remote" (*E* 6: 261). The essay describes how this "immunity from war" created a line of aesthetic continuity which was broken in 1914, when "suddenly, like a chasm in a smooth road, the war came" (261, 264). Intensely conscious of "things changing, of things falling, of death perhaps about to come," these essays all dramatise the idea of a gulf between the post-war literary climate and an inaccessible community of past writers held together by a spirit of "unabashed tranquillity" (*E* 6: 273; *E* 4: 239). Thus, if Woolf's vibrant literary journalism is fraught with a melancholic insistence on severed bonds and lost intimacy, this rhetoric emerged from her keen sensitivity to the effects of modern warfare and total war on the post-war literary imaginary.

Woolf's imagery of detachment, separation and loss – "of death perhaps about to come" – exemplifies what Robert B. Pippin has described as a specifically modernist "language of anxiety, unease, and mourning" (xii). In "Poetry, Fiction and the Future" (1927), she figures contemporary art as a "narrow bridge" detached from its foundations: "For it is an age clearly when we are not fast anchored where we are; . . . all bonds of union seem broken" (*E* 4: 438, 429). Her idea of a detached, free-floating artistic realm links the simultaneous loss and demolishment of literary "foundations and rules," and of the shared values upholding them, to the Georgians' fragmented aesthetic experiments, in which "Grammar is violated; syntax disintegrated" (*E* 3: 434). Woolf's observations converge with a claim once frequently made about modernist writers, one that is worth revisiting: that their insistence on formal experimentation evinces "dissatisfactions with the affirmative, normative claims essential to European modernization" (Pippin xi), which nonetheless betray nostalgia for a time when literary conventions were firmly grounded in unquestioned religious, moral and epistemological certainties. As a consequence, it was said – not irrelevantly – modernist writing abounds with "images of death and loss and failure" (xii), and forges in this melancholic idiom "a link between the dawning sense of a failure in the social promise of modernisation . . . and the appeal of a radically autonomous, self-defining cult of art" (35).[2]

But what would it have meant for Woolf, in the wake of the Great War, to mourn the confident promises of modernity, with its faith in history as progressing towards universal peace and prosperity? If Pippin's classic, aestheticist account of modernism converges with a no longer dominant critical image of Woolf and Bloomsbury, more recent scholarship has illuminated Woolf's engagement in some of the most vibrant interactions between Bloomsbury's political and aesthetic avant-gardes. Pippin's "problem of historical discontinuity" (10) has engaged politically oriented accounts of the First World War as an event of decisive influence on Woolf's aesthetic practice. Vincent Sherry, for one, reads Woolf's writing of the 1920s as a political response to British war-time politics and, more specifically, the Liberal party's use of public reason to justify Britain's involvement in the war. Addressing Pippin's notion of modernism as a "Culture of Rupture" (Pippin 29), Sherry adopts his view of the war as causing a radical break with Enlightenment values, manifest in the disruptive aesthetics of literary modernism. Sherry considers Woolf's anti-nationalism as central to a group of London modernists' "vanguard awareness" of the war as "a watershed between Enlightenment ideals . . . and their gruesome disillusionment," an awareness that informed these writers' understanding of the post-war period as "a specified Now . . . defined by a sense of itself as separate" (18–19, 17). Christine Froula, however, ascribes a different temporality to Woolf's, and Bloomsbury's, jointly political and aesthetic engagement with the destructive legacy of the war: in speaking of "the Bloomsbury Avant-Garde," Froula highlights the centrality of Enlightenment ideals to Bloomsbury's future-oriented efforts to rebuild European civilisation "on firmer ground and more lastingly," even as the Great War, at the height of modernity, had "destroyed the illusion that Europe was 'on the brink' of an international, economically egalitarian civilization committed to human rights, political autonomy and world peace" (9, 1).

As these alternative accounts indicate, Woolf's conflicted depictions of literary and political modernity cannot be straightforwardly described in terms of aestheticist nostalgia, nor in terms of the uncomplicated alignment of modernism and modernity suggested by the word "avant-garde," with its connotations of futurity and political commitment. What intrigues me here is the undeniable melancholic, retrogressive dimensions of the modernist "now," which, radically and temporally detached from modernity, must trouble political readings of Woolf's modernism, just as the melancholic vocabulary of destruction and irreversible separation surfaces in her otherwise sanguine post-war journalism. As Heather Love puts it in her thought-provoking study of a "backward modernism" (7) which refuses, through negative and politically non-productive affects such as melancholia, to turn its back on the persistence in the present of past violence, "backwardness is a feature of even the most forward-looking modernist literature" (6).

The question of mourning needs attention if we are to make sense of Woolf's ambivalent treatment of modernity as a historical trajectory entailing unprecedented violence, destruction and ruin, and yet, at the same time, enabling literary-political interventions against violence and war. While Woolf's melancholic register cannot be easily translated into Pippin's nostalgic aestheticism, it suggests that aspects of modernity have been lost and must be mourned by the modernist writer. But what exactly are these lost objects – certain epistemological and moral certainties, perhaps, or the possibility of their sharing? And what literary features attest to their mourning? We can only attempt to answer these questions, since we seem to be examining textual symptoms not of regular mourning, which is conscious and knowing, but of melancholia as defined in another post-war essay, Freud's "Mourning and Melancholia" (1917): "an object-loss which is withdrawn from consciousness," in which "one [patient or analyst; here, writer or reader] cannot see clearly what it is that has been lost" (245). Can we speak, in a psychoanalytic register, of an affective ambivalence by which the simultaneously loved and hated lost object is introjected as it were, unconsciously made part of, yet in grating conflict with, the writer's worldview and values, so that the reader's role is not that of the analyst, but of the cultural decipherer seeking to trace an ethical struggle in those melancholic textual features which would seem to indicate moral nihilism and socio-political withdrawal? These questions take us back to the problematic of intimacy and storytelling with which we began, and back from politics to the realm of ethics, via *Jacob's Room* (1922), Woolf's first novel to enact a definitive, and arguably melancholic, break with "the very foundations and rules of literary society" (*E* 3: 434).

Jacob's Room engages in complex ways with the impact of the Great War on the modernist literary imaginary. As numerous critics have observed, the novel's thematic concern with alienation, mourning and loss is reflected in its disruptive, fragmentary form. The broken narrative continuity of Woolf's first genuinely experimental novel, it has been argued, attests to a reflected engagement with the post-war legacy of loss and mourning.³ That is to say, the break with representational conventions is in itself depicted as a loss: formal innovation is configured as inherently melancholic. In *Jacob's Room*, expressions of mourning are simultaneously expressions of a pervasive crisis of storytelling. The elusive protagonist is lost and mourned from the novel's first pages: "'Ja–cob! Ja–cob!' shouted Archer, lagging on after a second. The voice had an extraordinary sadness" (4). This cry, reverberating throughout the text in the voices of various characters, conveys the tone of "extraordinary sadness" colouring a narrative in which loss has at least two aspects: Jacob Flanders, the young protagonist eventually lost in the war,⁴ is also a story lost to Woolf's narrator and readers. In constantly drawing attention to the narrator's failed efforts to access and represent "Jacob's room," a phrase which evokes the protagonist's interiority as well as his actual lodgings, the novel problematises the inefficacy of narrative description, omniscience and continuity in a post-war world.

My reading of *Jacob's Room* will depart from an earlier, poststructuralist critical tradition, which tended to emphasise Woolf's politically motivated rejection of realist novel conventions, and her exposure of their complicity with British militarism and patriotism. Thus, for William R. Handley, Woolf developed in *Jacob's Room* a fragmented, anti-realist fictional mode aimed at dismantling the nationalistic and patriarchal cultural narratives which fuel militarisation and war: "Woolf's subversion of narrative order" was "an act of aesthetic and political rebellion against hegemonic control as defined and practiced in both art and life" (113).⁵ In such accounts of Woolf's subversion of realist methods as a sign of her political commitment, there is little consideration of her persistent notion of a *loss* of literary conventions after the war. They leave two questions in particular largely unaddressed: if the novel's mournful expression implies a radical severing of bonds not only with nineteenth- and early twentieth-century realism, but with modernity's entire literary legacy, can its formal, arguably melancholic, fragmentation be said to inspire ethically responsible writing when, as we have seen, Woolf's contemporaneous essays describe a pervasive crisis in the capacity of post-war fiction to cultivate norms and values? And doesn't the ambivalent introjection characteristic of melancholia suggest an ethical interrogation of the modern novel's complicity with warmongering ideals (rather than a straightforward, political blaming of the realists)? I propose an affirmative answer to these questions, and an approach which will explore the melancholic poetics of *Jacob's Room* as the locus where Woolf's non-violent ethics and politics converge.

If Woolf has mourning of the war dead coincide with the loss of storytelling and novel conventions, joining thereby "the loss of a loved person" with "the loss of some abstraction" (Freud, "Mourning and Melancholia" 243), then this cluster engenders further and more obscure aspects of loss, all of which involve multiple forms of intimacy. The fraught relationship between the novel's descriptive title and a story eluding definition captures a pervasive concern with a constant slippage between lived experience and a language marked by diminished referential capacity. Considering the inefficacy of the letter form in the early twentieth century, the narrator reflects how modern letters are mere "phantom[s] of ourselves"; "speech attempted," in which only feeble traces of personality are retained: "The hand in them is scarcely perceptible, let alone the voice or the scowl" (*JR* 79). This passage stands in contrast to the sort of letter writing opening the novel, where Betty Flanders's tears merge with the ink of her written words: "Slowly welling from the point of her gold nib, pale blue ink dissolved the full stop; for there her pen stuck; her eyes fixed, and tears slowly filled them" (3). In the post-war years, the narrator seems to say, the possibility of such intimate channelling of affective states through writing "proceeding from . . . one's inmost self" ("intimate, *adj.* and *n.*," def. A.2) has been lost.[6] The problem of obstructed self-expression is also one of communication, in which scribbles on a page must fail to affect their recipients, that is, "To have an effect on the mind or feelings of (a person); to impress or influence emotionally; to move, touch" ("affect, *v.*²," def. 2.a):

> For centuries the writing-desk has contained sheets fit precisely for the communications of friends. Masters of language, poets of long ages, have . . . addressed themselves to the task of reaching, touching, penetrating the individual heart. Were it possible! But words have been used too often; touch and turned, and left exposed to the dust of the street. (*JR* 80)

This reflection surfaces in *Jacob's Room* as a more general grappling with the limits of written representation as a vehicle for creating intimacy. Letter writing functions in the novel as a figure for literary expression, in which the writer's dyadic address to the reader emulates an individual's intimate communication of thoughts, feelings and perceptions to another. However, the text insists on a Benjaminian correlation between broken communication, isolation and a foreclosure of intimacy. The conversations, scenes and relationships composing *Jacob's Room* are relentlessly fragmented or interrupted, not least by the narrator, who flaunts her position as a failed storyteller through an affective short-circuiting of dyadic communication in passages such as the cerebral reflection on letters, which, framed as a letter writer's address ("Let us consider letters . . ." [79]), breaks up one of the most overtly erotic sequences in the novel at the point of Jacob's sexual intercourse with Florinda, thereby foreclosing the reader's affective investment in the story.

But what lost forms of intimacy and storytelling are actually mourned by such literary treatment? Considered in the light of Woolf's post-war literary journalism, her modernist breakthrough in *Jacob's Room* would seem to be primarily concerned with the loss of an art form and its affective structures, whether those of letter writing or the novel, or, more radically, the loss of the intimate bonds enabled by written communication at large. However, this loss seems to imply another: the ghostly whispers of the disembodied, phantom letter writer – "speech attempted," in which "the voice" is "scarcely perceptible" – betray the loss of an affectively resonant vocal expression expelled by the modern novel. If Woolf speaks of a centuries-long usage of the writing-desk for the fundamentally impossible task of creating intimacy by means of the letter form, her first quintessentially modernist novel enacts Benjamin's later insight into vocal storytelling as an art eclipsed by two seemingly unrelated landmarks of modernity: the First World War and the rise of the modern novel. "Was it not noticeable at the end of the war that men returned from the battlefield grown silent – not richer, but poorer in communicable experience?" Benjamin asks, and goes on to locate the beginnings of this communicational crisis in the ascendant novel form, which "gradually removed narrative from the realm of living speech": "The birthplace of the novel is the solitary individual" (362, 364). If the narrator of *Jacob's Room* emerges as a Benjaminian, ghostly letter writer who mourns the loss of aural storytelling, conceived as an intimate, collective sharing of lived experience, this figure also anticipates Woolf's unfinished essays "Anon" and "The Reader."[7] Conceived in the midst of intense air raids on London in September 1940, these essays outline how the pre-modern cultural performances of Anon – the "common voice singing out of doors" – were increasingly marginalised with the rise of modern civilisation. While "Every body shared in the emotion of Anon's song, and supplied the story," the readers of written text "are at a remove from the thing treated. We are enjoying the spectacle of melancholy, not sharing its anguish" (*E* 6: 582, 581, 601).

To claim, as I do here, that the melancholic aesthetic of *Jacob's Room* figures the intimate transmission of affect enabled by storytelling as the lost origin of modernity is to align this text more with Woolf's late work than with her other writings of the 1920s, and such a reading of the novel out of its immediate context has political as well as ethical consequences. From the 1930s, Woolf came to interrogate political modernity with particular force, denouncing its imperialist and capitalist expansion as a violent and exploitative venture. In her last writings, this interrogation is extended to modern art. I have argued elsewhere that the melancholic textual features of her last novel *Between the Acts* (1941) highlight the complicity of modern literature from the sixteenth century onwards with the political violence she condemns in *Three Guineas*: the novel reveals how the modern privileging of eloquence and stylistic virtuosity brought about the eclipse of pre-modern cultural activity depicted in "Anon," thereby enabling the rise of a new, exceptionally violent civilisation ("Melancholic Translations"). Such insights can be detected as early as in *Jacob's Room*, if we attend to its fragmented narrative as Woolf's idiosyncratic expression of modernist, textual melancholia. The question of intimacy remains central to such a reading because, as I shall argue, Woolf exposes a ubiquitous nexus of intimacy and letters (in the broad sense of written texts and literary culture) as the very site where the complicity of literary modernity with the violence of political modernity becomes apparent. And this exposure emerges in the domain of ethics.

Throughout *Jacob's Room*, modern intimacy is depicted as bound up with the composition and deciphering of written texts. If we return to the narrator's reflection on letters, the practice of writing and reading letters – and, by extension, literature – is described there as a dyadic, intimate exchange in which interiority and affect can be shared by virtue of being put into writing, deciphered and known: "For centuries the writing-desk has contained sheets fit precisely for the communications of friends. Masters of language, poets of long ages, have . . . addressed themselves to the task of reaching, touching, penetrating the individual heart." For Woolf's contemporaries, however, "a doubt insinuates itself: . . . something whispers, Is this all? Can I never know, share, be certain?" These questions, which link the writer's effort to share experience with the attainment of knowledge and certainty, interrogate an established custom of letter composition in which intimacy, knowledge and the written communication of affect are taken to be interrelated and mutually constitutive. Despite its nostalgic guise, this expression of doubt confounds nostalgia in its articulation as a voiceless whisper – by whom? An anonymous letter, perhaps, a "phantom of ourselves, lying on the table," in which "the power of the mind to quit the body is manifest" (*JR* 80, 79–80, 79).

Articulated in the narrator's deliberate language, this doubt comes from an unknown elsewhere, as a manifestation of affectless, disembodied text. As such, it "insinuates itself" as a ghostly, ethical questioning of the narrator's eloquence and the kind of intimacy sought by modernity's "Masters of language": the "reaching, touching, penetrating [of] the individual heart." Apart from its association of intimacy with friendship and love, the trope of the penetrated heart exposes here the violence intrinsic to intimacy as action- and object-driven eros, not so much because of its allusion to sexual penetration, but because of Woolf's figuration, elsewhere, of "the individual heart" as a site of inviolable interiority (80). These lines take us to Lily Briscoe's musings about "the chambers of [Mrs Ramsay's] mind and heart," an interior space figured as "tablets bearing sacred inscriptions, which if one could spell them out would teach one everything" (*TL* 57). This notion of intimacy as an act of deciphering written text prompts Lily's erotically as well as aesthetically charged question: "What *art* was there, known to love or cunning, by which one pressed through into those secret chambers?" (emphasis mine). While the pressure of Lily's hand on Mrs Ramsay's knee spurs the intimate, yet ethically problematic act of pressing through into the loved one's "heart and mind," this interiority ultimately resists intimate reading, as Lily's quest is redirected to another, radically different form of intimacy: "it was not knowledge but unity that she desired, not inscriptions on tablets, nothing that could be written in any language known to men, but intimacy itself."

In this later novel, Woolf would depict a non-violent intimacy located beyond the breach of privacy implied by linguistic mastery, yet within the bounds of eros and a modernist aesthetic. Lily keeps her head on Mrs Ramsay's knee while she imagines intimacy as an extra-textual unity, and it is later, as she paints her Post-Impressionist portrait, that a question makes her recall the intimate scene: "But into what sanctuary had one penetrated?" (56). Woolf's first obviously modernist novel experiment, however, categorically severs erotic and affective object attachments between characters, between the narrator and Jacob – the lost object of her melancholic narrative – and between readers and text. In what follows, I shall argue that this refusal of intimacy as constructed by modernity reveals a quest for a new, non-violent mode of literary intimacy. "Yet letters are venerable," the narrator reflects, "for the journey is a lonely one, and if bound together by notes . . . we went in company, perhaps – who knows?" (*JR* 80). Would this be the company, perhaps, of the railway carriage in "Character in Fiction," this "common meeting-place" framed by a collective readership's "duties and responsibilities" (*E* 3: 431, 435) as fellow travellers and storytellers? If, on one level, the novel's broken narrative voices a nostalgic mourning of the novel form as a site for intimate encounters and the sharing of values, its melancholic dimension also reveals a mourning of archaic, extra-textual forms of intimacy expelled by political and literary modernity, and through this textual melancholia, I propose, Woolf creates an alternative, ethically viable contract between writer and reader.

Matricidal Modernity and the Persistence of Archaic Intimacy

This century's "melancholy turn" in literary and modernist scholarship has brought a productive focus on Woolf's socio-political treatment of loss and mourning. In this critical light, *Jacob's Room* has been considered a "modern elegy" as defined by Jahan Ramazani. Covering elegiac texts from Thomas Hardy and onwards, Ramazani claims that "by becoming anti-elegiac . . . and melancholic," these texts refuse an earlier, predominant notion of literature as a site for successful, or compensatory and consolatory, mourning (xi). In other words, the modern elegy becomes melancholic in a psychoanalytic sense by virtue of defining itself as radically detached from the premises of literary modernity's earlier stages: "it becomes anticonsolatory and anti-encomiastic, anti-Romantic and anti-Victorian, anti-conventional and sometimes even anti-literary" (1–2). Drawing on Ramazani's work, Tammy Clewell detects an "anticonsolatory practice of mourning" (199) in Woolf's inter-war fiction, and while previous scholarship had stressed the cultural, social and political (rather than merely personal) dimensions of Woolf's literary engagement with mourning and loss,[8] Clewell was among the first to read this engagement as a "sustained effort to confront the legacy of the war." In writing her elegiac novels *Jacob's Room* and *To the Lighthouse*, Clewell argues, "Woolf repeatedly sought not to heal wartime wounds but to keep them open" (198; see 198–99).[9] She invokes here a feature central to the modern elegy: a perceived necessity to "question the ethical grounds of recuperative art" (Ramazani 8). As Clewell insightfully puts it, Woolf's novels insist that post-war literature "can no longer responsibly serve the purposes of transcendence, consolation and redemption," since "the symbolic resources capable of offering consolation, ending mourning, and enabling the bereaved to cut their losses were the very same resources that led to the outbreak and legitimation of the Great War" (214, 202).

What Clewell invites us to see is that Woolf's break with modernity's consolatory literary models is not only, or perhaps even primarily, a political act but also an ethical one: successful mourning as psychoanalytically defined – the transposition of affective-libidinal investment from the lost other to a new other-as-object – emerges, in Woolf's writing, as an ethically problematic ideal because its violent reduction of others to replaceable objects sanctions the political violence of modern warfare (198–99). Clewell, then, made a substantial contribution to Woolf studies by bringing earlier, politically oriented readings such as that of William Handley, who addresses the problem that "Jacob has an exchange value in that his life is exchanged for national preservation" (Handley 116), into the realm of ethics.[10] Clewell's intervention has been followed by an expanding body of criticism exploring Woolf's post-war writing of loss and mourning at this juncture of ethics and politics. Madelyn Detloff, in *The Persistence of Modernism* (2009), and Sanja Bahun have offered particularly substantial accounts of Woolf's ethico-political uses of melancholia as a concept-symptom on the level of aesthetic form. Like Clewell, Detloff and Bahun consider Woolf's interrogation of the "dying of death" characterising the twentieth century: the "active denial" and "distinctly modern repression" of death from life (Clewell 201) which Freud addressed in his wartime text "Thoughts for the Times on War and Death" (1915), and which continued to structure compensatory responses to loss in the post-war years.[11] However, both complicate Clewell's notion of an uncompromisingly anti-consolatory melancholia. Detloff points out that Woof, among the modernists, was exceptionally aware that "If redemptive narratives... are suspect for their potential to turn loss into political gain, so too are narratives that refuse categorically the possibility of consolation" (*Persistence* 14).[12] Bahun, on her part, reads Woolf's writing as a modernist "practice of countermourning" (9) – Bahun's term for a historically charged, aesthetic response to the modern denial of death which integrates mourning and melancholia. Countermourning, in Bahun's definition, is a "memorial articulation of loss that is at the same time expressive and critical" because it "aims at 'therapeutic' engagement yet nevertheless utilizes the symptomatology of melancholia, thereby retaining (rather than recalling) the lost object, in all its uncognizability, as an integral part of the text and the reader's experience thereof." As Bahun astutely observes, melancholia, when thus conceived "as both a symptom-cluster and a tool in the cultural practice of countermourning, may have a far more active social function than commonly perceived, and ... modernists were acutely aware of this potential" (8, 8–9, 9).[13]

These ground-breaking accounts of Woolf's melancholic aesthetic as sociopolitically as well as ethically productive – and far removed from the vaguely defined historical escapism so commonly associated with modernist melancholia – inspire my reading of *Jacob's Room* as a melancholic, yet potentially redemptive quest for non-violent modes of literary intimacy and storytelling. In particular, I suggest that the novel retains rather than names or identifies a cluster of lost objects as traces on the level of form, and that this novelistic experiment constitutes an ethical practice because it resists the objectifying logic of substitution which informs literary modernity's ideals of eloquence and linguistic mastery. Bahun's distinction between modernist countermourning and nostalgia is central here: while countermourning exhibits symptoms of melancholia such as "compulsive self-reflexivity, epistemological and affective insecurity, and problematic relation to the 'logocentric' and symbolic processes (including, notably, difficulties in expressing what exactly has been lost)" – all of which pervade Woolf's text – nostalgia is "a mental state oriented toward a recognizable time-place in the past, which does not necessarily impede articulation or cognition" (21–22, 22). These categories enable a useful differentiation between, on the one hand, the explicit nostalgia, as articulated in Woolf's post-war journalism, for literary modernity's favoured modes of storytelling and intimacy, and, on the other, the melancholic textual features of *Jacob's Room*, which betray a loss of more obscure, archaic forms of intimacy and storytelling in a manner reminiscent of Woolf's late writings. Archaic in the double sense of pre-modern and pre-subjective, these constellations surface in the novel as traces of "the world beneath our consciousness . . . to which we can still return" ("Anon," *E* 6: 584). In seeking to examine these traces in terms of their literary and ethical significance, I revisit Julia Kristeva's *Black Sun: Depression and Melancholia* (1989), which offers an exceptionally compelling framework for uncovering the ethical dimensions of Woolf's first distinctly modernist novel.

Kristeva's work provides a theoretical model for understanding literary expressions of melancholia as an impossible mourning of primal intimacy and, as such, it holds particular significance in relation to traces of loss and radical separation in modernist texts.[14] Crucially with regard to *Jacob's Room*, Kristeva interprets signs of melancholia in literary writing as revealing an inability to successfully mourn a primal loss – the infant's separation from the mother – and a subsequent refusal of the linguistic mastery which would compensate for this loss. For Kristeva, linguistic articulation has a compensatory function insofar as "The symbol is established through a negation . . . of the loss" (*BS* 26). When expressing her/himself in words, the subject seems to be saying: "I have lost an essential object that happens to be, in the final analysis, my mother. . . . But no, I have found her again in signs, or rather since I consent to lose her I have not lost her (that is the negation), I can recover her in language" (43). "Upon losing mother and relying on negation," Kristeva writes, "I retrieve her as sign, image, word" (63). For the speaking subject, then, the spoken word becomes a comforting substitute for the lost mother. However, if the act of speaking can be said to negate loss and separation, literary works can disavow negation and, in analogy with depressed persons, "fall back on the real object [the Thing] of their loss, which is just what they do not manage to lose, to which they remain painfully riveted" (43–44). Such denial of negation "would thus be the exercise of an impossible mourning, the setting up of a fundamental sadness" (44). Both processes (negation and its rejection), Kristeva notes, make up the affective structure of any literary work: "Literary creation . . . bears witness to the affect – to sadness as imprint of separation and beginning of the symbol's sway; to joy as imprint of the triumph that settles me in the universe of artifice and symbol" (22). In other words, "if there is no writing other than the amorous, there is no imagination that is not, overtly or secretly, melancholy" (6).[15]

In its uncompromising severing of affective ties and pervasive mournful tone, *Jacob's Room* balances precariously between eros and melancholia. Death, loss and separation haunt the novel from the outset: Betty Flanders evokes her dead husband; Archer, unable to find his brother on the beach, cries out "Ja–cob! Ja–cob!" with "extraordinary sadness" (*JR* 4); and Jacob himself cannot reach the rock he takes to be his nanny, is "lost" and runs away sobbing with a skull in his arms (5). The intimate sphere created by the mother putting her sons to bed is as frail as the aster "trembl[ing] violently" next to a child's bucket in the garden; the storm at sea shakes the foundations of the lodging house with its "eternal conspiracy of hush and clean bottles" (7, 9), a phrase repeated twice as if the words themselves could form a protective shield against the destructive forces outside. The phrase upholds a negation of those forces, as do the soothing words Betty Flanders murmurs to ensure her children of the safety and inviolability of the nursery (7). However, this scene of intimacy is disrupted by an abrupt shift to a hyper-detached focalising perspective recalling the "Time Passes" section of Woolf's "elegy" *To the Lighthouse*,[16] a pattern recurring throughout the text: "For the wind was tearing across the coast. . . . And rolling dark waves before it, it raced over the Atlantic. . . . the aster was beaten [by the rain] to the earth" (8–9). It is as if vocal-linguistic utterance can only be either a melancholic expression of loss without a clear object (Archer's cry), or an ineffective effort to protect against loss, separation and destruction (his mother's words). From beginning to end, a persistent textual melancholia manifests itself, while its origin and objects remain as enigmatic to Woolf's reader as to her ghost-like narrator: "the little bays with the waves breaking unseen by any one make one remember the overpowering sorrow. And what can this sorrow be?" (40). In this, the novel's melancholic poetic features and their inability to negate or compensate for loss convey what Kristeva calls "sadness as imprint of separation"; the text itself seems "painfully riveted" to a cluster of objects including, as we shall see, objects so obscure and primal that they suggest Kristeva's "Thing." And like Kristeva's *Black Sun*, we shall note shortly, the melancholic narrative of *Jacob's Room* exhibits traces of an underlying, non-violent ethics.

In her capacity as psychoanalyst, Kristeva can establish that what has been lost is the mother-as-object, and that "Matricide is our vital necessity"; that is, the primary, violent act of expelling the mother as the origin of our being is necessary for our formation as autonomous individuals capable of erotic and intimate relations with others (*BS* 27; see 27–29). This act is one of representation – "The wager of conveyability [in Western metaphysics] is also a wager that the primal object can be mastered . . . by means of a torrent of signs" – which, Kristeva suggests, amounts to a form of ethical violence whereby to convey the lost mother is "to betray her, transpose her, be free of her" (67). However, she also speculates that it is ultimately not a cognisable object that has been lost, but a primal, archaic and unique "Thing" that, in melancholic (literary) expression, resists conveyance, translation, or violent betrayal through linguistic substitution (13; see 47–48, 64). As a psychoanalytic work, then, *Black Sun* adopts this field's dominant ideal of "'normal,' 'healthy,' or 'successful' mourning" (Ramazani 28), but it also resonates with modernist expressions and contemporaneous psychoanalytic accounts of melancholia, which, as Bahun has shown, contain rich ethical potential: as an experience of loss which defies articulation, melancholia in the entwined discourses of modernism and psychoanalysis "permanently questions the ego's self-sufficiency" and "powerfully testifies to the unappropriability of certain objects" (38).[17] Ewa Ziarek has argued convincingly that Kristeva's theory of melancholia evinces, or rather prepares the ground for, an ethics of psychoanalysis that would productively complement Levinas's philosophy of alterity and non-violence (70–75). Kristeva's account of matricide and maternal alterity, Ziarek claims, offers compelling insights into the violence inherent in Western metaphysics with its ideals of linguistic mastery and autonomous subjectivity. Such a potential ethics of psychoanalysis would necessitate a Levinasian focal shift from the ontological priority of the subject to the ethical primacy of the other, a shift already achieved in the melancholic state of being overwhelmed by an internalised, irreplaceable other (74–75).

If we follow Ziarek's illuminating reading of Kristeva, the ethical substratum of *Black Sun* revolves around a politically productive conception of melancholia as a refusal of matricide, the very first negation of loss which enables not only later, ethically violent modes of compensatory mourning but also (and here I venture beyond Ziarek) representational practices sustaining erotic and intimate object attachments, which tend to inscribe the lost other in an economy of exchangeability and replaceability. Notably, for Kristeva, the loss of the "Thing" is experienced as grief over "the disappearance of that essential being" (*BS* 5), that is, of an archaic mode of primary intimacy: the fusional union with the mother which precedes the subject's formation in the symbolic order of linguistic and social contracts, and which both enables (through linguistic mastery) and disrupts (in the case of melancholia) later intimate relations in the subject-object economy. Thus conceived, melancholia in literary texts arguably emerges as symptom-traces revealing an impossible mourning of intimacy as extra-linguistic presence, continuity and plenitude. In the melancholic refusal to substitute the latter mode of intimacy for the former, we can detect a critique, similar to that levelled by Jacques Derrida in "By Force of Mourning" (1996), of an ingrained tendency to transform the lost other into an object for the autonomous subject of Western philosophy and psychoanalysis. Clewell applies Derrida's insights into melancholic mourning as "the condition for our ethical orientation in the world" (Clewell 207) to Woolf's elegiac, fictional refusal of a wartime and post-war economy in which compensatory mourning and political aggression are mutually constitutive. Building on Clewell's work, I see this refusal as a radical exploration of primal intimacy, the Kristevan lost Thing, to which literary writing must remain riveted if it is to account for its historical complicity with ethically violent economies of intimacy and affect.

While the first chapter of *Jacob's Room* highlights the incapacity of spoken language to maintain a primordial intimacy between mother and child that would protect against loss and separation, its ethico-political implications emerge in a later scene at the close of Chapter 12, which echoes and returns, melancholically as it were, to the focal shifts at the end of Chapter 1 from the spirit-lamp burning feebly by the baby's cot to the hurricane "rolling dark waves before it," and back to the lodging house where "the garden went out. It was but a dark patch" (*JR* 8, 9). The later episode similarly enacts the disruption and eclipse of a scene of intimacy, between Jacob and Sandra Wentworth Williams at the Acropolis, by the narrator's ghostly voice: "Now one after another lights were extinguished. Now great towns – Paris – Constantinople – London – were black as strewn rocks. . . . the wind was rolling the darkness through the streets of Athens" (140–42). These poetic allusions to Foreign Secretary Edward Grey's famous remark on 3 August 1914, that "The lamps are going out all over Europe," foreshadow the outbreak of war depicted in Chapter 13,[18] which ends with further intensification of the poetic imagery – "Darkness drops like a knife over

Greece" – in a swift return from Greece and eros back to Cornwall, the site of primal loss, where the muted sound of guns wakes Betty Flanders (*JR* 154). For all its anticipatory foreshadowing, then, the repeated, politically charged images of a destructive force ushering in a dark age establish an immobile, melancholic temporality as defined by Kristeva: "[time] does not pass by, the before/after notion does not rule it, does not direct it from a past towards a goal. . . . an overinflated, hyperbolic past fills all dimensions of psychic continuity" (*BS* 60). In its compulsive iteration of the first chapter's eclipse of intimacy, the Acropolis episode returns to this scene, creating a frozen temporal horizon in which two events, the negation of primal separation (manifest in the mother's ineffective words of comfort) and the first full-scale manifestation of modern warfare, occur as in a continuum, as if the first somehow entailed the other. Woolf's technique here does not only achieve a melancholic break with modernity's melioristic belief in individual and historical progress (from primal dependency to autonomous subjectivity, from violence and barbarism to peace and enlightenment); it also conjures the loss of primal intimacy as the disavowed beyond of British and European modernity. The tenacious return from the Acropolis to the mother figure lays bare the historical moment in which "Darkness drops like a knife over Greece." As Angeliki Spiropoulou (62, 72) and Theodore Koulouris (10, 124) observe, Woolf interrogates persistently the "Greek" foundation of European civilisation and British imperialism, a particular Hellenist tradition centred on the values of classical Athens as a source of "sweetness and light" (Koulouris 49), and exposes its function as the cultural currency enabling the First World War. Koulouris writes:

> In its role as the originary cultural, political and intellectual designation of western literary imagination and philosophical thought, Greek constitutes for Woolf . . . a beacon which stands not only for the finest and most illustrious achievements of the British Empire, but also as (sic) a ghost, a "specter," which has helped promote and legitimise the ills and barbarism of twentieth-century European history. (10)[19]

In these passages from *Jacob's Room*, a more ancient spectre, the "Thing" eclipsed by modernity's literary, philosophical and political paradigms, undermines these paradigms' foundational status and reveals their inherent violence.[20]

Woolf's insights into modernity's unprecedented capacity for violence emerge even more forcefully through a dramatic reversal in the novel's chiaroscuro as the raging wind originating in Athens reaches its destination: the City of London's financial centre. While her depiction of the impending war as a double eclipse (of primal intimacy and the telos of enlightenment) entails a transition from light to darkness, a striking passage at the end of Chapter 12 figures the summer 1914 – "The height of the season"; "The height of civilization" (*JR* 144) – as the return of light and colour following a solar eclipse:

> But colour returns; runs up the stalks of the grass; blows out into tulips and crocuses. . . . The Bank of England emerges. . . . Sunlight strikes in . . . upon all the jolly trappings of the day; the bright, inquisitive, armoured, resplendent, summer's day, which has long since vanquished chaos; which has dried the melancholy medieval mists; drained the swamp and stood glass and stone upon it; and equipped our brains and bodies with such an armoury of weapons that merely to see the flash and thrust of limbs engaged in the conduct of daily life is better than the old pageant of armies drawn out in battle array upon the plain. (143)

This blending of prismatic colour and solar light differs conspicuously from Woolf's later depiction of a solar eclipse and its aftermath in "The Sun and the Fish" (1928), where, as Jane Goldman has demonstrated, the eclipse of the solar, masculine enlightenment subject and return of resplendent colour bring a compelling vision of feminist counter-enlightenment (*Feminist Aesthetics* 13–106). As during a pro-war demonstration on 4 August 1914, the day of Britain's declaration of war on Germany, the sun with its connotations of armament and militarisation in this composedly ironic passage is "almost too hot" (*JR* 150). And in analogy with the demonstrators "testifying to their faith, singing lustily," the weaponised "conduct of daily life" in the pre-war modern metropolis materialises out of a nexus comprising erotic instincts and global capitalism (this is the moment before dawn):

> People still murmur over the last word said on the staircase. . . . So when the wind roams through a forest innumerable twigs stir; hives are brushed; insects sway on grass blades; the spider runs rapidly up a crease in the bark; and the whole air is tremulous with breathing; elastic with filaments.
>
> Only here – in Lombard Street and Fetter Lane and Bedford Square – each insect carries a globe of the world in his head, and the webs of the forest are schemes evolved for the smooth conduct of business; and honey is treasure of one sort and another; and the stir in the air is the indescribable agitation of life. . . . There is a whir of wings as the suburban trains rush into the terminus. (143)

The filaments composing the interwoven spider and business webs suggest the nets of modernity as theorised by Maud Ellmann: the "networks of circulation and exchange"; "the webs of communication, commodities, and capital" (4, 2) through which the modern(ist) subject is precariously constituted, and thereby irrevocably severed from primal intimacy. These are also the webs of eros and linguistic mastery, so that in modernist writing, "it is absence that gives rise to ramifying networks in which language, money, and libido circulate"; "what is forfeited to circulation never returns, . . . the modernist wanderer is destined for dissemination rather than return" (5–6, 8–9).

However, while, for Ellmann, the loss of primal intimacy can only be articulated in modernist texts as a form of memorialising nostalgia,[21] the quiet textual melancholia of *Jacob's Room* interrogates the very course of the modern(ist) subject's inevitable entanglement, or entrapment, in modernity's nets. In the passages above, the resilient processes of inspiration, weaving and inventiveness, suggestive of literary as well as economic and technological productivity, sustain central tenets of modernity such as the "'demystification' of life" and faith in the civilisational benefits of a free market economy (Pippin 4). And yet, the transition from primary intimacy to libidinal relations also emerges as a particular constellation of eros, capitalism and modern warfare, in which erotic instincts or life drives, whether directly sexual or pertaining to intimate ties in a broader sense, do *not* "seek to preserve and unite" in Freud's sense of furthering the development of civilisation and operating against war ("Why War?" 356; see 359; see *Civilization and Its Discontents* 313).[22] Woolf's depiction of "the indescribable agitation of life" echoes two earlier sentences: "It is thus that we live, they say, driven by an unseizable force. They say that the novelists never catch it; that it goes hurtling through their nets and leaves them torn to ribbons" (*JR* 137). This "unseizable force," which threatens to tear apart not only the weave of the modernist novel but presumably also the filaments of modern civilisation, cannot be neatly conceptualised in terms of the primal aggressive instinct theorised contemporaneously by Freud and Klein. It seems more closely aligned with eros as the civilisational instinct composing the very fabric of modernity's webs, and as such, it carries within it the seeds of violence and (self-)destruction: "These actions [of young men willingly giving up their lives in war], together with the incessant commerce of banks, laboratories, chancellories, and houses of business, are the strokes which oar the world forward, they say" (136).[23]

Throughout the novel, the modern nets of capitalism and eros are epitomised by the world of letters, written texts and literary culture, for which, as we have seen, epistolary correspondence figures as a recurring metonym: "stamped now with English stamps, again with Colonial stamps . . . the post was about to scatter a myriad messages over the world" (*JR* 109). In their "task of reaching, touching, penetrating the individual heart" through an intimate communication of interiority to another, modernity's "Masters of language," writers of letters as well as literature, perpetuate a "habit of profuse communication" which is exposed as both ineffective and potentially violent (80, 109). Enrolled in the flow of language and capital, modern letters are shown to sustain an economy of substitution analogous to a Cambridge professor's volubility, which makes "the soul itself sli[p] through the lips in thin silver disks which dissolve in young men's minds like silver" (32). Here, letters in the sense of "the reading and study of written texts" as a scholarly practice, "the academic or literary world" ("letter, *n.¹*," def. 5.a), play a central role in turning interiority and indeed knowledge into digestible commodities, a practice which, as Rachel Hollander observes, forms a central target of Woolf's much discussed critique of the British university system as "an elitist male institution that leads to war" (64; see 55–56).

This economy precludes intimacy, ingeniously conceived as "a sort of spiritual suppleness, when mind prints upon mind indelibly" (*JR* 37). Intimacy by this definition would seem to imply two individuals' mutual capacity to affect one another, "To have an effect on the mind or feelings of (a person); to impress or influence . . . to move, touch" ("affect, *v.²*," def. 2.a), as if the one mind was the page ready to receive the imprint or impression of another. The printing metaphor is crucial in its designation of print technology as a precondition for modern intimacy, but also in its allusion to an archaic dynamic of impression and receptivity predating the mediation of the printed book, and the modern, literary construction of interpersonal intimacy as a currency or medium of exchange, in which interiority and affect are translated into textual entities to be deciphered and circulated as commodities. Woolf's beautiful image of a mind open, like a page of a book, to the imprint of another's story (of past experiences, thoughts, perceptions and emotions) differs notably from Lily Briscoe's idea of intimacy as an intrusive, erotically as well as aesthetically charged determination to decipher text inscribed in the "secret chambers" of the loved one's "mind and heart." Read alongside her metaphor of mind printing upon mind, Woolf's figuration of inviolable, untranslatable interiority as "tablets bearing sacred inscriptions" (*TL* 57) evokes a pre-modern opacity by which intimacy consists not in lucid penetration, but in a readiness to receive the inscrutable imprint of a life story as part of one's own. This "spiritual suppleness," which arises between Jacob and his interlocutor when their speech signifies as vocal sound rather than semantic content – "the words were inaudible" (*JR* 37) – suggests a Benjaminian notion of intimacy as the aural sharing of lived experience, one that Woolf would theorise later as the intimate transmission of affect enabled by Anon's song, but eclipsed with the circulation of print texts.

"Pure from all Body, Pure from all Passion": Non-Violence and the Imprint of Primal Sadness

If *Jacob's Room* interrogates the modern nexus of intimacy, letters and the medium of print as the locus where ethical violence as a specifically literary phenomenon converges with the violent outcomes of global capitalism and militarisation, the text also voices a yearning to extricate the novel from these webs. Later, in the midst of a second world war, Woolf would write: "It was the printing press that finally was to kill Anon. But it was the press also that preserved him" (*E* 6: 583). In the print text, she holds, we can "hear the voice of Anon murmuring still," the pre-modern storyteller's "wandering voice" surfacing as "the world beneath our consciousness . . . to which we can still return" (583, 591, 584). *Jacob's Room* displays an extraordinary use of print letters[24] as the privileged means by which to recover those archaic modes of intimacy and storytelling which are inscribed,[25] in the text's melancholic imaginary, as modernity's lost and inaudible origins. In this, the novel's inquiry into the ethical dimensions of literary intimacy anticipates Woolf's reflection, in a letter to her friend and lover Vita Sackville-West, about the proofs of her novel *Passenger to Teheran* (1926):

> Indeed, it is odd that now, having read this, I have picked up a good many things I had missed in private life. What are they, I wonder, the very intimate things, one says in print? There's a whole family of them. Its (sic) the proof, to me, of being a writer, that one expresses them in print only. (*L* 3: 291)

In writing *Jacob's Room*, Woolf demonstrated how the process of composing and reading print text can mourn, recover and create intimate modes which could not be conceived in intimate exchanges outside of the world of print.[26] One such mode emerges just after the image of a mind receiving the imprint of another:

> Simeon said nothing. Jacob remained standing. But intimacy – the room was full of it, still, deep, like a pool. Without need of movement or speech it rose softly and washed over everything, mollifying, kindling, and coating the mind with the lustre of pearl. (*JR* 37)

In Hollander's reading via Irigaray's effort to bring eros into the sphere of a Levinasian ethics, this passage resembles the orgasmic depiction of Clarissa

Dalloway's attraction to women in *Mrs Dalloway* (*MD* 27), and its androgynous sexual imagery (the female pool combined with the pearl colour of semen) suggests a non-appropriative, extra-linguistic expression of same-sex desire (Hollander 58–60). For all their erotic vibrancy, however, these lines strike me as genuinely innovational in how they depict intimacy as a libidinally charged atmosphere which precedes and exists independently of any erotic attachment. While Clarissa is overcome by an erupting wave of rapture, the atmosphere pervading a room like a gently rising wave is not unlike the free-floating "emotion of Anon's song," in which "Every body shared" to collectively "suppl[y] the story" (*E* 6: 581). "Without need of movement or speech," it exceeds the action- and language-driven reach of eros altogether to become "nothing that could be written in any language known to men, but intimacy itself" (*TL* 57). In its capacity to soothe and pacify ("mollifying") as well as excite and arouse ("kindling"), intimacy, conceived as an atmosphere, operates in "the enigmatic realm of *affects*" as defined by Kristeva: "moods are *inscriptions*" (*BS* 21, 22), the psychic representation of "archaic *energy signal[s]*" which alternatively sustains and dismantles semiotic and symbolic expression, and to which literary creation "bears witness" (21, 22). The literary transposition of affect "into rhythms, signs, forms" constitutes "the communicable imprints of an affective reality, perceptible to the reader (I like this book because it conveys sadness, anguish, or joy) and yet dominated, set aside, vanquished" (22). As Woolf put it in "The Reader," the second unfinished chapter of the book on English literature's history that was to open with "Anon," readers of print text "are at a remove from the thing treated. We are enjoying the spectacle of melancholy, not sharing its anguish" (*E* 6: 601).[27] And yet, in *Jacob's Room*, she explored the unique potential of print to create an atmosphere of intimacy through which affective imprints, "vanquished" through modernity's literary eloquence, might impress themselves, and act ethically, upon the reader.

From the first pages, the novel steeps the reader in an atmosphere pervaded by sadness, a pre-linguistic affect which, "dominated, set aside" (*BS* 22) by the text's poetic virtuosity, nonetheless disturbs this virtuosity through the eruption of primal, mournful cries and the obdurate presence of primeval landscapes. Gillian Beer has studied Woolf's exploration of a particular, modernist and psychoanalytic "analogy between ontogeny (individual development) and phylogeny (species development)," by which literary modernism and Freudian psychoanalysis imagined the unconscious "in the guise of the primeval" (Beer 6). And if Freud and Woolf both insisted on "the survival of what precedes consciousness, precedes history" (Beer 11), in *Jacob's Room*, this endurance materialises through the novel's melancholic expression: "'Ja–cob! Ja–cob!' shouted Archer.... The voice had an extraordinary sadness. Pure from all body, pure from all passion, going out into the world, solitary, unanswered, breaking against rocks – so it sounded" (*JR* 4). Figured as a wave breaking against "one of those ... rocks which emerge from the sand like something primitive" (5) – Jacob is oblivious to his brother's call while climbing one – Archer's naked cry holds the archaic imprints of sadness, a primal affect surging in the "noncommunicable grief" of melancholia (*BS* 3), which disintegrates the libidinal bonds sustained through intense emotions and impulses in the subject-object economy; the voice appears "pure from all passion," that is, from "any strong, controlling, or overpowering emotion, as desire, hate, fear etc." ("passion, *n*.," def. 6.a).

As such, the same cry – "Ja–cob! Ja–cob!" – intersects the narrative as one of the "recurring, obsessive litanies" characterising melancholic expression (*BS* 33). Unprotected from primal sadness, Kristeva's melancholic is "unable to find a valid compensation for the loss" (5). The cry for Jacob is voiced through Bonamy, left at the end with his friend's letters in an empty room, and silently, through Clara Durrant before Jacob's enlistment, where it pierces Mr Bowley's words of substitution: "Bonamy, Jacob – which young fellow was it?" (*JR* 146). Thus invoked, Jacob seems to activate the melancholic process by which new losses revive the original loss: "The linguistic signifier, which was a seeming, is then swept away by the disturbances like a sea wall by ocean breakers" (*BS* 64). In its excessive vocality, manifest on the page in its first iteration through the defamiliarising, splitting dash, the cry fails to semantically designate one particular lost object.[28] Instead, like Kristeva's reflections under her heading "Sadness Holds Back Hatred," it emits ethical overtones of a Levinasian kind:

> My sadness affect is the ultimate yet *mute* witness to my having, in spite of all, lost the archaic Thing of omnipotent ascendancy. That sadness is the final filter of aggressiveness ... not because of simple moral or superego decency, but because in sadness the self is yet joined with the other, it carries it within.... Sadness would thus be the negative of omnipotence, the first and primary indication that the other is getting away from me. (*BS* 64)

Suggestive of such pervasive sadness, the image of waves breaking against rocks is persistently repeated to create a text melancholically "ruled by primary processes" such as displacement, condensation and "vocal and gestural rhythms" (65). Herein lies its ethical force: while it exemplifies condensation both in a figurative and psychoanalytic sense, this image resists the metaphoric logic of displacement or substitution partly, through simile ("Like the blunt tooth of some monster, a rock broke the surface," *JR* 42), or entirely ("And then all night to hear the grinding of the Atlantic upon the rocks," 44).[29]

Such resistance to metaphoric displacement is self-consciously displayed by Woolf's narrator as she reflects on her role as a faltering storyteller in the context of the first modern, global war of its kind and scale: "Often have I seen them – Helen and Jimmy – and likened them to ships adrift, and feared for my own little craft. . . . And now Jimmy feeds crows in Flanders" (*JR* 83). As with Jimmy, whose fate the protagonist shares, the narrator approaches Jacob as a fellow character whose person, life and destiny cannot ethically be sublimated through aesthetic figuration. Instead, her attempts at figuration appear riveted to Jacob's overwhelming presence as, on the one hand, a little-known fellow human and, on the other, an irreplaceable lost other. Narrator and characters are all drawn to Jacob, the novel's elusive object of desire, "like the hawk moth, at the mouth of the cavern of mystery" (61). Woolf's repeated use of the image of the moth conveys this obsessive quest for the protagonist: "If you stand a lantern under a tree every insect in the forest creeps up to it"; "But something is always impelling one to hum vibrating. . . . Yet over him we hang vibrating" (25, 61). However, just as the cry for Jacob rings out "unanswered, breaking against rocks," so the insects drawn to the lantern must "knock their heads against the glass" (4, 25). For Hollander, such realisations of another's persistent opacity evince, throughout Woolf's writing, a non-violent, Levinasian ethics of restraint predicated on a subject's responsibility for the life of the unknowable other (43–45, 47). Dwelling on Woolf's suggestive diary entry about her brother's conversation with a German prisoner of war – "the existence of life in another human being is as difficult to realise as a play of Shakespeare when the book is shut. . . . The reason why it is easy to kill another person must be that one's imagination is too sluggish to conceive what his life means to him" (*D* 1: 186) – Hollander ascribes to both Levinas and Woolf "the view that the imaginative recognition of the infinite possibility represented by another person is incompatible with the ability to kill that person easily" (45). *Jacob's Room* has a strikingly similar image: "Each had his past shut in him like the leaves of a book known to him by heart; and his friends could only read the title" (*JR* 53).

I would add to Hollander's insightful observations that this non-violent ethics of the literary imagination takes shape, in *Jacob's Room*, through the novel's textual melancholia, manifest here in the related images of the mysterious cavern and the inaccessible book. Renouncing the realist narrator's omniscience, Woolf's narrator highlights the incapacity of the post-war novel to intimately transfer the imprint of one mind onto another,[30] and this refusal of literary intimacy betrays losses of an archaic kind. Imagining her storytelling position as that of a moth insensibly drawn to a place which is at once bright (a lantern) and dark (a cavern, and indeed Jacob is later likened to a shadow [*JR* 60]), she appears riveted not primarily to an object of libidinal or emotional attachment, but to the irreducible Thing figured by Kristeva (using Gérard de Nerval's metaphor) as a black sun: "an insistence without presence, a light without representation: the Thing is an imagined sun, bright and black at the same time" (*BS* 13). As a modern storyteller, Woolf's narrator is a melancholic "witness/accomplic[e] of the signifier's flimsiness, the living being's precariousness. . . . At this logical extreme, desire no longer exists. Desire becomes dissolved in a disintegration of transmission and a disintegration of bonds" (20).

How, then, can such melancholic storytelling create an ethics of non-violence? On this point, Judith Butler's philosophy of non-lethal mourning practices offers a compelling complement to Kristeva's theory of melancholia. "The disorientation of grief," Butler writes in *Precarious Life*, "posits the 'I' in the mode of unknowingness" (30). The experience of loss entails an inevitable, melancholic dislocation of the knowing and autonomous subject: my incapacity to know what *in* the other I have lost indicates "the unconscious imprint of my primary sociality," that is, the imprint of the primal ties preceding the separation of self and other (28; see 21–22). Butler ventures that inhabiting grief as a state of dispossession may counteract the ways in which loss, mourning and political aggression tend to fuel one another during wartime, restoring the subject's autonomy and the other's replaceability, and thereby eliminating "our collective responsibility for the physical lives of one another" (30; see 19–49). Like Butler's dispossession, Kristeva's black sun points towards an "archaic attachment" (*BS* 13): the primal intimacy eclipsed by the matricidal formation of the subject as autonomous. It seems to me that the black suns of *Jacob's Room* place Woolf's narrator, but also her reader, in a Butlerian and Kristevan "mode of unknowingness": arrested by the storyteller's inclusive pronouns – "something is always impelling one to hum vibrating"; "over him we hang vibrating" (*JR* 61) – we, too, become the moths irresistibly drawn to the locus which is at once a lantern and a cavern. Positioned as the moth-like recipients of the narrator's fragmented story, we are made receptive to the archaic imprints of another's irreducible presence.[31]

Thus acted upon, are we compelled to resist violence not only in encounters with those we know and love but also in our unwilled, intimate proximity to unknown and unknowable others? Potentially, insofar as we remain disoriented by the narrator's melancholic expression. According to Butler, grief "challenge[s] the very notion of ourselves as autonomous and in control. I might try to tell a story here about what I am feeling, but it would have to be a story in which the very 'I' who seeks to tell is stopped in the midst of telling. . . . My narrative falters, as it must" (*PL* 23). As Handley observes, Woolf's narrator rejects a "traditional and self-blinding notion of absolute individual autonomy" (112) habitually maintained in fiction through an omniscient narrator's mastery over an unbroken narrative, a form of mastery which is shown, throughout the novel, to serve the patriarchal and nationalistic ends of British war-time politics. But if Woolf's rejection of narrative omniscience and coherence can be seen as a political "rebellion" against militarisation and war-time nationalism (Handley 113), then the melancholic language in which this rejection is expressed raises an ethical imperative whose significance exceeds the early twentieth-century context. Like Butler's dispossessed subject, the narrator of *Jacob's Room* is consistently "stopped in the midst of telling" and challenges, thereby, the ideal of subjective autonomy sustaining not only realist writing[32] but also, more pervasively, the very fabric of modern letters.

The novel's fractured, melancholic storytelling practice amounts to more than a dislocation of subjective autonomy, however, particularly in how it interrogates the collective and ontological dimensions of affect-laden enunciation. Under her heading "Sadness Holds Back Hatred," Kristeva notes that the oceanic "surge of affect and primary semiotic processes comes into conflict, in depressive persons, with the linguistic armour . . . as well as with symbolic constructs (apprenticeships, ideologies, beliefs)" (*BS* 64–65). Such a conflict is embodied by the isolated, hyper-detached narrator of *Jacob's Room*: a "lucid observe[r]" condemned to "banishment, absence, void" (*BS* 54, 7). "Absent from other people's meaning," Kristeva explains, the melancholic subject attains a state of "supreme metaphysical lucidity" characterised by "the arrogant feeling of being witness to the meaninglessness of Being, of revealing the absurdity of bonds and beings" (4). By categorically positioning herself outside the novel's groups of characters, Woolf's narrator disrupts all manifestations of "bonds and beings," of ontologically grounded social ties between individuals. "Dods Hill dominated the village. No words can exaggerate the importance of Dods Hill," she remarks ironically (*JR* 11), thereby stressing her distance from the village community. Stealing into the village church by night, the narrator finds it empty, and yet it "seems full of people," echoing with the sound of five hundred years' unbroken ceremonies: "Their tongues join together in syllabling the sharp-cut words. . . . Plaint and belief and elegy, despair and triumph" (116). For the congregation, the collective enunciation of the ceremonial words reinforces not only the bonds of faith on which the community is based but also its ontological foundation: the individual members' joint articulation of passionate emotion. The narrator, however, typifies the modernist artist as melancholic: "This gloom, this surrender to the dark waters which lap us about, is a modern invention. Perhaps . . . we do not believe enough" (121). Refusing to subscribe to the characters' various symbolic, libidinal conventions,[33] Woolf's narrator resembles Kristeva's "radical, sullen atheist" who, like the melancholic modernist storyteller, is "deprived of meanings, deprived of values" and therefore unable to escape perpetual isolation (*BS* 5, 14).[34]

Might the narrator's refusal of "bonds and beings" amount to more than metaphysical or moral nihilism? Perhaps, if viewed through the lens of Ziarek's analogy between the melancholic's supreme lucidity and Kristeva's insights into the necessity of matricide as a precondition for autonomous subjectivity, both of which, Ziarek argues, can alert us to the violence pervading Western metaphysics (73, 75). If the melancholic is in some ways a lucid philosopher, then Kristeva herself emerges as "a philosopher of ethics on the scale with Levinas. And her diagnosis of 'the lack of meaning of Being' would issue a profound critique of ontology in order to establish ethics as the first philosophy" (Ziarek 71). Isn't this how we should understand the narrator's hyper-detachment and lucid exposure, discussed above, of modernity's nets of eros, capitalism and modern warfare, from which the circulation and affective economy of modern letters cannot be disentangled? Compelled to reproduce the poetic volubility of modernity's "Masters of language" (*JR* 89), Woolf's narrator nonetheless undermines its capacity for libidinal investment and thereby ontological grounding; the cold irony of the post-eclipse, pre-war passage empties the metaphoric sun of its progressive connotations and rousing force, while the metaphor for literary intimacy as an exchange of affect and interiority literally tinkles hollow: "the soul itself slip[s] through the lips in thin silver disks" (32). As an exhausted metaphor, the trope of the "armoured, resplendent, summer's day" (143) undercuts the capacity of "linguistic armour" and "symbolic constructs . . . ideologies, beliefs" (*BS* 64–65) to deny or protect against loss, as does the narrator's distancing framing – "they say" (*JR* 136) – of the belief that young men's sacrifice of their lives for the nation "together with the incessant commerce of banks . . . and houses of business, are the strokes which oar the world forward." In resisting the economy of substitution which links literary metaphor to the sacrificial logic of war, the narrator's storytelling exhibits the melancholic "imprint of [primal] separation and beginning of the symbol's sway" (*BS* 22). "Symbolic" for Kristeva refers to social as well as linguistic contracts, and with the melancholic erasure of "*symbolic impact* within the subject," symbolic values can no longer be internalised (37). The ultimate result of a subject ceasing, like Woolf's narrator, to be inscribed in the compensatory system of language, is a "symbolic breakdown."

In the novel's melancholic expression, such an impending breakdown occurs as a radical, modernist questioning of the representational capacity of language; the entire textual web of *Jacob's Room* is thus torn by the persistence of the primal Thing, which "will not be translated in order that it not be betrayed" (*BS* 53). While "verbal sequences turn up only if a trans-position is substituted for a more or less symbiotic primal object" (41), Woolf's fragmented narrative resists concatenation, thereby marking the ethical limits of translatability, of "sign systems distant from the site of pain" (42). Ramazani describes the modern elegy as offering "not so much solace as fractured speech" (ix), and according to Kristeva, the melancholic utterance is "repetitive and monotonous." Sentences are "interrupted, exhausted, come to a standstill" (*BS* 33). In Woolf's novel, these features become visible on the level of print as a set of formal signs of melancholia. These include "Interruptions in linguistic sequentiality," long and frequent silences and "nonrecoverable elisions" in syntactic structures (38, 34). Sentences in *Jacob's Room* are indeed interrupted, and silences in the form of ellipses or a blank space on the page frequently replace a story about to be told. Reporting from an evening at Clara Durrant's home, the narrator observes a type of ruptured speech – "Nothing settled or stayed unbroken. Like oars rowing now this side, now that, were the sentences that came now here, now there" (47) – which is illustrated a few pages later:

> Mr. Wortley passed them, smoking a cigar.
> "Every day I live I find myself agreeing . . ." he said as he passed them.
> "It's so interesting to guess . . ." murmured Julia Eliot.
> "When first we came out we could see the flowers in that bed," said Elsbeth.
> "We see very little now," said Miss Eliot. (49, ellipses in original)

This disruptive effect is intensified when a sentence which already expresses a sense of melancholic isolation forms a separate paragraph, isolated, as it were, on the page: "'Ja–cob! Ja–cob!' Archer shouted"; "So Clara left him" (4, 76). As Kathleen Wall remarks about the novel's fractured form: "It is as if the form does not merely reflect loss but marks the traces of that loss on the novel's textual skin" (308).

By enacting formally some defining symptom-traces of melancholia, Woolf's text achieves what Kristeva terms a *"dissociation of [aesthetic] form* itself, when form is . . . abstracted, disfigured, hollowed out," a process unleashed when an "abyss . . . separates language from affective experience" (*BS* 27, 54). Signifiers, when *"not bound* to semiotic imprints (drive-related representatives and affect representations)" are experienced as empty, creating an "artificial, unbelievable language" marked by a massive "loss of reference" (52, 44). In *Jacob's Room*, such loss of reference emerges in Woolf's persistent disconnection of her novel's form and materiality from its affective content. Through its many omissions and disruptions of narrative sequence, the novel conveys a melancholic, and arguably modernist, view of aesthetic form as dissociable from affective and libidinal investments. Such libidinal voiding of the literary medium is achieved in the midst of what appears to be a vivid depiction of a Soho market:

> The street market in Soho is fierce with light. Raw meat, china mugs, and silk stockings blaze in it. . . . Shawled women carry babies with purple eyelids; boys stand at street corners; girls look across the road – rude illustrations, pictures in a book whose pages we turn over and over as if we should at last find what we look for. Every face, every shop, bedroom window, public-house, and dark square is a picture feverishly turned – in search of what? It is the same with books. What do we seek through millions of pages? (*JR* 83–84)

The market scene vanishes as we become aware that *Jacob's Room* is a material object composed by illustrations and pages, and in the process of reading, our affective investment in the novel's content is disrupted by the narrator's relentless quest for a lost object, or Thing. The interrupted erotic encounter between Jacob and Sandra is similarly replaced with an account of the form and outline of the Acropolis, the venue of their meeting:

> But to return to Jacob and Sandra.
> They had vanished. There was the Acropolis; but had they reached it? The columns and the Temple remain; the emotion of the living breaks fresh on them year after year; and of that what remains? (141)

This textual separation of the first line from the description of the Acropolis stresses the gap between the vanished story and the solid shape of a site existing independently of the scenes played out there. In its emphasis on architectural form and structure at the expense of the affective intensity of a scene that literally evaporates into thin air, the passage casts literary contracts as "abstracted" or "hollowed out," to use Kristeva's terms. In the melancholic mode, erotic and libidinal expression fails: such affective currents, too, break against obdurate stone, but not the prehistoric rocks receiving waves of primal sadness. If the Parthenon is "likely to outlast the entire world," this is because its dazzling architecture – "perhaps it is beauty alone that is immortal" – appears as the ideal aesthetic form, inspiring, yet independent from libidinal and emotional attachments: "Although the beauty is sufficiently humane to weaken us, to stir the deep deposit of mud – memories, abandonments, regrets, sentimental devotions – the Parthenon is separate from all that" (130). The formalist connotations of this reflection are unmistakable, and like the painterly analogy above between book pages and pictures, they evoke a particular work on aesthetics which Woolf engaged as she was writing *Jacob's Room*: Roger Fry's essay collection *Vision and Design* (1920) and, in particular, his Post-Impressionist manifesto "An Essay in Aesthetics" (originally published in 1909). I shall end this chapter with a consideration of Woolf's novel as a unique modernist experiment in which melancholic expression and a formalist aesthetic converge. While melancholia and Bloomsbury formalism both tend to be associated with a separation of art and aesthetics from libidinal ties and moral obligations, I propose that Woolf's joining of these radically different representational modes forms a compelling ground for the novel's non-violent ethics.

Formalism, Melancholia and the Ethics of Affective Detachment

Critics have long observed that the post-war, modernist crisis of representation also encompasses moral principles as well as the ethical role of literature. Martin Halliwell's study of modernism and morality is concerned with the "renunciation of moral certainty... exemplary of the modernist stance" (16), and as Hollander notes, *Jacob's Room* "both portrays and enacts the crises of knowledge and ethics that followed the Great War" (42). At the same time, as we recall, Woolf thought it necessary to remind her contemporaries that novelistic storytelling is a matter of "duties and responsibilities" in which the reader is implicated (*E* 3: 435–36), and several scholars have detected the formation of a novel ethics in *Jacob's Room*.[35] Indeed, the ethical turn in Woolf and modernist criticism has brought a welcome focus on the novel's achievement of a process which Melba Cuddy-Keane ascribes to the paradigmatic modernist text: an "enactment [of] what much current ethical theory urges in theory: a dwelling in between questionableness and answerability, between the uncertain and the 'ought'" (217). And yet, the text's pervasive melancholia of the writing process continues to raise the question whether Woolf's first manifestly modernist novel experiment does not ultimately convey a resistance to ethical contracts. In particular, those melancholic textual features which categorically separate the novel's form from its affective content evoke Roger Fry's aesthetic theory, in which the formal dimensions of art emerge as not only separable but also emphatically detached from the moral obligations of life.

In "An Essay in Aesthetics," Fry advocates a feature of Post-Impressionist painting described in a 1917 lecture (published in *Vision and Design* as "Art and Life") – "the re-establishment of purely aesthetic criteria . . . the rediscovery of the principles of structural design and harmony" (*VD* 8):

> Art, then, is an expression and a stimulus of th[e] imaginative life, which is separated from actual life by the absence of responsive action. Now this responsive action implies in actual life moral responsibility. In art we have no such moral responsibility – it presents a life freed from the binding necessities of our actual existence. (15)

When considered not as an illustrational representation of life, but as the process of eliciting aesthetic emotion through formal design, art forms an autonomous realm detached from moral contracts. Aesthetic and moral responses to an artwork are incompatible, Fry argues, and aesthetic contemplation eliminates the need for responsive, and thus responsible, action. Since art "appreciates emotion in and for itself," the spectator watching an accident at the cinema will not "pass at once into actions of assistance" (19) and can therefore feel "pity and horror . . . quite purely" (14). Similarly, "The picture of a saint being slowly flayed alive" will not produce the "sensations of sickening disgust that a modern man would feel if he could assist the actual event; but they have a compensating clearness of presentment to the consciousness." A precondition for Fry's theory, then, is a curious sort of quasi-detached observation: "In the imaginative life . . . we can both feel the emotion and watch it" (19).

While few contemporary Woolf critics would argue that her writing embraces Fry's privileging of artistic design over the moral commitments and emotional responses of life, any consideration of her aesthetic strategies in *Jacob's Room* must take into account her position vis-à-vis Bloomsbury formalism. In particular, the novel's treatment of loss and affective detachment attests Woolf's vivid engagement with Fry's aesthetic theory. This engagement is present from the outset: the novel's first pages enact some of the tenets outlined in "An Essay in Aesthetics." The opening scene is first presented through the tearful gaze of Jacob's mother, then the focalising perspective abruptly shifts:

> But a stamp? She ferreted in her bag; then held it up mouth downwards; then fumbled in her lap, all so vigorously that Charles Steele in the Panama hat suspended his paint-brush.
>
> Like the antennae of some irritable insect it positively trembled. Here was that woman moving – actually going to get up – confound her! He struck the canvas a hasty violet-black dab. For the landscape needed it. It was too pale. (4)

Summed up in Steele's brushstroke, Betty Flanders's composition of her tear-stained letter is transformed into a painter's object. Even Archer's melancholic cry is subsumed by the artist's detached observation: "Steele frowned; but was pleased by the effect of the black – it was just *that* note which brought the rest together." In Steele's composition, expressions of grief and sadness are subordinated to what Fry called "the principles of structural design and harmony." As a painter privileging aesthetic form, Steele may be able to, as Fry puts it, "both feel the emotion and watch it."

The opening of *Jacob's Room* leads us to ask to what extent the novel's melancholic features, such as affective detachment and the narrator's metaphysical lucidity, can be said to enact the premises of Fry's essay. A much-debated passage from *A Room of One's Own* comes to mind:

> a novel starts in us all sorts of antagonistic and opposed emotions. Life conflicts with something that is not life. . . . On the one hand, we feel You – John the hero – must live, or I shall be in the depths of despair. On the other, we feel, Alas, John, you must die, because the shape of the book requires it. Life conflicts with something that is not life. (83)

This sense of a conflicted relationship between "shape" and "life" pervades Woolf's critical writings on the novel genre as well as her own novels. As Lee Oser remarks, her fictional characters "shuttle between . . . mimesis and abstract form, as Woolf confronts the divide between realism and formalism that occupies her in *A Room of One's Own*" (92). Yet it seems to me that these lines reach beyond such divides by making a keen observation, triggered by Woolf's insights into modernist formalism, about a vacillation inherent to the novel form: as a distinctly modern literary genre, the novel must both seek and fail to forge affective ties between reader and text. Later, in "Anon" and "The Reader," she theorised the modern, autonomous individual's separation from pre-modern modes of intimate storytelling, and as we have seen, the lucid narrator of *Jacob's Room* explores the loss of a primal, extra-textual transmission of affective imprints: intimacy conceived as a mind printing upon another. Woolf knew as early as the 1920s that the readers of her elegiac fiction must occupy Steele's contemplative position, "enjoying the spectacle of melancholy, not sharing its anguish" (*E* 6: 601). What, for Woolf, were the ethical implications of this insight? And what does she mean by writing, in her essay "On Not Knowing Greek" (1925), that "In the vast catastrophe of the European war our emotions had to be broken up for us, and put at an angle from us, before we could allow ourselves to feel them in poetry or fiction" (*E* 4: 47–48)? As in the passage from *A Room of One's Own*, the echoes of Fry in this reflection are unmistakable and demand close attention to the ethical motivations for Woolf's work.

Before we look further into the ethical complexities of the melancholic-formalist aesthetic particular to *Jacob's Room*, it is worth reviewing a pervasive critical tendency to align Woolf's formalism with the aesthetic tenets of Bloomsbury, and with a broader modernist rejection of collective moral standards in favour of individualistic re-conceptions of ethics as an aesthetic category.[36] Modernist efforts to dismantle epistemological certainties have long been understood as a transposition of authority from communal moral contracts to an autonomous and self-grounding artistic sphere, a process which grew out of "a sense that modernity's official self-understanding – enlightened, liberal, progressive, humanistic – had been a misunderstanding" (Pippin 31).[37] From this not entirely superseded perspective, what I take to be melancholic aesthetic features, the textual devices which throughout *Jacob's Room* transmit an acute sense of loss and alienation, could be said to endorse perhaps not moral nihilism, but the particular moral and artistic individualism advocated by those Bloomsbury members who fervently endorsed G. E. Moore's ethical philosophy. While Woolf and Fry were never among Moore's most ardent admirers, Tom Regan stresses affinities between Fry's thought and Moore's view of aesthetic contemplation as an intrinsic good, and dwelling on Woolf's early engagement with Moore, he concludes that Woolf and Fry never sought "to contribute to the larger world of social justice" (9; see 20–22).[38] (Michael Lackey, however, points out that Woolf became far more critical of Moore "around the year 1920" [94], that is, at the time she was writing *Jacob's Room*.) More recently, Edward P. Comentale has claimed that the Bloomsbury painters and writers were directly influenced by Roger Fry's formalism and Moore's ethics, and that the "elitist aestheticism" and moral individualism of the group masked an imposition of the bourgeois cultural codes sustaining modern capitalism (50; see 47–64).[39] Oser concurs that Woolf's aesthetic formalism closely follows Moore's tenets, and that it thereby exemplifies the modernist "stylizing [of] ethics" in which ethics was brought into the domain of aesthetics (16; see 85–101).

The persistent (though no longer dominant) stance represented by these critics raises many questions. Must the aesthetic practice of the Bloomsbury members influenced by Fry and Moore be seen as reproducing their views on the relationship between art, morality and ethics? How tenable is the argument that the formalism and aesthetic contemplation advocated by the group, when put into practice by Woolf, created self-grounding literary works detached from ethical obligations in the larger, socio-political community? To answer these questions, we need to perceive how Woolf's engagement with Fry's aesthetic theory led her to explore a state of contemplative detachment which, in and through *Jacob's Room*, joins the visual artist with the modern spectator and reader. In his essay "The French Post-Impressionists," which appeared as "The French Group" in the *Catalogue of the Second Post-Impressionist Exhibition* (1912), Fry claims that these artists

> do not seek to imitate form, but to create form; not to imitate life, but to find an equivalent for life. By that I mean that they wish to make images which by the clearness of their logical structure, and by their closely-knit unity of texture, shall appeal to our disinterested and contemplative imagination with something of the same vividness as the things of actual life appeal to our practical activities. (*VD* 167)

In Post-Impressionist art, then, the aesthetic effect of a set of formal devices creates a compensating counterpart to life. By creating rather than imitating form, we can infer, the aesthetic realm becomes a parallel life where norms, values and ethical frameworks can be equally created. It is easy to see why this logic strikes critics as anything but "disinterested": Fry may well have dismissed Moore's *Principia Ethica* (1903) as "sheer nonsense" (1Regan 22), but his notion of art as an equivalent for life leaves open the possibility that, as for Moore, the contemplation of intrinsically valuable aesthetic qualities (rather than actions prompted by moral obligations) can create an ethics by which to live. *Jacob's Room* interrogates these aspects of Fry's formalism too. Making her way around London, Woolf's narrator does not merely observe the crowd dropping out of St Paul's Cathedral: "Nothing could appear more certain from the steps of St. Paul's than that each person is miraculously provided with coat, skirt, and boots; an income; an object" (*JR* 55). The description given here is a curious one; it is as if these characters were formed, conjured up on the spot. And rather than *describing* the view of an early London morning in the politically charged post-eclipse passage, the narrator seems to *create* it: "But colour returns; runs up the stalks of the grass; blows out into tulips and crocuses; solidly stripes the tree trunks.... The Bank of England emerges" (143). We seem to be facing here the gradual completion of a painting, watching an artist at work.

What, then, does such approximation of the reader's, the painter's and the spectator's perspective tell us about Woolf's aesthetic treatment of ethical and political questions such as those raised by the post-eclipse episode, in which the return of vibrant colour recomposes modernity's resplendent weave (or canvas) of eros, capitalism and war? For Oser, the "aesthetic soaring" of her fiction evinces an unreserved dedication to formalist, painterly principles. Commenting on her modernist manifesto "Modern Fiction" (1925), Oser remarks that "It is painterly to describe 'life' as 'a series of gig-lamps symmetrically arranged.' Life is not an aesthetic phenomenon – unless you are an aesthete" (92). Such assessments tend to overlook the inter-medial complexities of Woolf's writing, and the pressing ethical questions arising from her idiosyncratic combination of textual and painterly perspectives. Fry associated art primarily with the plastic arts, the medium of painting in particular, and for both Woolf and Fry, literary writing is by definition representational and maintains, therefore, a close connection to the psychological, emotional and ethico-political ties composing life. Fry's categories are frequently repeated, but also complicated, in Woolf's essays. Thus, in "Life and the Novelist" (1926), she distinguishes the writer of novels, who is "terribly exposed to life," from artists who "partially at least, withdraw; they shut themselves up for weeks alone with a dish of apples and a paint-box" (*E* 4: 400). A later essay, "Why Art To-Day Follows Politics" (1936), explicitly associates the writer's exposure with political commitment:

> Obviously the writer is in such close touch with human life that any agitation in it must change his angle of vision.... But why should this agitation affect the painter and the sculptor, it may be asked? *He is not concerned with the feelings of his model but with its form.*... The artist on his side held [in times of peace] that since the value of his work depended upon freedom of mind, security of person, and immunity from practical affairs ... he was absolved from political duties. (*E* 6: 75–76, emphasis mine)

The rhetorical difference between these statements reflects a changing cultural climate. The later essay looks back from the 1930s on a period stretching from the first Post-Impressionist Exhibition in 1910 to the end of the 1920s, in which it was still possible for plastic artists to think of their art as "immun[e] from practical affairs." Woolf's 1920s fiction combines the writer's sensitivity to socio-political problems with the artist's detached contemplation, a peace-time activity whose political value, even or especially in times of war, she came to defend in works such as *Three Guineas* and "Thoughts on Peace in an Air Raid." In this, her novels of this period take on a far more reflected and critical engagement with Fry's (and Moore's) ideas than Oser, Comentale, Regan and others allow, and if we are to fully appreciate the *ethical* dimensions of this engagement, we need to consider her fictional treatment of emotion and affect. As Lauren Berlant observes, "affect, the body's active presence to the intensities of the present, embeds the subject in an historical field, and . . . its scholarly pursuit can communicate the conditions of an historical moment's production as a visceral moment" ("Intuitionists" 846). Among Woolf's 1920s novels, the figure of the artist more concerned with formal design than with the emotions expressed or conveyed by her subject-matter is particularly visible in and behind *Jacob's Room*. Positioned as Woolf's modern readers/spectators, we are implicated in this formal-affective paradigm, and thereby, as we shall see, in the novel's melancholic poetics with all its ethical complexities.

In Woolf's first obviously modernist novel, aesthetic detachment is melancholic insofar as it entails an uncompromising severing of intimate, affective object attachments between characters; not only between the narrator as a failed, modern storyteller and her fragmented story but also, and importantly, between Woolf's reader and her novel's textual content. As an aesthetic effect of the book's formal qualities, this melancholic detachment creates a striking contrast to the nostalgic mode of an essay often considered alongside *Jacob's Room*: "On Not Knowing Greek." It seems remarkable that this essay should have been written after the novel; the former's nostalgia cannot be comfortably dissociated from a passage describing the post-war loss of the classical glorification of heroic sacrifice as a pervasive cultural ideal, an ideal fiercely rejected by *Jacob's Room*.[40] If the novel's non-violent ethics resides in its melancholic poetics, then the tonal and generic differences between these texts highlight the particular capacity of the modernist novel to create anti-war ideals. In thus exemplifying the fictional print text as a formalist equivalent for life, where affective and ethical ties can be discomposed and created anew, *Jacob's Room* also prompts detached, aesthetic contemplation of the emotional and libidinal investments (such as those described in the essay) which justify and enable war, and of the modern novelist and reader's inescapable involvement in such libidinal economies. A comparison of the two texts via Fry's aesthetic theory may help elucidate these points.

In notable contrast to the textual melancholia of *Jacob's Room*, Woolf's reflections on affect and emotion in "On Not Knowing Greek" betray nostalgia: "a mental state oriented toward a recognizable time-place in the past, which does not necessarily impede articulation or cognition" (Bahun 22). However, unlike those of her post-war essays which express nostalgia for literary modernity's favoured modes of intimate storytelling, the lost object of "On Not Knowing Greek" is classical Greek culture, conceived as "the origin and paradigm of Western thought and civilisation" (Spiropoulou 61). As Spiropoulou notes, this essay vacillates between Woolf's usual resistance to such nostalgia and its dwelling on ancient Greece as the inaccessible origin of Western modernity (66, 68). At the heart of this ambivalence lies Woolf's distinction between the affective economy of the novel as a modern art form, and the capacity of pre-modern, collective performances to forge social and moral bonds through extra-textual affective transmission. Her association of the latter with classical Greece has many affinities with the archaic storytelling practice she theorised later, in "Anon," as modernity's lost origin: in the earlier essay, too, she stresses the creative performance out of doors, where "a great fund of emotion is ready prepared" for "something emphatic, familiar, brief, that would carry, instantly and directly, to an audience" (*E* 4: 40). Crucially, Woolf ventures that "it is not because we can analyse [Greek literary characters] into feelings that they impress us. In six pages of Proust we can find more complicated and varied emotions than in the whole of the *Electra*," while in Sophocles's tragedies,

> we are impressed by . . . heroism itself, by fidelity itself. . . . the original human being is to be found there. Violent emotions are needed to rouse him into action, but when thus stirred by death, by betrayal, by some other primitive calamity, Antigone and Ajax and Electra behave the way in which we should behave thus struck down; the way in which everybody has always behaved. (42)

The Greek dramatists, for whom "every sentence had to explode on striking the ear," are found to lack the novelist's and the reader's license to convey and contemplate nuanced affective states in the private transaction of writing and deciphering print text (45). And yet, the essay implies that it was only after the First World War that writers and readers could really begin to analyse passionate emotions by dissociating them from instinctive or unreflected action:

> Accustomed to look directly and largely rather than minutely and aslant, it was safe for [the Greeks] to step into the thick of emotions which blind and bewilder an age like our own. In the vast catastrophe of the European war our emotions had to be broken up for us, and put at an angle from us, before we could allow

ourselves to feel them in poetry or fiction. . . . But the Greeks could say, as if for the first time, "Yet being dead they have not died. . . . for hastening to set a crown of freedom on Greece we lie possessed of praise that grows not old." (47–48)

Before the war, Woolf suggests, modern letters tended to retain the collective economy of emotional impression particular to classical Greece – "we are impressed . . . by heroism itself, by fidelity itself" – in which literary-affective imprints of social values could be a force spurring morally just, and frequently violent action. Koulouris has related Woolf's reflections on Greek volubility in this essay to her critical engagement, throughout her work, with the classical values of heroism and fidelity as mobilised in pre-war Britain through the cultivation of sentiments such as *dulce et decorum est pro patria mori* (115–16, 118, 124), sentiments inspired by the Greek ideals of the eloquent poet-warrior, male homosociality and eros as sacrificial love (110): "the heroic relinquishing of life for the benefit of the love-object" (110; see 97–131).

Despite its troubling nostalgia, then, "On Not Knowing Greek" offers some thought-provoking insights into the moral and political stakes of affective transmission and detachment as specifically literary phenomena. This dimension of the essay echoes Fry's writing on the aesthetic contemplation of violent emotions detached from their objects and the instinctive re/actions they habitually cause. "An Essay in Aesthetics" presents three situations where self-preservation or moral responsibility determines a sequence, inevitable in life (*VD* 15), in which intense emotions triggered by an object spark instinctive, responsive action. The first sequence is threat (encountering a wild bull) which triggers fear followed by flight; the second is observing an act of violence which elicits "sickening disgust" and then paralysis; and the third, seeing an accident, triggers "pity and horror" which "pass at once into actions of assistance" (13, 19, 14). In art, with its inherent distance from these "binding necessities" of life, such chains become broken up: "Morality . . . appreciates emotion by the standard of resultant action. Art appreciates emotion in and for itself" (15, 19). For Fry, as we have seen, this distance frees aesthetic creation from moral *and* ethical obligations, terms which he uses interchangeably about the opposite view, that art must "forward right action" (15). In Woolf's work, however, we can discern a productive, ethical (not moral) potential in the aesthetic detachment of overpowering emotion from responsive action as theorised by Fry, whereby "we get, in the imaginative life, a different set of values, and a different kind of perception" (13). Specifically,

> the need for responsive action hurries us along and prevents us from ever realising fully what the emotion is that we feel. . . . In short, the motives we

actually experience are too close to us to enable us to feel them clearly. They are in a sense unintelligible. In the imaginative life, on the contrary, we can both feel the emotion and watch it. (19)

Moore, too, insisted on the ethical value of aesthetic contemplation as a way towards unsettling the inexorability of moral rules of action. If patriotism and self-sacrifice were among the moral virtues rejected by Moore and Bloomsbury at large (Regan 245), might we not begin to examine how Woolf's selective appropriation of Fry's tenets shaped an ethical project with repercussions beyond the intimate sphere of friends and lovers to which Moore's ethics is limited?[41] Read alongside "On Not Knowing Greek," Fry's lines above describe a mode of critical perception particular to modern art which, for Woolf, crystallised during the post-war years into an arguably ethical sense that "our emotions had to be broken up . . . and put at an angle from us" (*E* 4: 47–48). Her essay also indicates something which she had already demonstrated powerfully through *Jacob's Room*: that the most effective site where emotional investments can be taken apart and scrutinised in terms of their ethico-political consequences is the literary text, enriched by the affective detachment characterising the plastic arts.

Indeed, the melancholic aesthetic of *Jacob's Room* attests to the ethical necessity of examining modernity's literary-affective attachments; the "sidelong, satiric manner" of "looking [at emotions] minutely and aslant," which Woolf associates with the writing of Wilfred Owen and Siegfried Sassoon (*E* 4: 48, 47), also defines her novel. As a hyper-detached, modernist storyteller, the narrator depicts the First World War's unprecedented mass sacrifice of human life in two visual scenes tellingly stripped of affective motivations and responses:

> The battleships ray out over the North Sea, keeping their stations accurately apart. At a given signal all the guns are trained on a target which . . . flames into splinters. With equal nonchalance a dozen young men in the prime of life descend with composed faces into the depths of the sea. Like blocks of tin soldiers the army covers the corn field, moves up the hillside, stops, reels slightly this way and that, and falls flat, save that, through field-glasses, it can be seen that one or two pieces still agitate up and down like fragments of broken match-stick.
>
> These actions, together with the incessant commerce of banks . . . and houses of business, are the strokes which oar the world forward, they say. (*JR* 136)

The sardonic framing of these almost farcical tableaus in the second paragraph prompts the reader-observer's separation of the sacrificial acts from the libidinal investments which make them possible, thereby revealing their absurdity as well as their inevitability in the capitalist order of modernity. A further frame is given in the subsequent paragraph, which opens: "It is thus that we live, they say, driven by an unseizable force" (137). I have suggested that Woolf depicts this force not as an inherently destructive drive, but as the sum of erotic attachments ensuring the uninterrupted operation of global capitalism and modern warfare. This is "the indescribable agitation of life," the incessant weaving of modernity's capitalist, libidinal and representational webs which is likened to the industrious activity of insects: "Only here – in Lombard Street . . . the webs of the forest are schemes evolved for the smooth conduct of business; and honey is treasure of one sort and another" (143). Evoking Fry's insights into the ways in which emotional as well as moral agitation tends to trigger instinctive, unreflected action in life, Woolf's restless insects suggest the political and financial agitation on the brink of Britain's involvement in the war and, more specifically, the mobilisation of patriotic love to stir young men to enlist.

Spinning their webs in the dark, the insects execute a night-time activity whose scope and consequences are withdrawn from the reader's conscious and visual faculty, yet as ubiquitous as the air we breathe: "the whole air is tremulous with breathing, elastic with filaments." Enmeshed in these obscure nets, the narrator's subsequent textual weave, or canvas, brings the dazzling, painterly vision of the Bank of England and London's financial centre into being: "But colour returns. . . . Sunlight strikes in . . . upon all the jolly trappings of the day; the bright, inquisitive, armoured resplendent, summer's day." However, a tonal discord marks this vision as an effect of Woolf's nuanced chiaroscuro, where the glorious sunlight is not only blinding in its glaring brilliance but also obscured by the insects' incessant weaving, which is blind in the double sense of lacking sight and discernment, and concealed from sight, enfolded in darkness: "There is a whir of wings as the suburban trains rush into the terminus." For Fry, the depiction of light and shade is one of the "emotional elements of design," that is, one of the formal methods by which an artist arouses aesthetic emotion (*VD* 23; see 23–24). In Woolf's textual use of this formal element, a combination of tonal and visual disharmony inspires a complex affective response, an aesthetic emotion distinct from any "state or display of strong emotion . . . among a large group of people in response to a person, thing, event, etc." ("sensation, *n.*," def. 3.a). Disoriented by this aesthetic emotion, at once hot and chilling, the reader nonetheless attains some of the narrator's detached lucidity: we are incited to both feel the pre-war sensation of elation and observe it as the very fabric of modernity's bewildering webs, and thereby to perceive the absurdity of the destructive and self-destructive actions they demand.

In *Jacob's Room*, then, as in Fry's aesthetic theory, the creative procedure by which heightened physical sensation is transformed into dispassionate, contemplative "aesthetic feeling" makes possible the observing subject's lucid examination of their emotional states (*VD* 26). Unlike Fry, however, Woolf insists on the ethico-political necessity of this process. In this, her novel attempts something known in contemporary theory as affective mapping. The text repeatedly contrasts orderly maps of physical space to modernity's webs – we perceive the material "filaments," not the network as a whole – and the emotional fabric composing them: "The streets of London have their maps; but our passions are unchartered" (*JR* 143, 82). The painterly passage above enacts with particular intensity Woolf's later reflection that the Greeks' emotions towards war, as the very origin of literary and political modernity, must "blind and bewilder an age like our own" (*E* 4: 47). Woolf would concur, I think, with Jonathan Flatley's insight, in *Affective Mapping: Melancholia and the Politics of Modernism* (2008), that modernity made not only Jamesonian cognitive mapping difficult but affective mapping also, especially because of its unparalleled, new and disorienting experiences of loss (79). As for Woolf, affective disorientation has political implications for Flatley:

> Just as the lack of a cognitive map of one's social space is crippling for effective political activity, so too is the lack of an affective map, for several reasons. Our most enduring and basic social formations – patriarchy, say, or capitalism itself – can only be enduring to the extent that they are woven into our emotional lives in the most fundamental way. . . . Because our social formations work through affect, resistance to them must as well. (78–79)

If this is the case, what kinds of affects might offer productive resistance to the warmongering ideals sustaining the modern nexus of global capitalism and patriarchal militarisation? Flatley proposes that modernist aesthetic practices which express "a non-depressing, politicizing melancholia" (8), and the particular lucidity characteristic of such melancholia, might enhance a socio-politically committed project of affective mapping through their capacity to bring about the reader's (Benjaminian) self-estrangement (in the sense of Brechtian defamiliarisation): "being able to treat oneself as an object, so that one is able to subject one's emotional life [and affective attachments] to analysis, reflection, and direction" (80; see 6). Within Woolf's oeuvre and apart from her late novel *Between the Acts*, this possibility becomes particularly compelling in *Jacob's Room*, even if, as I see it, the novel's affective mapping operates primarily in the domain of ethics.

We have seen how *Jacob's Room* works on the reader like Archer's solitary cry: in conveying the affective imprint of primal sadness, the book appears "pure from all passion" (*JR* 4), from "any strong, controlling, or overpowering emotion, as desire, hate, fear etc." ("passion, *n.*," def. 6.a), and this textual melancholia resists the ethically violent, matricidal economy of substitution which underpins modern warfare as well as the world of letters. Might this melancholic transmission of sadness without an object, which reactivates the loss of primal intimacy, also enable a form of affective mapping? Can the novel's lucid insights into the violent workings of capitalism and literary eloquence really emerge from its melancholic aesthetic mode, when melancholia, as "an object-loss . . . withdrawn from consciousness" (Freud, "Mourning and Melancholia" 245), by definition prevents cognitive understanding of the melancholic affect and its attachments? To address these questions, we might return to Fry's thoughts on the aesthetic effects of light and shade: "Our feelings towards the same object become totally different according as we see it strongly illuminated against a black background or dark against a light" (*VD* 24). Fry's reflection appears to have shaped Woolf's ambivalent portrayal of her protagonist: as the novel's lost object and Thing, we recall, Jacob is depicted as a lantern placed in a dark forest, but also as a cavern, dark but mysteriously lit by some radiance which attracts the moth-like narrator and reader. What ethical insights might Woolf's reader gain by becoming one of the insects blindly hitting the lantern's glass, or the moth hovering over "the mouth the cavern of mystery" which is Jacob's life and person (*JR* 61)?

As a lost object of desire or mourning, a light against a dark background, Jacob is treated with melancholic ambivalence by the narrator: as a loved person (Betty Flanders's son, or Woolf's brother Thoby, on whom Jacob's character is modelled), Jacob also embodies the nexus of militarisation and modern letters denounced by the narrator. As has often been pointed out, the main target of her critique is the elite university education provided to a small section of the young men of Jacob's generation (including Woolf's brother, who died of typhoid fever in 1906, the year Jacob goes to Cambridge), which saw themselves as the inheritors of Greek classical culture with its glorification of heroic sacrifice.[42] Such readings tend to emphasise the narrator's distance from Jacob: her intermittent hostility and scorn (Clewell 203–5),[43] or her emphatic positioning of herself as an outsider of his circle (Zwerdling, "Woolf's Satiric Elegy"; Spiropoulou 68–69). However, if we follow Freud's early description of melancholia, the melancholic's affective ambivalence evinces not distance, but "an *identification* of the ego with the abandoned object" ("Mourning and Melancholia" 249), a return to an earlier way of relating to others, prior (Kristeva would say) to the subject's matricidal formation as autonomous. If Jacob, as our lantern and object of desire, is the very embodiment of the arrogant 'I' of Western civilisation, might we not realise, the moment we "knock [our] heads against the glass" (*JR* 25), that we too remain melancholically tied to this model of the subject and the violence it enables? And yet, just as the self-reflective narrator seeks to extricate herself from the capitalist and literary webs in which she remains caught, Woolf's reader might emerge transformed from this singular reading experience, with a new capacity to critically examine "the ego as altered by identification" ("Mourning and Melancholia"). The lantern paragraph, introduced by an ellipsis, significantly interrupts the narrative account of an "orderly procession" at Cambridge – "what certainty, authority controlled by piety, although great boots march under the gowns" (*JR* 24) – tearing the textual weave with its quiet, melancholic tonality:

> ... If you stand a lantern under a tree every insect in the forest creeps up to it – a curious assembly, since though they scramble and swing and knock they heads against the glass, they seem to have no purpose – something senseless inspires them. One gets tired of watching them, as they amble round the lantern and blindly tap as if for admittance. . . . Ah, but what's that? A terrifying volley of pistol-shots rings out. . . . A tree – a tree has fallen, a sort of death in the forest. After that, the wind in the trees sounds melancholy. (25, introductory ellipsis in original)

As in the later visual analogy between the forest's webs and those of modern capitalism, we are made to observe ourselves in the industrious, senseless insects, whose weaving and tapping display blind libidinal attachments. In the passage above, our alertness to this undiscerning blindness is intensified by the analogy between the sound of a tree falling and that of a weapon being fired; the latter makes the former appear as sharp as it might to someone whose aural perception is keener than the visual. And like the narrator, whose acute ear detects the nuanced, melancholic timbre of the wind and Archer's cry, we are made receptive by this training of our perceptual faculties to the imprint of primal sadness, an affect which colours this passage and indeed the text as a whole.

If our heightened affective receptivity as readers of *Jacob's Room* alerts us to our entanglement in modernity's webs by making us scrutinise or map our passionate object attachments, it also captures us in more archaic ties through which we may become something other than autonomous. As a subtler affect than the intense passions elevated since the Greek origin of literary and political modernity (the villagers' ceremonial verbalisation of collective emotion in *Jacob's Room* recalls Woolf's description of classical drama in "On Not Knowing Greek"), the novel's melancholic sadness takes us from ontology, morality and unthinking action into the realm of a post-Levinasian ethics.[44] In particular, Woolf manipulates our affective relation to her lost protagonist in passages where he emerges as "dark against a light" (*VD* 24), thereby displacing us from our ontological attraction to the light of the 'I'. Just before Jacob is likened to a dark cavern emitting the radiant light of a unique existence, a portrait suggestive of the Kristevan Thing which is a sun at once bright and black (*BS* 13), his resistance to objectifying, intimate reading makes him appear as a shadow: "In any case life is but a procession of shadows, and God knows why it is that we embrace them so eagerly, and see them depart with such anguish, being shadows. . . . For . . . we know nothing about him. Such is the manner of our seeing. Such the conditions of our love" (*JR* 60). Just as a shadow must elude a loving embrace, Jacob escapes the libidinal investments we tend to confer on a literary character. In becoming "an insistence without presence, a light without representation" to which the reader can only relate melancholically (*BS* 13), he reactivates the intimate modes of attachment and impression forming "the conditions of our love" or erotic attachments, yet eclipsed by our formation as autonomous subjects and by modernity's dissemination of print texts. As Flatley observes, Freudian psychoanalysis, with its emphasis on libidinal (and primarily sexual) bonds, lacks a substantial theory of affect, and affect remains undertheorised in psychoanalysis more generally (44, 50–51). However, Kristeva's transformative insights into literary melancholia can make us perceive a non-violent ethics at the heart of the fragmented, melancholic poetics of Woolf's first distinctly modernist novel experiment. At once disorienting and hyperlucid, *Jacob's Room* inspires resistance to the affective economy of modern letters, and to the modern reader's inevitable implication in the ethical and political violence sustained by this economy's disavowal of primal ties. Through its formal markers of loss and emotional detachment, *Jacob's Room* reveals Woolf's formidable effort to re-establish an ethical ground for the post-war novel by means of a radical transformation of literary intimacy.

2

"An Inner Meaning Almost Expressed": Introspection as Revolt in *Mrs Dalloway*

In September 1923, one year after finishing *Jacob's Room*, Woolf wrote, full of excitement, about the new novel she was composing:

> You see, I'm thinking furiously about Reading & Writing. I have no time to describe my plans. I should say a good deal about The Hours, & my discovery; how I dig out beautiful caves behind my characters. . . . The idea is that the caves shall connect, & each comes to daylight at the present moment – Dinner! (*D* 2: 263)

Woolf's pleasurable discovery and tantalising address mark a breakthrough in her conception of literary intimacy. While the moth-like narrator and reader of *Jacob's Room* must "hum vibrating . . . at the mouth of the cavern of mystery" (*JR* 61), her subsequent novel seduces the reader to embark on a delightful excursion into its characters' "beautiful caves" of interiority: of thoughts, memories and sensations. This invitation is not mediated by an omniscient narrator, though; experimenting with focalisation and free indirect discourse, Woolf created, in *Mrs Dalloway*, a narrative voice alternatively separate from and merging with the voices of the focalising characters, thereby immersing her reader in moments of suspended subjectivity – radically intimate moments in which the individual self cannot be comfortably distinguished from the other and outside. If the fragmented, melancholic narrative of *Jacob's Room* marks the loss of literary intimacy, the exuberant, intensely pleasurable poetics of *Mrs Dalloway* affirms its jubilant recovery. And yet, as the related images of the primeval, mysterious cavern and glistening caves intimate, each novel reveals a distinct quest for primal forms of intimate attachment, and for modes of being prior to the formation of the 'I' as a self-sufficient entity, in a thought-provoking challenge to the violence sanctioned by the pervasive ideal of absolute subjective autonomy.

This challenge is articulated in two radically different modes of poetic expression: the affective detachment and voiding of metaphoric figuration in *Jacob's Room* gives way, in *Mrs Dalloway*, to an abundant proliferation of affectively charged metaphors. If Kristeva is right that "Literary creation . . . bears witness to the affect – to sadness as imprint of separation and beginning of the symbol's sway; to joy as imprint of the triumph that settles me in the universe of artifice and symbol" (*BS* 22), we could say that the transition from *Jacob's Room* to *Mrs Dalloway* marks a trajectory from primal sadness to triumphant joy. However, the linguistic mastery asserted through metaphoric substitution is constantly resisted also in the later novel, but not through oceanic waves of primal sadness. What erupts in the vibrant poetics of *Mrs Dalloway* is the "fountain of creative energy" (*AROO* 131) which transports the writer from the realm of intense creative pleasure into the region of bliss or *jouissance*, where the mastery and unity of the writing self momentarily dissolves in a Kristevan "reuniting with affect" (*IR* 26), that is, with the somatic, pre-verbal sensations and emotions repressed by any social-linguistic order dominated by the figure of the strictly autonomous 'I.' I shall argue, in this chapter, that writing *Mrs Dalloway* enabled Woolf to develop an aesthetic practice of intimate revolt: a form of artistic creation in which systematic social, political and ethical violence is resisted not primarily through the indignant exposure of such violence, but through the very act of writing poetically and, more specifically, through the pleasure particular to poetic introspection.

In *Mrs Dalloway* as in *A Room of One's Own*, lyrical introspection is playfully dislodged from the Western model of subjective autonomy with which it has so long been associated; on the contrary, it breaks the mould of the masculine, self-possessed 'I.' Through a poetic lyricism which surfaces in Woolf's prose as much as in her political argument, the later text dispels the obstacle imposed on the post-war novelist by writers whose protest against the increasing gains of the women's movements, as Woolf insightfully argues, help sustain a militarised, capitalist-imperialist civilisation marked by perpetual war (*AROO* 49–50). Disturbed in her reading of the fictional Mr A's prose by "a straight dark bar, a shadow shaped something like the letter 'I'" (130), Woolf's narrator reflects:

> But why was I bored? Partly because of the dominance of the letter "I" and the aridity, which, like the giant beech tree, it casts within its shade. Nothing will grow there. And partly for some more obscure reason. There seemed to be some obstacle, some impediment in Mr A's mind which blocked the fountain of creative energy and shored it within narrow limits. (131)

The creative fountain suggests the writer's experience of *jouissance*, an unspeakable pleasure and affective intensity which Woolf perceives to be foreclosed in the (masculine) self-assertion dominating not only the work of the Edwardians but also, and just as pervasively, literary expression in the post-war years (*AROO* 131–32). Indeed, the essay's political argument hinges on Woolf's insistence that a genuine literary resistance to the ubiquitous violence sustained by the arid 'I' must proceed through a new form of poetic prose, in which the "fountain of creative energy" is unblocked.

This insight had materialised, a few years earlier, in the intensely sensual poetics of *Mrs Dalloway*. Throughout the process of writing the novel, Woolf made continuous introspective notes in her diary about something like an orgasmic fountain about to erupt. On 13 June 1923, she reflects: "Often now I have to control my excitement – as if I were pushing through a screen; or as if something beat fiercely close to me. What this portends I don't know. It is a general sense of the poetry of existence that overcomes me" (*D* 2: 246). One year later, she asks herself: "What was I going to say? Something about the violent moods of my soul. How describe them, even with a waking mind? I think I grow more and more poetic. Perhaps I restrained it, & now, like a plant in a pot, it begins to crack the earthenware" (304). The two passages mark a notable shift from an overwhelming sense of the "poetry of existence," figured as the sensation of something beating fiercely and close, to a concern with poetic creation, where the word "poetic" describes the writer's urge to depict the intense emotions aroused by this sensation. In a later entry, on 13 December 1924, Woolf observes about her new novel: "it seems to leave me plunged deep in the richest strata of my mind. I can write & write & write now: the happiest feeling in the world" (323). At stake in this entry is not only the question of describing "extraordinary emotions" or "violent moods" (246, 304) but also the writer's pleasure in "pushing through" the "screen" of consciousness through the process of writing poetically. This process is suggested by the lyrical sentence "Perhaps I restrained it, & now, like a plant in a pot, it begins to crack the earthenware"; the earthenware of the writer's soul or mind "begins to crack" in the moment of writing the metaphor ("& now").

The enraptured language in which Woolf records her creative transport from intense physical pleasure to bliss found its way into the poetic prose of *Mrs Dalloway*, and the novel enacts this transition repeatedly from the opening lines:

> Mrs Dalloway said she would buy the flowers herself.
> For Lucy had her work cut out for her. The doors would be taken off their hinges; Rumpelmayer's men were coming. And then, thought Clarissa Dalloway, what a morning – fresh as if issued to children on a beach.

> What a lark! What a plunge! For so it had always seemed to her when, with a little squeak of the hinges, which she could hear now, she had burst open the French windows and plunged at Bourton into the open air. (*MD* 4)[1]

But can this poetics of pleasure and blissful transport really, as I claim here, be considered a mode of socio-political critique, let alone a form of literary revolt and non-violent resistance? The question bears asking, notably because such a poetics no doubt seems at odds with Woolf's much discussed determination, when writing the novel, to "criticise the social system, & to show it at work, at its most intense" (*D* 2: 248). There is a wealth of criticism particularly on the systemic violence inflicted by the shell-shocked soldier Septimus Smith's medical doctors, whose lethal healing practices, in wartime, would send soldiers back to the front and, after the fraught Versailles peace, drive patients to suicide through a coercive process of socialisation, as in Septimus's case. Woolf's own phrasing – "I want to criticise the social system, & to show it at work" – might serve as an apt description of the methodology pervading some of the most substantial readings of *Mrs Dalloway*. It also suggests the paranoid mindset which Eve Kosofsky Sedgwick has memorably contrasted to reparative, pleasurable modes of reading, writing and knowing.

In *Touching Feeling: Affect, Pedagogy, Performativity* (2003), Sedgwick observes how, at the turn of the twenty-first century, what Paul Ricoeur once called a "hermeneutics of suspicion" – a paranoid reading practice aimed at exposing and revealing systematic yet supposedly hidden oppression, violence and injustice – had become a "monopolistic program" (144), a theoretical methodology whose privileged status has entailed the routine dismissal of alternative, pleasure-driven critical practices centred on positive affects such as joy. Melanie Klein's paranoid and depressive *positions* inspire Sedgwick's "interes[t] in doing justice to the powerful reparative practices that . . . infuse self-avowedly paranoid critical projects, as well as in the paranoid exigencies that are often necessary for non-paranoid knowing and utterance" (128–29). In particular, Sedgwick dwells on the relevance of Klein's depressive position as the source of a reparative, pleasure-seeking mode:

> discussions of the depressive position in Klein [tend] to emphasize that that position inaugurates ethical possibility – in the form of a guilty, empathetic view of the other as at once good, damaged, integral, and requiring and eliciting love and care. Such ethical possibility, however, is founded on and coextensive with what Foucault calls "care of the self," the often very fragile concern to provide the self with pleasure and nourishment in an environment that is perceived as not particularly offering them. (137)

For Sedgwick, the reparative strategies inaugurated by the depressive position form a compelling model for ethical, reparative and pleasurable modes of experiencing and understanding literary texts, and indeed the world at large.[2] She stresses that "to practice other than paranoid forms of knowing ... does *not*, in itself, entail a denial of the reality or gravity of enmity or oppression," and that "it is sometimes the most paranoid-tending people who are able to, and need to, develop and disseminate the richest reparative practices" (128, 150).

Sedgwick's insights offer an incisive lens for reviewing the development of Woolf's modernist prose from *Jacob's Room* to *Mrs Dalloway*. In Kleinian terms, the melancholic poetics of *Jacob's Room* can be said to reactivate the infant's depressive position, "a melancholia in *statu nascendi*"; for Klein as for Kristeva, melancholia betrays the subject's "fear of losing the one irreplaceable object, his mother, whom he still mourns at bottom" (Klein 352). I have suggested that in mournfully re-enacting the loss not only of the mother-as-object, but of the very first mode of being constituting primal intimacy, the textual melancholia of *Jacob's Room* at once exposes the systemic violence sustained by the matricidal webs of modernity, and seeks (in voicing the affect of primal sadness) to recreate or repair those archaic intimate and affective attachments which modernity violently disavows. Inspired by Kristeva's *Black Sun* (1989), my reading of the novel needed to be simultaneously paranoid and restorative, as per Sedgwick, in order to illuminate the deep intersections between these modes in Woolf's writing. These interactions are equally deep in the pleasurable aesthetic of *Mrs Dalloway*, which, like Klein's pleasure-seeking mode, emerged from a depressive position – that of *Jacob's Room*.

As I turn my attention from the first novel to the second, I would like to underline the extent to which Sedgwick's thesis – that "it is sometimes the most paranoid-tending people who are able to, and need to, develop and disseminate the richest reparative practices" (150) – holds true for Woolf, and for her composition of *Mrs Dalloway* in particular. I will pursue a trajectory from the socio-political sphere, through a discussion of influential and insightful paranoid interpretations of the novel, to ethics, where I hope to land in a reparative reading drawing on Kristeva's and Judith Butler's respective theories of violence, intimacy and introspection. In its poetic creation of psychological depth, *Mrs Dalloway* achieves the plunge into the "dark places of psychology" advocated in "Modern Fiction" (*E* 4: 162), and as we shall see, Woolf locates intimacy in the suspension of subjective perspectives enabled through the blissful act of exploring the life of the mind. Indeed, the novel attains its critical edge, its cutting (paranoid) exposure of systematic political and ethical violence, not despite but through its pleasurable exploration of intimacy and interiority. This claim departs definitively from Alex Zwerdling's largely unchallenged separation of the contemplative, introspective strand of Woolf's writing from her novels' socio-political engagement.[3] My aim in this chapter is to show that in Woolf's hands, the lyrical, introspective probing of psychological depth, and the joyful "reuniting with affect" (*IR* 26) it entails, becomes a vehicle for social critique as well as a non-violent ethics. In *Mrs Dalloway*, I argue, Woolf developed an ethics of intimate introspection which fervently opposes a "social system" founded on the violent ideal of absolute subjective autonomy and a concomitant disciplinary imperative to suppress affective intensity.

Several critics have contextualised the medical authorities denounced in the novel and, in particular, their insistence on the need for traumatised patients to practice self-control and emotional restraint. Thomas C. Caramagno, Elaine Showalter and Hermione Lee have all pointed out that Woolf's personal experience of authoritarian medical doctors and ineffective treatments shaped her representation of Sir William Bradshaw and Dr Holmes in *Mrs Dalloway*. In the nineteenth-century medical tradition to which most of Woolf's physicians belonged, manic-depressive illness was treated as a neurotic disease in which manifestations of "excessive emotionalism" were to be cured with self-discipline (Caramagno, *The Flight of the Mind* 14). Caramagno notes that Woolf was advised early on against "losing control of her emotions" and that she repeatedly reproached herself for such loss of control in her diaries and letters (15).[4] In her study of attitudes to shell shock, "war neurosis" or "male hysteria" in post-war Britain, Showalter stresses that the Victorian ideal of self-discipline also inspired treatments of "hysterical soldiers who displayed unmanly emotions or fears" (*The Female Malady* 167–70): "Septimus's problem is that he feels too much for a man. His grief and introspection are emotions that are consigned to the feminine" (192–93).[5] Showalter makes a crucial point in observing that Woolf links Septimus's expressions of intense emotion with the act of introspection. Septimus is advised repeatedly by his doctors to "take an interest in things outside himself" and to "think as little about [him]self as possible"; "health," Holmes tells his patient, "is largely a matter in our own control. Throw yourself into outside interests; take up some hobby" (*MD* 18, 83, 78). Bradshaw and Holmes thus enforce a psychological norm of strict rationality and emotional restraint when they ask Septimus to take an interest in "things outside" instead of exploring his inner life. In these and other passages, Woolf reveals how the medical establishment with which she was intimately familiar viewed introspection as a threat to the rational, civilised self because the act of looking inwards involves the unbridled expression of affect and emotion.

Moreover, the psychological imperative to suppress intense emotions is depicted as central to a coercive form of socialisation. Caramagno writes about Woolf's doctor George Savage, whose medical approach was inspired by the American physician Silas Mitchell:

> Savage, like Mitchell, evaluated his patients' progress in terms of their submission to his conservative view of reality: the patient was asked to relinquish control to the doctor, to follow directions without question. Because Savage identified sanity with social conformity, he denigrated the value of self and brushed aside the patient's experience of her illness. (16)[6]

For medical authorities like Savage and Mitchell, the physician in control functions as a model for the patient by pointing out the patient's lack of control. This assumption forms a target of Woolf's brilliant satire in *Mrs Dalloway*: "receiv[ing] the impress of Sir William's will," his patients are made to watch him "go through, for their benefit, a curious exercise with the arms, which he shot out, brought sharply back to his hip, to prove (if the patient was obstinate) that Sir William was master of his own actions, which the patient was not" (86). As a pervasive social ideal, self-control, or the mastery of emotions as well as (bodily) action – what Bradshaw terms "proportion" – enables a forceful mechanism of social exclusion: "Worshipping proportion, Sir William not only prospered himself but made England prosper, secluded her lunatics, forbade childbirth, penalized despair, made it impossible for the unfit to propagate their views until they, too, shared his sense of proportion" (84).[7] Bradshaw emerges here as a representative of the patriarchal and patriotic social establishment critiqued in *A Room of One's Own* and *Three Guineas*, where Woolf polemically casts educational, legal and military authorities as forming what she refers to in her diary as one "social system." As Lee observes, Woolf offers in *Mrs Dalloway* "a political reading, ahead of Foucault, of the conspiracy between social engineering, the restraint of the mentally ill, and the patriarchal self-protection of the establishment" (193).[8]

Insofar as Woolf set out to "criticise the social system, & to show it at work" when writing *Mrs Dalloway*, her novel demonstrates with cutting efficiency how the jointly psychological and social norm of self-control was also operative in post-war Britain on a political level; through the act of telling his patients to practise emotional restraint, William Bradshaw "ma[kes] England prosper." In two influential readings of *Mrs Dalloway*, Alex Zwerdling and Christine Froula focus on Woolf's lucid insight that in the politically turbulent inter-war years, the ideal of self-control served as a means for strengthening national identity.

The memory of the recent war, a rapid disintegration of the British Empire, the tensions between nations following the Treaty of Versailles and the emergence of totalitarian formations in Europe all posed threats to Britain as a nation in the 1920s. As Zwerdling points out, the novel's representatives of the governing class advocate a "repression of instinct and emotion" which "has everything to do with the ability to retain power. . . . But the calm is only on the surface; there is turbulence beneath" ("*Mrs. Dalloway* and the Social System" 72). Froula goes further than Zwerdling in her analysis of psychic repression as bound up with socio-political forms of domination. In Froula's psychoanalytic reading, *Mrs Dalloway* "indicts post-war nationalisms that, while pretending to battle external threats to peace and security, actually produce enemies, dominators, and war by an unacknowledged violence within" ("Postwar Elegy" 139).[9] As Froula emphasises in *Virginia Woolf and the Bloomsbury Avant-Garde*, Woolf shared John Maynard Keynes's assessment of the Versailles Treaty as a display, on behalf of the Allied powers, of the aggressive nationalisms which had led to one war and would bring about another.[10]

Such paranoid readings (in Sedgwick's sense) have played a crucial role in foregrounding Woolf's exceptionally keen awareness that, in the inter-war years, psychological and interpersonal violence was deeply intertwined with violence in the public, socio-political sphere, and that in a nationalistic social order, the disciplinary repression of affect and emotion institutes oppression, coercion and violence. They have also made it possible to appreciate the ways in which Woolf's modernist aesthetic resists nationalist aggression by virtue of dismantling the ideal of absolute subjective autonomy. As Rebecca Walkowitz observes, Woolf knew "that social norms are embedded in traditions of literary style and that literary style is embedded in the politics of national culture" (84),[11] and her inter-war experiments with modernist form (for Walkowitz a form of "cosmopolitan style") deliver a critique of militaristic patriotism through a "Decentering [of] the first-person point of view" (80). If we follow Walkowitz's (paranoid) critical approach, then, social critique for Woolf operates on the level of aesthetics as a relentless questioning of the 'I' asserted by the novelist Mr A in *A Room of One's Own*, an 'I' which is at once the product of a militarised, nationalistic society and what upholds it. However, if we cease to see exclusively through the paranoid theoretical lens, which until recently dominated socio-political readings of *Mrs Dalloway*, we can begin to appreciate the extent to which Woolf's suspicion of self-control and emotional restraint engendered a constructive, reparative poetics which operates through, yet exceeds a critique of the autonomous subject and its attendant social order.

Woolf's interrogation of the psychological, social and political ideal of being master of oneself and one's actions also shaped her thought-provoking configurations of intersubjectivity and ethics. On this point, Judith Butler's theory of ethical violence is central to my reading of *Mrs Dalloway* notably because it makes autonomous subjectivity both a political problem and a matter of intersubjective relations. Eighty years before *Precarious Life*, Butler's first book-length inquiry into the connections between a psychological ideal of unlimited subjective autonomy and the militaristic foreign policy adopted by the US government after 9/11, Woolf demonstrated in *Mrs Dalloway* how the same ideal sustained British nationalism in the inter-war years. But Woolf's novel anticipates Butler's theory also by suggesting that the political violence of aggressive nationalisms is coextensive with the ethical violence one individual is capable of inflicting on another. For Butler, a "deman[d] that we manifest and maintain self-identity at all times" leads the self-assertive subject to impose its worldview, norms and values on others. Conversely, Butler argues, ethical as well as socio-political violence can be countered through the suspension of the first-person perspective (*GAO* 42). We shall see, in the subsequent sections, how the introspective lyricism of *Mrs Dalloway* resists the forms of violence preoccupying Butler. While the text lucidly casts the disciplining of affect as a cause of ubiquitous ethical and socio-political violence, Woolf realised her ambition to "criticise the social system" through a creative, reparative mode which she frequently referred to, while composing the novel, as poetic. Indeed, *Mrs Dalloway* illuminates the extraordinary potential of poetic introspection to bring about a momentary loss of "egoic mastery" (*GAO* 64) in dyadic encounters, and a concomitant, joyful suspension of the first-person point of view. Throughout the text, this suspension is imagined as a mode of intimacy and achieved through Woolf's aesthetic and ethical practice of intimate revolt.

Insofar as *Mrs Dalloway* affirms and celebrates the affective undercurrents of psychic life, it is poetic in Julia Kristeva's sense of the term. In *Revolution in Poetic Language* (1984), Kristeva theorises the productive dialectic through which the literary representation of conscious and unconscious, symbolic and pre-symbolic processes engenders what she calls poetic language. As Kristeva puts it, this dialectic is "neither absolutizing the thetic into a possible theological prohibition, nor negating the thetic in the fantasy of a pulverizing irrationalism" (*RPL* 82). Semiotic or primary processes thus "for[m] the signifier, logically anterior to the grammatical sequences the Cartesian subject generates, but synchronous with their unfolding"; they *"function synchronically within the signifying process of the subject . . . of cogitatio"* (42, 29). The process through which a poetic "pulverization" of coherent linguistic structures succeeds in "cracking the socio-symbolic order, splitting it open," is a phase in a dialectic of accumulation and dispersal, a dialectic which is possible only within and through the subject's thetic positing of their autonomy in the symbolic order of a social community (88, 79). What the poetic "semiotization of the symbolic" (79) enables, then, is an aesthetic practice which is transformative because it resists absolutising social structures in which norms and values are upheld through a total repression of the semiotic by the symbolic. Social critique for Kristeva operates in literary production as a suspension of subjective autonomy; in the moment an individual is put "in process/on trial" through the writing of poetic language (22), the symbolic order in which s/he is inscribed is called into question.

When Toril Moi in her introduction to *Sexual/Textual Politics* proposed a Kristevan reading of Woolf's work, her emphasis was rather different. Her somewhat reductive summary of Kristeva's notion of revolutionary poetic writing – "the [semiotic] fragmentation of symbolic language . . . comes for [Kristeva] to parallel and prefigure a total *social* revolution" (11) – exemplifies a broader, poststructuralist tendency to locate Woolf's critical poetics in her textual subversion of symbolic repression.[12] Moi's approach was developed by Makiko Minow-Pinkney in her book-length study of Woolf and Kristeva, which ascribes to Woolf's experimental novels "a feminist subversion . . . of the very definitions of narrative, writing, the subject – of a patriarchal social order" (*Virginia Woolf and the Problem of the Subject* x). For Minow-Pinkney, *Mrs Dalloway* problematises the repression of the pre-linguistic union with the mother by the rational, unified subject in the symbolic.[13] While Minow-Pinkney's field-defining scholarship does not overlook the importance of the thetic in the Kristevan dialectic, it is marked by what she takes to be a privileging in Kristeva's work of the moment of semiotic eruption.

Moi and Minow-Pinkney transformed the field of Woolf studies in foregrounding a radical poetic capacity to undermine the univocal perspective of any symbolic (jointly literary and socio-political) order dominated by the writer's strictly coherent 'I', but they perform rather selective readings of both Kristeva and Woolf when claiming that *Mrs Dalloway* disrupts linear and coherent models of consciousness and narrative, and that the novel's opposition to authoritarian power structures is achieved primarily through such disruption.[14] If this assumption can be said to privilege the unconscious over the conscious, the emotional over the rational and pre-Oedipal attachments over Oedipal resolution, I propose that the novel's critical poetics emerges, like Kristeva's poetic language, from a conception of the symbolic and presymbolic dimensions of the psyche as coextensive and interdependent. That is to say, Woolf developed through the form and style of *Mrs Dalloway* a mode of social critique which proceeds through a joyful exploration of interiority and depends on a poetic interplay of conscious and unconscious processes. Rather than achieving a relentless subversion of the symbolic 'I,' Woolf's aesthetic practice fundamentally reconstructs the individual subject by promoting and inviting self-reflective introspection, which is central to the Kristevan dialectic between symbolic and semiotic. My departure from the theorised line of Woolf scholarship inaugurated by Moi and Minow-Pinkney might seem slight, a mere shift of emphasis, but I believe that a pleasurable, reparative attention to Woolf's introspective, affectively charged poetics as a form of intimate revolt might revive and continue a critical project left incomplete.

In my attempt at such a reparative reading of *Mrs Dalloway*, I shall draw on Kristeva's two-volume series *The Powers and Limits of Psychoanalysis*, comprising *The Sense and Non-Sense of Revolt* (2000) and *Intimate Revolt* (2002), in which social critique emerges as a mode of intimacy rather than (exclusively) a form of transgression or subversion. The aesthetic culture of revolt explored by Kristeva depends primarily on "thought as return, as search … 'going in quest of oneself'" (*IR* 6). What Kristeva terms intimate revolt is the process, central to avant-garde art, in which introspection, the act of looking inwards, enables a momentary return to a pre-symbolic way of relating to the world. In *The Sense and Non-Sense of Revolt*, she explores the Latin etymology of the word "revolt," showing that meanings such as "return" and "turning back" preceded the contemporary political meaning of "a rejection of authority" (1–4). Intimacy for Kristeva is "similar to the life of the mind, that is, the activity of the thinking ego," and "where we end up when we question apparent meanings and values" (*IR* 43). Crucially, the textual practice of revolt or critique is intimate, in the Latin superlative sense of "the most interior,"[15] because it achieves a "reuniting with affect" (44, 26). "We all have a sensorial cave," Kristeva writes, and the critical poetics she theorises is fundamentally concerned with "revalorizing the sensory experience" (54, 5). In this sense, "the intimate obtains a depth far beyond that of the thinking ego thinking of itself" (51). Thus conceived as a form of self-presence or presence of mind, intimacy, Kristeva argues, is necessary for the individual subject's capacity to call formative social values into question. Because it suspends the autonomous 'I' and, with it, the norms sustaining the social order in which the subject is inscribed, the act of intimate revolt is "a protest against already established norms, values, and powers" (1). The Kristevan aesthetic revolt is not, then, "the actual, concrete form of acting-out . . . in the form of violence, inflicted or sustained," but a "new symbolic form" based on self-reflexivity and introspection (*SNR* 24).

The idea of introspection as enabling a return to a pre-subjective mode of being is also central to Butler's ethical theory of accountability. In *Giving an Account of Oneself*, Butler theorises an introspective form of social critique operative in dyadic encounters between two individuals – the privileged realm of ethics. For Butler, the self-reflective act of giving an account of oneself suspends subjective autonomy, and this suspension makes possible a critique of the norms and values forming an individual in a socio-cultural community. During the process of giving an account of oneself to another, Butler holds, the speaker returns momentarily to a state in which 'I' cannot be distinguished from 'you.' Further to that, an individual whose first-person perspective is dislocated in the presence of an irreducible other is compelled not to commit the ethical violence of imposing their worldview on that other. In this sense, the giving of an account is an ethical act. Both Butler and Kristeva, then, highlight the extent to which an individual's inner life – thoughts, perceptions and emotions – shapes and is shaped by that individual's historically conditioned worldview. Likewise, for both, the communication of interiority, whether through intimate revolt or the act of giving an account of oneself, enables an interrogation of formational social norms and moral values. Their considerable differences notwithstanding, Kristeva's and Butler's respective theories of introspection as a non-violent form of return, or turning back, makes it possible to read *Mrs Dalloway* in a new light. They can make us see three things in particular, which I shall address in what follows: that Woolf configures interiority as enmeshed in the normative horizon shaping individuals in a violent socio-political order; that her aesthetic practice in *Mrs Dalloway* cultivates intimacy as defined by Kristeva – a "reuniting with affect" achieved through the poetic exploration of the life of the mind; and, finally, that the novel's poetics of intimate revolt both critiques the ethically violent imperative to suppress intense emotion and emphasises the individual subject's accountability before another.

Self-Control, Aggression and Ethical Violence

Insofar as Woolf's aesthetic practice in *Mrs Dalloway* can be read as an ethical, non-violent form of social critique, the novel anticipates *A Room of One's Own* stylistically as well as conceptually. Published four years after *Mrs Dalloway*,

Woolf's essay questions "male society and its values (militarism, hierarchy, authoritarianism)" (DuPlessis 40) by exposing the self-possessed writing of the unitary 'I' as a strategy for "enforc[ing] male values" (*AROO* 133). A counter-strategy is articulated in the opening pages:

> I am going to do what I can to show you how I arrived at this opinion about the room and the money. . . . Perhaps if I lay bare the ideas, the prejudices, that lie behind this statement you will find that they have some bearing upon women and some upon fiction. (4)

In thus retaining the face-to-face address particular to the essay's original lecture form,[16] Woolf holds her narrator accountable before her addressee as one individual before another (the imagined dyad of textual intimacy), but also before a collective (the speaker or storyteller's audience). Following this opening address, with its implied opposition of accountability and self-reflection to (proto-)fascist, "self-assertive virility" (134), the narrator begins her story:

> Here then was I . . . sitting on the banks of a river a week or two ago in fine October weather, lost in thought. . . . Thought – to call it by a prouder name than it deserved – had let its line down into the stream. It swayed, minute after minute, hither and thither among the reflections and the weeds, letting the water lift and sink it, until – you know the little tug – the sudden conglomeration of an idea at the end of one's line: and then the cautious hauling of it in, and the careful laying of it out? (5–6)

The passage dramatises playfully the idea of introspection, the act of looking inwards, as a self-reflective and potentially self-critical gesture. The metaphorical dimension of the narrative complicates the narrator's intention to demonstrate, through logic and reason, the unfolding of her political argument. The images of looking into the depths (of the mind) – the capturing of a thought, the "hauling of it in" and the "laying of it out" – illustrate a process that could not be described literally, precisely because it eludes the controlling grasp of conscious reflection. Throughout *Mrs Dalloway*, too, metaphors of deep water indicate psychic depths, as in Peter Walsh's reflection about "our soul . . . our self, who fish-like inhabits deep seas and plies among obscurities threading her way . . . over sun-flickered spaces and on and on into the gloom, cold, deep, inscrutable; suddenly she shoots to the surface" (*MD* 136). In Kristeva's theory, metonomy and metaphor are both central to the aesthetic practice in which the simultaneous unfolding of unconscious and conscious, symbolic and pre-symbolic processes makes the autonomous subject a subject-in-process (*RPL* 28, 59). Woolf's fishing metaphor in *A Room of One's Own* appears to produce precisely this dialectic.

Strictly within a symbolic framework of address, the narrator's poetic images point to the unconscious psychic dimension which shapes the line of thought to be presented for the reader's examination. Writing against a violent social order which promotes the assertion of the first-person perspective, Woolf posits a way of making critical statements and arguments through self-reflective and introspective fictional practices. In other words, *A Room of One's Own* begins by articulating a critical poetics which takes as its starting point the modernist "assumption that a part of human psychic life – what James termed 'the hidden self' and Virginia Woolf described as the 'hidden depths' of the psyche – escapes our conscious knowledge" (Micale 9).[17]

This poetics is also intensely sensual and pleasurable, as in Woolf's more overtly sexual use of the alluring fishing metaphor in her 1931 Speech to the London and National Society for Women's Service (published posthumously in revised form as "Professions for Women"). In this speech, the scene of the speaker or storyteller's address to a female audience becomes a seductive account of the novelist's "desire to be as unconscious as possible" in order "that nothing may disturb the flow, that nothing may interrupt the mysterious nosings about, feelings rounds, darts and dashes and sudden discoveries of that very shy and illusive fish the imagination" (*E* 5: 642, 643):

> I imagine [the female novelist] really in an attitude of contemplation, like a fisherwoman, sitting on the bank of a lake with her fishing rod held over its water. . . . she was letting her imagination down into the depths of her consciousness while she sat above holding on by a thin but quite necessary thread of reason. . . . The novelist is sitting on the shores of the lake, holding the little line of reason in her hands when suddenly there is a violent jerk; she feels the line race through her fingers. The imagination has rushed away; it has taken to the depths; it has sunk – heaven knows where – into what dark pool of extraordinary experience. . . . The novelist has to pull on the line and haul the imagination to the surface. The imagination comes to the top in a state of fury.
>
> "Good heavens!" she cries – "how dare you interfere with me! How dare you pull me out with your wretched little fishing line?" And I – that is the reason – have to reply, "My dear you were going altogether too far. Men would be shocked." Calm yourself, I say, as she sits panting on the bank – panting with rage and disappointment. . . . In fifty years I shall be able to use all this very queer knowledge that you are ready to bring me . . . about women's bodies for instance – their passions. (643–44)[18]

In *Mrs Dalloway*, pleasurable, contemplative introspection is juxtaposed to an ethically violent privileging of acts and events. As we have seen, the psychiatrist

Sir William Bradshaw's ideal of absolute self-control forecloses introspection; Septimus is told to "think as little about [him]self as possible," and Bradshaw's "curious exercise with the arms" exemplifies for his patients the healthy state of being master of one's mind and actions (*MD* 83, 86). The performance of this exercise is not only a mechanism of social exclusion. By imposing the restrictive norm of composure and self-control on Septimus, his doctors also inflict a form of ethical violence on him in the sense that to disregard Septimus's interiority is to fail to recognise him as a psychologically complex, and therefore inviolable, subject. In her 1920 review "Freudian Fiction," Woolf contrasts psychoanalysis, conceived as a science, to the realm of literature. As Elizabeth Abel notes, this review depicts the application of psychoanalytic theory to fiction as "a colonization of the literary field that transforms 'characters' into 'cases' through the application of a doctrinal 'key' that 'simplifies rather than complicates'" (17). Such reduction of psychologically complex minds to cases, or objects of study, shapes William Bradshaw's medical practice; his interpretative "key[s]," to use Woolf's own term, are proportion and self-control. By contrast, Woolf demonstrated, in composing *Mrs Dalloway*, what she argues for in "Freudian Fiction": the unique capacity of fiction to represent psychological complexity. In so doing, she began to explore a (psychoanalytic) depth model of the psyche into the remotest and therefore, paradoxically, most intimate regions where self-control must be relinquished. For Woolf as for Kristeva, the intimate or inmost, conceived as individual psychic life, comprises the unconscious, and therefore the strange and unknown. As S. K. Keltner observes, intimacy throughout Kristeva's *oeuvre* "signals not what is most familiar to me, but the strangeness pervading what is most familiar" (61), and the extent to which the same holds true for Woolf has yet to be explored.[19]

In the very act of creating intimate depth through poetic literary writing, Woolf's aesthetic practice resists the ethical violence of objectification. By contrast, Bradshaw's disregard for interiority is linked in the novel to his ethically problematic notion of the subject as strictly autonomous and in control, which is associated with his barely hidden aggression. In this sense, *Mrs Dalloway* anticipates Butler's observation that aggression and violence follow from the "deman[d] that we manifest and maintain self-identity at all times and require that others do the same" (*GAO* 42). Septimus remarks about the medical establishment of which Bradshaw and Holmes are representatives: "They scour the desert. They fly screaming into the wilderness. The rack and the thumbscrew are applied" (*MD* 83). Septimus's metaphors – the bird of prey, the instruments of torture – suggest that aggressive instincts and violent coercion are indistinguishable from the "proportion" of his doctors' psychological ideal. A similar image is used in *A Room of One's Own* to describe male professors who possess "money and power, but only at the cost of harbouring in their breasts an eagle, a vulture ... the instinct for possession, the rage for acquisition" (49). By associating figures of high social standing with predatory birds, these passages evoke the psychoanalytic theories of aggression which were largely contemporaneous with the composition and publication of *Mrs Dalloway*. Lyndsey Stonebridge writes about Freud's *Civilization and Its Discontents* (1929), which elaborates on his theory of the death drive in *Beyond the Pleasure Principle* (1920), that the "scandal" of the later work "rests with [Freud's] image of a super-ego which does not simply repress murderous desires but draws from them and repeats their ferocity with all the violence that it at the same time prohibits" (7). Melanie Klein's theory of primary aggression endorsed Freud's notion of the death drive, and Stonebridge examines the influence of Klein's work on numerous British accounts, in the 1920s and '30s, of instinctive aggression as a cause of violence and war.[20] The psychoanalytic notion of the individual's violent instincts as inextricable from public and political violence thus structures Woolf's images of establishment figures as birds of prey; William Bradshaw embodies civilisation as well as its discontents.

However, Woolf's fictional account in *Mrs Dalloway* of the causes of violence focuses less on the eruption of aggressive drives in the form of violence directed outwards than on the psychic mechanism of repression. As Zwerdling and Froula have pointed out, Woolf shows that unlimited self-control as a social (and moral) value – a norm which shaped British nationalism in the inter-war years – causes violence because it is sustained through repression. In this, her novel arguably engages the psychoanalytic problem that non-violence as a moral stance requires the super-ego's aggression turned inwards, towards the ego. For Freud, the earliest ethical commandment – "Thou shalt not kill" – originated in primal violence ("Thoughts for the Times" 81–86), and other non-violent moral imperatives (such as "Love thy neighbour as thyself" 337) are dictated by a "cultural super-ego" which, analogously with the super-ego's aggression towards the ego, brings about an internalisation of the aggressive instinct (*Civilization* 336–37). Within the Freudian schema, the civilisational capacity of art is feeble; the intensity of the satisfactions gained through artistic creation is "mild as compared with that derived from the sating of crude and primary instinctual impulses" (267).

The psychoanalytic impasse by which moral injunctions against violence necessitate either an ultimately ego-centred form of self-preservation (whereby

I seek to preserve the life of the other, to whom I am bound, only to ensure my own survival) or self-destruction (aggression against the self, as in melancholia) also pervades the work of Melanie Klein. Butler addresses precisely this impasse in her recent responses to Klein's and Freud's theories of morality and aggression, where she attempts to imagine a non-violent ethics capable of reversing the psychoanalytic primacy of the ego. Such an ethics, for Butler, would entail a mode of self-preservation originating in the desire to preserve the life of those (intimate and unknown) others who remain a formative, indistinguishable part of the self (*FW* 44–47, 174–77; "The Desire to Live"). I shall return, in the last section of this chapter, to the relevance of Butler's ethical reversal for Woolf's post-war experiments in poetic prose. For now, I will note that Woolf's novel prompts a Butlerian interrogation of the psychoanalytic conception of civilisation's discontents, a theoretical model which locks morality and modern civilisation in an eternal struggle between libidinal and destructive drives, Eros and Death. However, while Butler accepts the psychoanalytic axiom that "aggression is coextensive with being human," I see *Mrs Dalloway* as representative of Woolf's 1920s writing in how it depicts aggression as less a primal instinct than the consequence of a particularly violent civilisation sustained by the repressive, ethically violent ideal of self-mastery. In this, the text's revolt against psychic repression cultivates "a certain ethical practice, itself experimental, that seeks to preserve life better than it destroys it" (*FW* 177).

Throughout *Mrs Dalloway*, Woolf highlights the capacity of literary representation to further or, alternatively, resist the repressive norm of self-control. The first possibility is the focus of a passage which outlines the true character of Bradshaw's "proportion" as a psychological ideal with socio-political implications:

> Proportion, divine proportion, Sir William's goddess, was acquired by Sir William walking hospitals, catching salmon, begetting one son in Harley Street by Lady Bradshaw. . . . Worshipping proportion, Sir William not only prospered himself but made England prosper, secluded her lunatics, forbade childbirth, penalized despair, made it impossible for the unfit to propagate their views until they, too, shared his sense of proportion. (84)

This passage is striking because it is conveyed not, as is most of the novel, through a focalising character, but through the voice of an omniscient narrator. As we have seen, Woolf emphasised, in *Jacob's Room*, the complicity of (Edwardian) realist omniscience with war-time patriotism and militarism. The passage above achieves the same end through imitating realist strategies. By embedding the sharp critique of the second sentence in the psychiatrist's and the realist narrator's tone of disinterested observation, these lines highlight the discord between the ideal of strict rationality and the violent impulses it conceals, not least in how they mimic a syntactically orderly depiction of external events ("walking hospitals, catching salmon, begetting one son"). We recall Woolf's ethically and politically charged critique, in "Character in Fiction," of Arnold Bennett and H. G. Wells's privileging of acts and events at the expense of interiority. In Kristeva's theory, violence occurs in "the time of acts" (*IR* 21), that is, the time of the symbolic. This is also the temporal order of representational modes in which symbolic reason and logic repress the semiotic dimension of psychic life. From this perspective, a non-violent poetics may well be articulated through literary writing which promotes interiority and introspection.

As the passage above also makes evident, William Bradshaw's ideal of proportion "ma[kes] England prosper" particularly because the private and dyadic exchanges between Bradshaw and his patients are inextricably bound up with the public and political realm of British nationalism. Walkowitz writes about Woolf's short story "The Mark on the Wall" (1917): "It is about the refusal . . . to *separate* the political 'facts' of a European war (casualties and official reports) from the disarray of a living room in England" (86). The same can be said about *Mrs Dalloway* insofar as the novel shows the patriotic, militarised "social system" to be "at work, at its most intense" (*D* 2: 248) in intersubjective spaces such as Clarissa Dalloway's living room. In a dramatisation of a covertly hostile encounter between Clarissa and Peter Walsh, Woolf depicts the aggression which inevitably arises as two individuals assert their subjective perspectives without recognising the interlocutor's different viewpoint. The encounter is staged as a battle between the two, in which each struggles to defend a self-image threatened by the other's questioning presence. Clarissa's question "Well, and what's happened to you?" is followed by images of enmity and warfare:

> So before a battle begins, the horses paw the ground; toss their heads; the light shines on their flanks; their necks curve. So Peter Walsh and Clarissa, sitting side by side on the blue sofa, challenged each other. His powers chafed and tossed in him. He assembled from different quarters all sorts of things; praise, his career at Oxford; his marriage, which she knew nothing whatever about; how he had loved; and altogether done his job. (*MD* 37–38)

The metaphor of horses on a battlefield suggests at once beast-like instinct – the aggressive impulses which the two characters barely manage to suppress – and the battlefield as a site of nations at war. The idea of a battle is accentuated by

Peter and Clarissa's respective handling of sharp objects (a pocket-knife and a needle) capable of inflicting violence. Feeling his own worldview undermined by Clarissa's high social standing ("there's nothing in the world so bad for some women as marriage" [35]), Peter fingers his knife:

> So it is, so it is, he thought, shutting his knife with a snap.... And this has been going on all the time! he thought; week after week; Clarissa's life, while I – he thought; and at once everything seemed to radiate from him; journeys; rides; quarrels; adventures; bridge parties; love affairs; work; work, work! and he took out his knife quite openly, his old horn-handed knife which Clarissa could swear he had had these thirty years – and clenched his fist upon it. (35, 37)

The abrupt shift of focalising perspectives in the following paragraph highlights further the friction and hostility of the encounter:

> What an extraordinary habit that was, Clarissa thought; always playing with a knife. Always making one feel, too, frivolous; empty-minded; a mere silly chatterbox, as he used. But I too, she thought, and, taking up her needle, summoned, like a Queen whose guards have fallen asleep and left her unprotected ... summoned to her help the things she did; the things she liked; her husband; Elizabeth; her self, in short, which Peter hardly knew now, all to come about her and beat off the enemy. (37)

In playing the two viewpoints off against each other, the text exposes the aggressive impulses which at every moment threaten to ruin the pleasant surface of a conversation between two old friends. This account of aggression is delivered through Woolf's experiments with focalisation and narrative perspective; the clash of perspectives is conveyed not as a descriptive report of the (sympathetic) conversation, but through the narrator's juxtaposition of two sharply conflicting worldviews. In this way, the formal arrangement of the scene exposes the structure of intersubjective encounters predicated on a "deman[d] that we manifest and maintain self-identity at all times," as Butler puts it (*GAO* 42). Interestingly, however, this arrangement gains its revelatory force notably through Woolf's idiosyncratic, intimate mode of focalisation. While the distinct voice of the realist third-person narrator shapes the social values and normative horizon of the text in question, the voice of Woolf's narrator merges, gently and alternately, with Clarissa's and Peter's introspective viewpoints, neither of which is privileged.[21] Operating as an intimate aesthetic performance rather than as detached narrative statement or (realist) description, Woolf's formal devices here foreground the interconnectedness of ethical violence and the violence of war.

The dyadic exchange between Peter and Clarissa also plays out in what Kristeva calls "the time of acts" (*IR* 21). Feeling his self-image threatened, Peter assembles to his defence a list of achievements: "praise, his career at Oxford; his marriage" (*MD* 38). Throughout the scene, similar claims to things done and achieved underpin Peter's and Clarissa's acts of self-assertion, which coincide conspicuously with their defensive and potentially threatening toying with sharp objects: "rides; quarrels; adventures; bridge parties; love affairs; work; work, work! and he took out his knife quite openly. . . . But I too, she thought, and, taking up her needle, summoned . . . to her help the things she did" (37). Woolf here conveys an insight central to Kristeva's theoretical paradigm – that the aggressive assertion of the symbolic 'I' is likely to lead to violence in the social and political time of acts. In the next section, I engage Kristeva's theory of intimacy to propose that Woolf developed in *Mrs Dalloway* a modernist aesthetic which evinces political and ethical commitment because it radically reconfigures the individual subject. Through its aesthetic figuration of rational and emotional, symbolic and pre-symbolic dimensions of the psyche as mutually constitutive and simultaneously operating, the text opposes the ethically violent act of asserting the first-person perspective in one-to-one encounters without apprehending the other's perspective or worldview.

In this sense, *Mrs Dalloway* confronts a restrictive social community sustained through the violent exclusion of subjects who are not considered "master[s] of [their] own actions" (*MD* 86), but the novel's social critique originates in the realm of ethics; for Woolf, to write in opposition to social and political conformism is to insist that such mastery can only be partial because of the alluring, intimate depths waiting to be conveyed by one subject to another in the dyadic encounter. As we shall see next, the non-violent ethics of *Mrs Dalloway* promotes intimacy as blissful self-presence. For Kristeva, we recall, the political practice of intimate revolt proceeds through the poetic writing of interiority. In a productive interplay of the bodily/sensual/pre-verbal and the rational/reflective/linguistic capacities of the psyche, intimate revolt for Kristeva "suspends the time of acts" (*IR* 21). This definition of revolt illuminates the fundamentally reparative dimension of Woolf's critical poetics. Against the repressive, ubiquitous ideal of self-control and the systemic violence it sustains, *Mrs Dalloway* cultivates an intensely pleasurable ethics of intimate introspection which has political potential because it suspends the time of violence and the subject's autonomy. I would like to go even further and venture that Woolf reverses a common notion of intimacy as something continuous that unfolds over time, and violence as sudden and disruptive; in *Mrs Dalloway*, it is violence that is constant by virtue of being systematic, hence the transformative capacity of intimacy conceived as a form of revolt.

"Reuniting with Affect": Intimacy, Bliss and Revolt in the Timeless

We saw, at the outset of this chapter, how Woolf's introspective diary notes about the pleasurable process of writing *Mrs Dalloway* both recorded and realised an enraptured transport from overwhelming physical sensations and intense emotions into the region of *jouissance*: the blissful climax attained in the poetic act of conveying such sensations and emotions in words. The creative pleasure Woolf associates with an orgasmic "fountain of creative energy" (*AROO* 131) is the kind of bliss which, according to Kristeva, erupts when the "unity of the speaking being, sealed by consciousness" is put "on trial" in poetic language. In *The Powers and Limits of Psychoanalysis*, Kristeva emphasises the "condition of renewal and joy" immersing the writer in revolt (*SNR* 18), in whom the suspension of the first-person perspective produces "a jouissance, the pleasure of sensory meaning or of the sensory in meaning" (*IR* 48). The "centrifugal forces of dissolution and dispersion" at work in *jouissance*, she claims, are "indispensable to the faculty of representation and questioning" (7). Conversely, it is "through retrospective questioning . . . through inquiry or analysis" that poetic art enables an intimate return to the pre-subjective. This is how, for Kristeva, intimacy can be "a continuous copresence between the sensible and the intelligible" (10, 47), while intimate revolt is an "attempt to find a representation (a language, a thought, a style) for this confrontation with the unity of law, being, and the self to which man accedes in jouissance" (10). Because it enables such confrontation, the activity of writing and/or thinking "can become . . . a constant calling into question of the psyche as well as the world" (*SNR* 19).

According to Kristeva, then, it is through the writer's experience of *jouissance* that his or her autonomous self and the social structure in which s/he is inscribed can be called into question. In this sense, the critical aesthetic practice of revolt both depends on and achieves an intimate "reuniting with affect" (*IR* 26). Kristeva stresses continuously the importance of "remain[ing] attentive to our inner states" and of "naming/thinking the unrepresentable sensations of the soul" (52). Such naming or thinking, she argues, materialises through the detached organisation of affect in literary form and style; discussing Marcel Proust's writing, Kristeva observes that "the strictly Proustian effect resides in the passage from what is felt to what is formulated" (58). Woolf, an avid reader of Proust, uses terms strikingly similar to Kristeva's "copresence between the sensible and the intelligible" when describing *À la recherche du temps perdu*, in which she sees a "union of the thinker and the poet" (*E* 5: 68).²² And in a letter to Roger Fry, dated 3 October 1922, Woolf asks with astonishment about the first volume of *La Recherche*: "How, at last, has someone solidified what has always escaped – and made it too into this beautiful and perfectly enduring substance? One has to put the book down and gasp. The pleasure becomes physical" (*L* 2: 566). In another letter to Fry, of 6 May the same year, she writes ardently of Proust as a source of inspiration for her own novel experiments:

> But Proust so titillates my own desire for expression that I can hardly set out the sentence. Oh if I could write like that! I cry. And at the moment such is the astonishing vibration and saturation and intensification that he procures – theres (sic) something sexual in it – that I feel I *can* write like that, and seize my pen and then I *can't* write like that. (525)

Woolf appears here as a precursor of Kristeva, Roland Barthes and Sedgwick, all of whom acclaim Proust's writing as a prime example of a simultaneously pleasure-driven and critical literary mode. For Sedgwick, *Time Regained* inspires "a strong theory of positive affect" centred on pleasure and joy, one that may provide a complementary alternative to the paranoid imperative (138), while Barthes refers to Proust's volumes as "*the* reference work" for his theory of literary bliss or *jouissance* as "shock, disturbance, even loss," the climax attained through the reader's transport from the "euphoria, fulfillment, comfort" of pleasure (36, 19, 19). The text of bliss for Barthes does for the reader what it does for Kristeva's writer in revolt: "the simultaneously erotic and critical value of textual practice" (all too often "forgotten, repressed, stifled" in literary critical and theoretical practices) momentarily "unsettles the reader's historical, cultural, psychological assumptions . . . values, memories, brings to a crisis his relation with language" (Barthes 64, 64, 14).

We shall return shortly to the bliss Woolf produces in her reader, and to the synthesis it inspires of thought and affect, lyrical effusion and aesthetic detachment, ecstatic pleasure and non-violent revolt. Among the characters in *Mrs Dalloway*, Clarissa resembles an artist as defined by Kristeva. "She plunged," we read, "into the very heart of the moment, transfixed it – there" (*MD* 31). Capable of both taking sensual pleasure in moments of *jouissance* and arranging them through strategies of conscious thought, Clarissa simultaneously "plunge[s] into" and "transfixe[s]" these moments in a blissfully poetic, metaphoric passage, indeed "one of the most emblematic modernist descriptions of female eros" (Frost):

> Only for a moment; but it was enough. It was a sudden revelation, a tinge like a blush which one tried to check and then, as it spread, one yielded to its expansion, and rushed to the farthest verge and there quivered and felt the world come closer, swollen with some astonishing significance, some pressure of rapture, which split its thin skin and gushed and poured with an extraordinary alleviation over the cracks and sores. Then, for that moment, she had seen an illumination; a match burning in a crocus; an inner meaning almost expressed. (*MD* 27)

Clarissa then proceeds to analyse this orgasmic experience: "But this question of love (she thought, putting her coat away), this falling in love with women. Take Sally Seton; her relation in the old days with Sally Seton, had not that, after all, been love?" (28). The word "love" here is devoid of what Kristeva terms sensory meaning and located in a distant past, and through the act of arranging her coat, Clarissa arranges or "transfixes" what is now the "question of love" in the symbolic time of acts.

How are we to understand this poetic transport from enraptured pleasure into orgasmic *jouissance* via the affectively detached aesthetic framing of the moment of bliss? Both lesbian and psychoanalytic readings of the passage have tended to see this framing as a form of narrative containment evincing the repressive, heteronormative disciplining of women's sexuality and same-sex intimacy in the early twentieth century.[23] Such readings have also focused predominantly on character rather than the political capacities of Woolf's poetics of *jouissance*; this is the tendency even in Bonnie Kime Scott's reading of the orgasmic passage in her aptly entitled chapter, "Woolf's Rapture with Language" (10–12). A welcome focal shift emerges in Laura Frost's forthcoming essay on modernist depictions of female orgasm. Frost illuminates the socio-political implications of a typical, introspective and metaphoric aesthetic mode which, like Woolf's, imagined the female climax as a mysterious, unbounded inner sensation distinct from the self-contained, definitive physical experience associated with male orgasm. It was precisely this elusive, boundless quality as figured in the introspective modernist imaginary ("an inner meaning *almost* expressed" [italics added]) which, Frost argues, made female orgasm in the first decades of the twentieth century susceptible to systematic biopolitical management aimed at regulating women's agency and autonomy.

In light of this development, we could ask whether Woolf's erotic climax in *Mrs Dalloway* does not ultimately resist what Frost calls "orgasmic discipline," not only because it is "Inspired by another woman, and self-alleviating" (Scott 11) – queer and lesbian orgasm largely eluded biopolitical regulation, Frost notes – but precisely through its detached aesthetic framing in the first and last sentence of the passage cited above. While Clarissa's act of introspection can perhaps do little to suspend or expand her historically specific normative horizon, in which same-sex desire as well as female orgasm required management, the intimate conflation of her voice with the poetic utterance of a skilled storyteller (the narrator) and writer (Woolf herself) in the figurative, orgasmic sentence arguably unleashes a process of intimate revolt, what Kristeva calls "naming/thinking the unrepresentable sensations of the soul" (*IR* 52), which depends as much on the writer and reader's physical pleasure as their sensory-affective detachment. This process may indeed be subversive because Woolf's invitation to experience the physical sensation of female orgasm, enabled through metaphoric figuration as well as its definitive framing in the time of acts ("Only for a moment"; "Then, for that moment"), exceeds the amorphous and private inner experience (Clarissa's, or Woolf's) which made female orgasm so susceptible to biopolitical co-optation in this period.

It is, Woolf suggests, through the intimate act of writing and reading poetic fiction that the momentary dissolution of the self in orgasmic *jouissance* as an aesthetic experience can bring about a politically subversive revolt against repressive social values and regimes. The introspective diary entry of 19 June 1923, where Woolf states her intention to "criticise the social system," begins with the idea that fiction writing should proceed from "feeling things deeply." "But now," she asks herself,

> what do I feel about *my* writing? – this book, that is, The Hours, if thats (sic) its name? One must write from deep feeling, said Dostoevsky. And do I? Or do I fabricate with words, loving them as I do? No I think not. In this book I have almost too many ideas. I want to give life & death, sanity & insanity; I want to criticise the social system, & to show it at work, at its most intense – But here I may be posing. (*D* 2: 248)

The passage suggests a direct connection between socio-politically committed writing and the communication of interiority; Woolf's concern that she "may be posing" in her critical effort is also an anxiety that her "fabricat[ing] with words" may somehow be dissociated from "deep feeling." If Woolf, in writing *Mrs Dalloway*, sought to question social structures (and strictures) through what Kristeva terms a revalorisation of sensory experience, her diary also suggests that form, style and structure would be crucial to this project. Further down in the same entry, Woolf sees strong potential in the novel's "so queer & so masterful" design: "The design is certainly original, & interests me hugely" (249). Later in the composition process, she reflects: "I think writing must be formal. The art must be respected. This struck me reading some of my notes here, for, if one lets the mind run loose, it becomes egotistic; personal, which I detest.... At the same time the irregular fire must be there; & perhaps to loose it, one must begin by being chaotic" (321). Woolf suggests, in these diary entries, that through the rigorous aesthetic devices of formally experimental, introspective and poetic representation, the "irregular fire" of the writer's intense emotions becomes in the fictional text something other than the unreflected, ego-centred expression of the coherent 'I.'

Woolf's conception of poetic creation as the communication of sensory experience and heightened emotion in the written word has clear affinities with Kristeva's theory of revolt: "the ultimate goal of art is perhaps what was once celebrated as incarnation. I mean by that the desire to make one feel – through abstraction, form, color, volume, sensation – a real experience" (*SNR* 11). In *Intimate Revolt*, Kristeva observes similarly that "When he finds a language for this opaque, nonverbal, sensory experience ... Proust succeeds where the autistic fails" (54). The idea of writing as at once incarnation and communication is realised in *Mrs Dalloway* by the aeroplane which advertises toffee in spelling out the word, letter by letter, in the sky. Soaring "up and up, straight up, like something mounting in ecstasy, in pure delight," the plane leaves behind a trail of white smoke shaped like "a T, and O, an F" (*MD* 24), letters with no intrinsic meaning or given correspondence to one another. The mesmerised spectators on the ground nonetheless expect a message to be delivered by the potentially nonsensical writing. "So, thought Septimus, looking up, they are signalling to me. Not indeed in actual words; that is, he could not read the language yet" (18). In Septimus's psychotic state, the letters, repeated by the nursemaid next to him, are void of semantic meaning and received as sound and sensory pleasure in pure incarnation:

> It was toffee; they were advertising toffee, a nursemaid told Rezia. Together they began to spell t ... o ... f ...
> "K ... R ..." said the nursemaid, and Septimus heard her say "Kay Arr" close to his ear, deeply, softly, like a mellow organ, but with a roughness in her voice like a grasshopper's, which rasped his spine deliciously and sent running up into his brain waves of sound, which, concussing, broke. (19, ellipses in original)

For Septimus, the aeroplane communicates not through what Kristeva terms symbolic meaning, but through the very process of writing; its message or signal emerges not from the linguistic sequence "t . . . o . . . f," but in the physically felt effect of the written letters.[24]

Septimus's psychotic receptivity plays a central role in the affectively charged communicational mode which Woolf created in writing *Mrs Dalloway*. In the aeroplane scene, other characters react physically to the very movement of the vehicle as it shapes letters in the sky. Responding not to what is being written, Mrs Dempster responds nonetheless, despite herself, as it were: "It swept and fell. Her stomach was in her mouth. Up again" (24). Equally central, however, is the structural arrangement of potentially meaning-bearing sequences. Throughout the episode, the writing in the sky is understood to communicate something only because it appears as letters in a sequence, even if its semantic meaning remains a question: "and it soared up and wrote one letter after another – but what word was it writing?" (18). It is through this question, asked repeatedly by the spectators, that they engage in what they take to be a communicative situation. The aeroplane transmits the "ecstasy" and "pure delight" of the act of writing because "a T, and O, an F" are arranged in that particular order.[25] The written communication described in this episode is also enacted through Woolf's very practice of writing poetically. While Septimus hears the nursemaid's words "close to his ear . . . with a roughness in her voice like a grasshopper's, which rasped his spine deliciously," his ecstatic pleasure is transmitted to the reader in a syntactically coherent poetic sequence designed by Woolf, in which syntactic mastery coincides with alliteration and pure sound. In this, the sequence exemplifies the text of bliss as conceived by Barthes – the dyadic site where the writer seduces the reader in creating a critical cut between the "edges" of literary-linguistic mastery and its dissolution (6–7), in this case through the aesthetic device of "vocal writing": "a text where we can hear the grain of the throat, the patina of consonants, the voluptuousness of vowels, a whole carnal stereophony" (66).[26]

In thus arranging and communicating intense physical sensations, Woolf problematises the state of "experimental psychosis" which, in Kristeva's theory, is attained by writers and, we could add, readers of poetic text: "It is through the archaeology of his unity, conducted in the material of language and thought itself, that the subject reaches the hazardous regions where this unity is annihilated" (*IR* 10). If psychosis is necessary for the poetic language of intimate revolt, this language is not psychotic. Septimus, who is unable to order and communicate his inner life, does not respond to the aeroplane's signals as a subject in the symbolic. The message he deciphers is his experience that "leaves were alive; trees were alive. And the leaves being connected by millions of fibres with his own body, there on the seat" (*MD* 19),²⁷ but he himself cannot formulate it. "[F]umbling for his card and pencil" (57), he must ask his wife to write down, as he speaks, a myriad observations, visions and overwhelming sensory experiences which to her can only be "very beautiful" or "sheer nonsense" (119). Perceiving himself as indistinguishable from the world around him, Septimus is incapable of taking part in communication and social exchange. "[Q]uite alone, condemned, deserted," he is an "outcast, who gazed back at the inhabited regions, who lay, like a drowned sailor, on the shore of the world" (79). As Froula observes, Septimus is expelled by "a society that scapegoats him for bringing home the murderous aggression it would disavow, that projects its aggression upon him" ("Postwar Elegy" 148).²⁸ If intimate revolt against such aggressive projection proceeds through the communicative sharing of intense emotion in poetic language, Septimus cannot be a writer in revolt. Torn between chaotic physical sensations and affectively detached reasoning – "he could reason; he could read . . . he could add up his bill," but "he could not feel" (75) – Septimus is acutely receptive to what Woolf calls "the poetry of existence" (*D* 2: 246), yet incapable of writing poetically. As Septimus's example ultimately reveals, the critical textual practice Woolf developed in composing *Mrs Dalloway* depends fundamentally not on a permanent dissolution of subjective autonomy, but on the writer's and reader's experience of *jouissance* within the communicative, intersubjective context of the symbolic order.²⁹

In *Mrs Dalloway*, the poetic, introspective process of intimate revolt is also enacted on a temporal level. The novel creates a Bergsonian distinction between linear time – what Kristeva terms the time of acts – and the time of the mind. Woolf's metaphor for writing interiority, "dig[ging] out beautiful caves," is extended through the related image of the "tunnelling process," which suggests a technique for conveying an immersion in memories (*D* 2: 263, 272). Critics have long read *Mrs Dalloway* as favouring inner time, what Bergson calls *durée*. Mary Ann Gillies, for one, traces Bergson's privileging of *durée* over *l'étendu* in British modernist texts, all the while conceding that, for Bergson, the experience of inner time must be spatialised in the clock time of communication and social relations; a complete immersion in *durée* would be "an isolated existence bordering on madness," a "solipsistic escape into the self" (13). For Woolf, Gillies suggests, such spatialisation occurs through writing and, more specifically, the writing of the moments of heightened sensitivity which Woolf herself called "moments of being" (59).³⁰ According to Gillies, "Woolf's original moment is one in which time, as clock time, ceases to exist and time, as *durée*, takes centre stage" (59); Woolf's moments of "being" or "pure *durée*," she argues, "bring about a conflation of times" in which "past and present time . . . literally coexist" (109). More recently, Teresa Prudente's book-length study of Woolf and the experience of time retains the critical focus on moments of "exit" from linear temporality. Woolf's treatment of the process of memory, Prudente claims, "transcends [linear time] in an instantaneous co-presence of past and present" (25). In the theoretical paradigm stretching from Bergson to Paul Ricoeur, memory functions in Woolf's fiction "not as a linear act of thinking," but rather as "an immersion in the past, . . . in which the sensorial more than the rational elements are fundamental" (26).[31]

While Prudente admits that for Woolf, linear and a-linear time are "complementary temporal directions, . . . co-existent and interacting in the subject" (35, 38), and while Gillies observes in *Mrs Dalloway* a "union" of *durée* and *l'étendu* (115), neither attempts a reading of this interaction as politically or ethically constructive. After all, as Prudente observes, Woolf exposes in *Mrs Dalloway* the convergence of linear time with the violence and coercion underlying William Bradshaw's ideal of absolute self-control: "Shredding and slicing, dividing and subdividing, the clocks of Harley Street nibbled at the June day, counselled submission, upheld authority" (*MD* 87). Is there a critical dimension to the novel's configuration of temporality other than this exposure? In response to critics like Prudente, we could ask: what critique of a violent social order is possible if the (ontologised) moments of "exit," in which clock time is suspended, are ultimately inscribed in the temporal sequence that sustains the ethical violence of coercion? I would like to consider the possibility that Woolf makes productive use of temporal linearity as a vital part of her novel's non-violent revolt, and more specifically, that her poetics of bliss or *jouissance* depends on the intimate "copresence between the sensible and the intelligible" (*IR* 47), which is also the copresence of the time of acts and its suspension. In this, my Kristevan approach to politicised novel experiments with temporality diverges from Caroline Levine's intriguing call for a new kind of formalist attention to the conflicting or colliding temporal rhythms shaping a literary work as a particularly charged site for political activity.[32]

Kristeva points out that the Freudian timeless, the temporality enabling revolt, is radical in a way the Bergsonian *durée* is not. While Bergson and Freud both conceptualised "an extrasubjective and extraexistential temporality that is the true challenge to thought" (*IR* 29), Bergson's qualitative duration is "always an immediate given of *consciousness*," whereas the linear temporality suspended by the Freudian *Zeitlos* is precisely "consciousness-time, a certain course of psychical events" (*IR* 29, 28). Kristeva stresses Freud's definition of rebellion as a momentary "access to the archaic," to the realm of "'non-time,' the 'timeless' . . . time undone" (*SNR* 16). That is, for Kristeva via Freud, conscious meaning is suspended in a "return" to the time of the unconscious, and in the timeless state "we revisit nothing less than our intimate depths" (*IR* 12). This process takes place in "a temporality heterogeneous to linear time (*Zeitlos*), thus opening each human manifestation (act, speech, symptom), beyond consciousness, toward unconscious/prepsychical/somatic/physical continuity" (32). It is in this sense that the Kristevan revolt in the timeless "suspends the time of acts" (21).

The revolutionary *Zeitlos*, Kristeva emphasises, is a "time outside time, . . . where time rejoins the timeless" (*IR* 25; see *SNR* 16). If, when immersed in the time of the unconscious, "we rupture the chain of values and current events," it is because the timeless depends fundamentally on the temporal (*IR* 25). In other words, the time of revolt "relies on the linear time of consciousness in order to inscribe a rift there, a breach, a frustration: this is the scandal of the timeless" (30). "Scandal" here is defined etymologically as "detainment": the timeless state does not subvert but *detains* linear temporality (31), and this detainment, or suspense, is the precondition for Kristevan revolt. Crucially, the *jouissance* experienced through psychoanalysis or the writing of poetic language is "not (only) a certain transgressive relationship to the Law but indeed this intersection of time and the timeless" (38).[33] In Woolf's novel, the moments of suspense or being create the possibility of *jouissance* in a state where time and the timeless coincide. Consider the following lines about Clarissa's reaction when hearing that she has not been invited to Millicent Bruton's lunch party:

> But she feared time itself, and read on Lady Bruton's face, as if it had been a dial cut in impassive stone, the dwindling of life; how year by year her share was sliced; how little the margin that remained was capable any longer of stretching, of absorbing, as in the youthful years, the colours, salts, tones of existence, so that she filled the room as she entered, and felt often, as she stood hesitating one moment on the threshold of her drawing-room, an exquisite suspense, such as might stay a diver before plunging while the sea darkens and brightens beneath him, and the waves which threaten to break, but only gently split their surface, roll and conceal and encrust as they just turn over the weeds with pearl.
> She put the pad on the hall table. She began to go slowly upstairs. (*MD* 26)

The passage displays an alluring contradiction; Clarissa remains convinced that time, "cut in impassive stone," is now inexorably linear, inflexible and incapable of expanding or "stretching," while Woolf suggests the opposite by manipulating the sentence. If the grammatical sentence is a static unit with a linear progression from capital letter to full stop, then the long sentence above is stretched and pleasurably suspended through innumerable subclauses, semi-colons and commas.[34] The time of the sentence, described as static, is similarly suspended; the past tense conveying Clarissa's (supposedly past) moments of "exquisite suspense" ("and felt often, as she stood hesitating") is, throughout the novel, the tense of the narrative present. As Minow-Pinkney notes, Woolf's use in *Mrs Dalloway* of the past tense (instead of the past perfect) to describe events of the past achieves a blurring or fusion of times, a "transcendence of narrative linearity" (57; see 56).[35]

However, it is not only the dividing line between past and present that becomes indistinct as we read about Clarissa on the threshold of her drawing-room; the blissful effect of simultaneity conveyed by the passage is also produced by an intersection of linear and timeless, conscious and unconscious temporalities. The image of the hesitating diver, a metaphor of the conscious, autonomous self on the verge of dissolving in *jouissance* ("the waves which threaten to break"), exemplifies the threshold linking the two temporalities in poetic language. If, as Kristeva holds, poetically metaphoric and rhythmical writing enable an intimate "reuniting with affect" (*IR* 26), then the passage above illuminates the at once temporal and timeless dimension in which such writing takes place. Indeed, the long sentence reveals the necessity of temporal and narrative linearity for the vital coexistence of semiotic and symbolic time in revolt. The sentence is inscribed in the narrative time of acts (Lady Bruton's lunch party; walking upstairs) and its syntactic structure, while manipulated, remains unbroken. The very rhythm of the poetic sentence is engendered by Woolf's meticulous punctuation and syntactic mastery. In this respect, *Mrs Dalloway* defies one of Kristeva's few remarks about Woolf. In an interview from 1974, Kristeva suggests that, as a woman writer, Woolf sees language as if "from a foreign land," which is why her texts cannot be fully poetic in Kristeva's sense: "Virginia Woolf describes suspended states, subtle sensations and, above all, colors . . . but she does not dissect language as Joyce does" ("Oscillation" 166). Kristeva's later emphasis on precisely "suspended states" – the Freudian timeless and the writer's *jouissance* – calls for a re-evaluation of her earlier assessment of Woolf's writing. Reading *Mrs Dalloway* alongside Kristeva's notion of intimate revolt might, then, reveal the extent to which the novel's experimental poetics operates like the politically resonant avant-garde aesthetic theorised by Kristeva.

Throughout *Mrs Dalloway*, (ontological) moments of being are portrayed, through Woolf's poetic language, as simultaneously linear and a-temporal (exceeding ontology); the characters' brief return to the pre-symbolic is inextricable from the novel's framework of striking clocks. This is how Peter, overcome by "the strangeness of standing alone, alive, unknown, at half-past eleven in Trafalgar Square," suddenly experiences an "exquisite delight; as if inside his brain, by another hand, strings were pulled, shutters moved, and he, having nothing to do with it, yet stood at the opening of endless avenues" (44). Peter's exquisite delight is a strikingly passive emotion, which brings about a momentary surrender of identity and subjective autonomy: "I haven't felt so young for years! thought Peter, escaping (only of course for an hour or so) from being precisely what he was, and feeling like a child who runs out of doors" (44–45). The passivity characterising *jouissance* is also conveyed by the aesthetic framing of Clarissa's orgasmic moment. The poetic sentence beginning "It was a sudden revelation, a tinge like a blush which one tried to check and then, as it spread, one yielded to its expansion" stands in contrast to the following sentence: "Then, for that moment, she had seen an illumination; a match burning in a crocus; an inner meaning almost expressed" (27). The pronoun "one," which in the first sentence substitutes the personal pronoun "she" in the second, suggests an experience similar to Peter's "escap[e]" from autonomous subjectivity. Two distinct moments, one of "yield[ing]" to the "expansion" of *jouissance* and one of containing this expansion in linear time, emerge here as simultaneous. My understanding of Woolf's productive simultaneity thus differs considerably from Martin Hägglund's recent case for appreciating how she depicts "the violent passage of time . . . at work even in the most immediate and fully experienced moment" (57); while Hägglund reads this paradigmatic modernist temporality in *Mrs Dalloway* as inherently traumatic (62–75), I see it as primarily reparative and pleasurable.[36]

How, then, does Woolf transmit the aesthetic experience of bliss, which both originates in and exceeds intense emotion, to her reader, so that the process of reading *Mrs Dalloway* may become an act of intimate revolt? The reading practice elicited by this text, and indeed by Woolf's novels from *Mrs Dalloway* to *The Waves*, might be best described via Barthes's idea of a convergence of two ways of reading: one which "sticks to the text . . . with application and transport" (12), and another, in which we must yield to the physical sensation of *jouissance*:

> The pleasure of the text is not necessarily of a triumphant, heroic, muscular type. . . . My pleasure can very well take the form of a drift. *Drifting* occurs whenever . . . by dint of seeming driven about by language's illusions, seductions, and intimidations, like a cork on the waves, I remain motionless, pivoting on the *intractable* bliss that binds me to the text (to the world). (18)

This simultaneity of applied, intimate reading and the blissful dissolution of the reading, drifting self into the erotic body of the text is immediately political insofar as parallels can be drawn between, on the one hand, our pleasurable receptivity to the lines describing Peter's "escap[e]" and Clarissa's "yield[ing]" and, on the other, Woolf's description, in *A Room of One's Own*, of the enraptured, creative mind in revolt against "self-assertive virility" (*AROO* 134) as androgynous. Woolf takes Coleridge's statement that "a great mind is androgynous" to mean "that the androgynous mind is resonant and porous; that it transmits emotion without impediment; that it is naturally creative, incandescent, and undivided" (128). Or, in Kristevan terms, the androgynous writer writes poetically. The act of "transmit[ting] emotion without impediment" in writing suggests a return to a pre-gendered, "undivided" state in which, as Emily M. Hinnov points out in her Kristevan approach to Woolf's androgyny, "the 'masculine' and 'feminine' sides of our being are melded" in "a sense of wholeness" prior to the construction of gender identities (22). This aesthetic mode of giving up gendered distinctions is, however, possible only within a social order in which such distinctions are firmly in place; Woolf speaks of a "fusion" (*AROO* 127) of the two sides in (symbolic) terms such as "collaboration" and "marriage of opposites" (136). In this way, Woolf's idea of androgyny resembles Kristeva's conception of intimacy as "a continuous copresence between the sensible and the intelligible – a true continuity, beyond division" (*IR* 47).[37]

"Odd Affinities She Had with People She Had Never Spoken To": The Intimate Opacity of the Account

Throughout *Mrs Dalloway*, the intimate mode of self-presence which momentarily suspends autonomous subjectivity has ethical implications because it shapes intersubjective contexts of address and accountability; intimate suspension is even central to Woolf's non-violent ethics. In her pleasurable depiction of moments of rupture, and rapture, in which an individual re-experiences pre-subjective fluidity, Woolf suggests that such moments may counter the ethically violent act of coercively imposing one's worldview on others. In this respect, a productive dialogue can be imagined between *Mrs Dalloway* and Judith Butler's *Giving an Account of Oneself*, where Butler argues that "If violence is the act by which a subject seeks to reinstall its mastery and unity, then nonviolence may well follow from the persistent challenge to egoic mastery" (64). While Kristeva emphasises the revolutionary potential of *jouissance*, Butler theorises a fundamental affinity between what she terms primary relationality, the introspective account, and the ethical imperative of refusing the violence of which a coherent 'I' is capable.

In *Giving an Account of Oneself*, Butler turns to psychoanalysis and its concern with "chart[ing] primary relational dispositions and scenes, articulating the scenes of address in which selves variably emerge" (55). For Butler, the intersubjective moment of address, in which two individuals give and receive social recognition, is ethical insofar as it re-enacts relational scenes prior to our formation as defensive and potentially violent subjects. "The ego," Butler writes, "does not come into being without a prior encounter, a primary relation, a set of inaugural impressions from elsewhere. . . . the ego is not an entity or substance, but an array of relations and processes, implicated in the world of primary caregivers" (58–59). Consequently, the moment of address, in which "I give an account of myself *to you*," recreates "prior, and more archaic, forms of address" (50). In this sense, to give an (introspective) account of oneself is to recognise that we are constituted through primary relations, and that these relations persist in intersubjective, dyadic encounters. Because of this persistence, an ethically valid account cannot take the shape of an unbroken narrative delivered by a coherent 'I.' That is, 'I' cannot speak of "my unconscious" since 'my' pre-symbolic attachment to others "defies the rhetoric of belonging" (53, 54); primary impressionability "is a domain in which the grammar of the subject cannot hold" (78). Butler thus draws on the intellectual resources of psychoanalysis to conclude that since "conscious experience is only one dimension of psychic life . . . we cannot achieve by consciousness and language a full mastery over those primary relations of dependency and impressionability that form and constitute us in persistent and obscure ways" (58).

For Butler, to give an account of oneself is to apprehend the unconscious, relational dimension of psychic life and, in the process, recognise the ethical limits of coherent narrative. This dimension, which she refers to as a subject's opacity, calls for "an ethical bearing toward the other"; "it is precisely by virtue of the subject's opacity to itself that it incurs and sustains some of its most important ethical bonds" (20). Because of my opacity to myself, 'I' am compelled to give others "a certain kind of recognition." Butler's ethics, then, is based on the acknowledgement of "our shared, invariable, and partial blindness about ourselves" (41). In *Mrs Dalloway*, what Clarissa calls "the privacy of the soul" (107) inspires recognition as theorised by Butler. Like *Jacob's Room*, Woolf's subsequent novel foregrounds the individual subject's incapacity to know and represent the inner life of another, but *Mrs Dalloway* also configures the individual self as unknowable. "And there is a dignity in people," Clarissa reflects, "a solitude; even between husband and wife a gulf; and that one must respect" (101). With this statement, Clarissa formulates something like a notion of all individuals as psychologically complex, opaque and therefore inviolable subjects. In a different context, Peter admits that Clarissa "ha[s] her reserves," and that all he can make of her inner life is "a mere sketch" (66). An ethical imperative to respect the other's opacity can also be traced on a formal and stylistic level in the novel: as we shall see, imagery, metaphor, focalisation and narrative perspective operate similarly to Peter's "sketch," and it is this aesthetic dimension that extends Woolf's non-violent ethics beyond intimate bonds as conventionally defined (here marriage and friendship). In composing *Mrs Dalloway*, Woolf developed an aesthetic which resists what Butler terms "egoic mastery" (*GAO* 64) in the narrative or storytelling act because it affirms the primary ties disavowed by the writer casting the shadow of his 'I' across the pages of his fiction. While *Jacob's Room* articulates an ethics grounded in the unknowability of the other and emerging from the formational loss of primal intimacy, *Mrs Dalloway* locates ethical relations in the strange, yet intimate "dark places of psychology" (*E* 4: 162) which continue to suspend the introspective subject's autonomy in dyadic encounters beyond the intimate sphere of kinship, friendship and love.

Metaphoric figuration is one device by which the novel illuminates the ethical consequences of acknowledging the obscure and ungraspable processes of subject formation. Consider the following passage, in which Elizabeth Dalloway, strolling about in the strand, decides that "she would like to have a profession":

> It was the sort of thing that did sometimes happen, when one was alone – buildings without architects' names, crowds of people . . . [would] stimulate what lay slumberous, clumsy, and shy on the mind's sandy floor, to break surface, as a child suddenly stretches its arms; it was just that, perhaps, a sigh, a stretch of the arms; an impulse, a revelation, which has its effects forever. (*MD* 116)

Inserted in a more descriptive sequence, which gives Elizabeth's thoughts and feelings in the third person as her own, the aquatic metaphor and generic pronoun imply that her decision emerges from unconscious processes of which Elizabeth herself is unaware. Woolf uses metaphor throughout *Mrs Dalloway* also to suggest that an individual's opacity to him/herself is fundamentally relational. Clarissa's "transcendental theory," as Peter calls it, is a theory of human relations which resembles Butler's notion of primary relationality. Reflecting on her dissatisfying sense of "not knowing people; not being known,"

Clarissa is nonetheless aware of "Odd affinities she had with people she had never spoken to": "sitting on the bus going up to Shaftesbury Avenue, she felt herself everywhere; not 'here, here, here'; and she tapped the back of the seat; but everywhere. . . . So that to know her, or any one, one must seek out the people who completed them" (129). Clarissa's theory suggests that an intimate exposure to others prior to and beyond the formation of 'I' and 'you' complicates not only 'my' attempt to know 'you' but also the subject's capacity to know itself as bounded and irrevocably separate from others – intimates as well as strangers. Clarissa, it seems, apprehends the relations which continue to form and compose the self in unconscious ways: "since our apparitions, the part of us which appears, are so momentary compared with the other, the unseen part of us, which spreads wide, the unseen might survive, be recovered somehow attached to this person or that" (129–30). On this point, Clarissa's realisation resonates with Butler's insight that our opacity to ourselves "establishes the way in which we are constituted in relationality" (*GAO* 64).

Clarissa, however, can only apprehend "the unseen part" of her "which spreads wide"; Woolf's metaphoric transformation of an abstract inner state into something concrete which can be "recovered" and "attached" refers to a psychic dimension which resists conscious thought and literal description. The image of the spreading self points back to an earlier passage:

> somehow in the streets of London, on the ebb and flow of things, here, there, she survived, Peter survived, lived in each other, she being part, she was positive, of the trees at home; of the house there, ugly, rambling all to bits and pieces as it was; part of people she had never met; being laid out like a mist between the people she knew best, who lifted her on their branches as she had seen the trees lift the mist, but it spread ever so far, her life, herself. (*MD* 8)

Compare this passage to Septimus's experience of his self as unbounded:

> But they beckoned; leaves were alive; trees were alive. And the leaves being connected by millions of fibres with his own body, there on the seat, fanned it up and down; when the branch stretched he, too, made that statement. The sparrows fluttering, rising, and falling in jagged fountains were part of the pattern; the white and blue, barred with black branches. (19)

Through the shared metaphor of the infinitely spreading self, the mist or pattern merged inextricably with trees, branches and other solid objects, Woolf points to a shared state – Septimus's psychotic receptivity and Clarissa's apprehension of a primary fluidity persisting in intersubjective relations – connecting two characters who have indeed never met. Numerous critics have observed that Woolf intended Septimus to be Clarissa's "double," and the many affinities between the two characters have been pointed out.[38] If, as Kristeva holds, metaphoric language enables a return to pre-symbolic fluidity and if, as Butler claims, this state is inherently relational, then Woolf's use of shared metaphors to connect Clarissa's and Septimus's characters might well be said to affirm the absence of intersubjective boundaries in what Clarissa calls the "unseen part" of the psyche. This assumption could not be conveyed through description or literal statement: Clarissa's relational theory is performed, or realised, through the shared metaphors connecting her and Septimus's characters.

The performative poetics of *Mrs Dalloway* also promotes accountability in Butler's sense of the term. According to Butler, an account of oneself resembles the "self-disclosing speech act" which in the psychoanalytic transference is both "an effort to communicate information about oneself" (descriptive) and "the recreation of a primary relationality" (performative) – a double dynamic of the transference (*GAO* 50). This, Butler holds, is operative in other scenes of address, which "draw me back to the scene of not knowing, of being overwhelmed" (59). In the process of addressing an account of oneself to another, the self-narrative becomes a transference and counter-transference, "a rhetorical deployment of language that seeks to *act upon* the other"; "I am doing something with this telling, acting on you in some way. And this telling is also doing something to me, acting on me, in ways that I may well not understand as I go" (51). On the other hand, full articulability should not be considered the ultimate goal of introspective self-narration in and beyond the realm of psychoanalysis, "for that goal would imply a linguistic and egoic mastery over unconscious material that would seek to transform the unconscious itself into reflective, conscious articulation" (58).

An ethically valid account, then, must be performative; it must have the capacity to interrupt or suspend what Butler terms the "egoic mastery" of linear and purely literal or descriptive narratives. This insight is illustrated in *Mrs Dalloway* by the encounter between Clarissa and Peter, where Peter's visit surprises Clarissa in the midst of mending her dress. The two friends ask each other for a narrated account of their respective life stories since the moment of parting thirty years earlier. As we have seen, Clarissa's question "Well, and what's happened to you?" is delivered and received in what Kristeva calls the time of acts, and so Peter responds by narrating a sequence of things done and achieved: "praise; his career at Oxford; his marriage" (37, 38). Clarissa and Peter can be said to act on one another with their respective accounts in the sense that the moment of telling is one of exposure, in which self-identity is perceived as precarious and frail. However, instead of acknowledging the primary impressionability formative of the ego, both assume defensive and aggressive positions. Feeling his story undermined as he tells it, Peter nonetheless relies on his narrative to defend his threatened self-image: "he was a failure, compared with all this. . . . Clarissa's life; while I – he thought; and at once everything seemed to radiate from him; journeys; rides; quarrels; adventures; bridge parties; love affairs; work; work, work!" (37). Clarissa, in her turn, formulates something like an account of her life:

> "Do you remember the lake?" she said, in an abrupt voice, under the pressure of an emotion which caught her heart. . . . For she was a child throwing bread to the ducks, between her parents, and at the same time a grown woman coming to her parents who stood by the lake, holding her life in her arms which, as she neared them, grew larger and larger in her arms, until it became a whole life, a complete life, which she put down by them and said, "This is what I have made of it! This!" (36)

Clarissa's emotionally charged memory of the lake causes a momentary suspension of linear time, a moment in which the times of her childhood, her years with Peter and the narrative present exist simultaneously. Through the metaphor of her life as an ever-expansive entity, Clarissa makes an introspective attempt at accounting for this simultaneity which, she perceives, shapes her self in inscrutable ways. Her narrative remains unaddressed, however, and its ethical validity is interrogated by the subsequent remark, delivered in free indirect discourse: "And what had she made of it? What, indeed? Sitting there sewing this morning with Peter" (36). These questions may express Clarissa's effort to acknowledge the momentary dislocation of her self and worldview; they may, also and more likely, convey the narrator's observation that she fails to do precisely that. Both characters' self-narratives, potentially an opportunity for accepting the ethical limits of absolute subjective autonomy, work instead to reinforce the aggressive hostility of the encounter.

Woolf's use of free indirect discourse also illustrates the ethical violence inflicted by a self-assertive subject on another, as in the following sentence inserted into a conversation between Bradshaw and Septimus:

> "So that you have nothing to worry you, no financial anxiety, nothing?"
> He had committed an appalling crime and been condemned to death by human nature.
> "I have – I have," he began, "committed a crime—" (82)

The source of this statement is not immediately apparent. As Kathy Mezei remarks about free indirect discourse, its "confusion of voices" forces the reader to ask: "who is speaking here?" ("Who is Speaking Here" 66). In *Mrs Dalloway*, she notes, Woolf goes particularly far in "attributing discourse to many different voices and undermining distinctions between them or between narrator and focalizers" (85). Who, indeed, is speaking in the passage above? If read as the authoritative remark of an omniscient narrator, the sentence in free indirect discourse reiterates a late nineteenth-century medical rhetoric which depicts mental illness as well as criminality as the degeneration of a healthy "human nature."[39] But the statement could, alternatively, be attributed to Septimus himself, in which case the narrator's voice merges intimately with his to give up the position of control and self-mastery accorded the omniscient narrator. From this second perspective, Woolf's use of free indirect speech as a mode of intimate storytelling enables her sharp critique of an ethically violent medical discourse internalised by Septimus. In other words, the intimate merging of voices in the novel has implications for how we read Woolf's political and ethical position. Ultimately, Woolf's free indirect speech prompts the question not only about who is speaking here but also about what close relationship between intimacy, ethics and social critique emerges when the narrator's and characters' voices appear indistinguishable, and how this paranoid, yet reparative, merger might act ethically on the reader.

Indeed, throughout *Mrs Dalloway* Woolf suspends distinctions between narrator and focalisers to resist ethical violence and create an intimate, reparative mode of engaging with literary texts. Rather than advancing an "indeterminacy of voice," as Mezei claims (66), the blurring of perspectives engendered through Woolf's focalising techniques compels the reader to identify a vibrant multiplicity of viewpoints, each of which is irrevocably individual. Roxanne J. Fand's dialogic approach to Woolf is illuminating in this respect. Fand adopts Mikhail Bakhtin's theory of the novel as "a 'dialogic' interplay of voices that resist unification by a single authorial voice" to argue that Woolf's writing exemplifies Bakhtin's "'polyphonic' model," in which "multiple and conflicting voices... [are] negotiating with each other from their unique fund of subject-positions" (18, 26, 33).[40] In *Mrs Dalloway*, such a plurality of voices is created notably through the chain or series of focalisation, a device enabled by the merging of the narrator's perspective with those of numerous focalising characters, many of whom are strangers to one another. As Septimus and his wife Rezia walk through Regent's Park, focalisation alternates between the two, until the couple becomes part of Maisie Johnson's consciousness: "Both seemed queer," who in turn becomes an object of Mrs Dempster's perception: "That girl . . . don't know a thing yet" (22, 23). In these brief focalising passages Woolf offers glimpses of the four characters' interiority, all the while drawing a nuanced and psychologically sensitive portrait of each.[41] These portraits complicate the reductive absorbing of one perspective by another which is at play here; because the chain is potentially infinite, because no voice is given the final say, the integrity of each perspective is restored or repaired. Seduced into repeated, brief yet breathtakingly intimate moments of immersion in psychologically complex minds, Woolf's reader is alerted by the abrupt shifts in focalisation that denying this complexity is ethically problematic. This reading experience is characteristic of the novel as a whole. In composing *Mrs Dalloway*, Woolf developed a poetics concerned with restoring the integrity of individual psychic life, and intimacy, the blissful suspension of conflicting viewpoints and the subject's autonomy, shapes the novel's ethics as much as its introspective modernist aesthetic. By inviting us into its "beautiful caves" of interiority, *Mrs Dalloway* revolts against the ubiquitous violence sustained by a systematic disregard for each individual's fundamental, alluring opacity.

3

Post-Impressionist Intimacy and the Visual Ethics of *To the Lighthouse*

We have seen how the reparative, introspective poetics of *Mrs Dalloway* furthers a non-violent ethics in which the suspension of subjective autonomy, conceived as a momentary return to a pre-subjective lack of boundaries between 'I' and 'you,' brings about recognition of the opacity marking the integrity, and therefore inviolability, of individual psychic life. Woolf's idea of an ethics based on an intimate suspension of the first-person perspective before an irreducible other is developed in *To the Lighthouse*, where it is articulated more explicitly as a question of intimacy as well as aesthetics. Post-Impressionist artist Lily Briscoe realises that Mrs Ramsay, the model for her painting, "lock[s] up within her some secret which certainly Lily Briscoe believed people must have for the world to go on at all," an insight which induces her to ask: "How then . . . did one know one thing or another thing about people, sealed as they were?" (*TL* 57, 57–58). "Sealed" like a "secret," the individual Lily is about to portray is inscrutable, unknown and unknowable, but Lily's recognition of Mrs Ramsay's unknowability cannot be distinguished from her simultaneous wish for what she calls intimacy. "What device," she asks herself, "for becoming, like waters poured into one jar, inextricably the same, one with the object one adored?" The image suggests a bodily and spiritual union: it figures two individuals' experience of seeing, perceiving and thinking as one. Rather than seeking to know and decipher Mrs Ramsay's inner life – "it was not knowledge but unity that she desired . . . intimacy itself" – Lily longs for a radically intimate state in which interiority can be shared (57).

In *The Way of Love* and *Sharing the World*, Luce Irigaray theorises an ethics of love and affection in which a Levinasian respect for another subject's absolute alterity is bound up with a desire to be "inextricably one," to use Lily's phrase, with this other. Irigaray defines intimacy as a brief return to a primary mode of being in which intersubjective boundaries dissolve. In "some conjunction of being-within and being-with," she writes, self and other may "seem to be returned to this natural site where they were in communion with one another through the same air, the same breath, the same energy, uniting them through a sharing of the surrounding world. At least this would be their quest" (*SW* 70). However, physical proximity for Irigaray "is also always remoteness" (99). Even in ephemeral moments of intimate unity, another subject has an irreducible singularity – an inner life, a worldview and a project – and must, therefore, remain "still unfamiliar, . . . incomprehensible to [my] mind, still unknown and not representable" (92). Irigaray's theory posits the necessity of being both near and remote; human relations can be ethical, she claims, only insofar as they encompass the possibility of intimate union as well as irrevocable distance. In this chapter, I illuminate compelling parallels between Irigaray's philosophy and Woolf's *To the Lighthouse* to argue that Irigaray's theory enables a nuanced understanding of the ethical relations conceptualised in the novel. Modelled on Lily Briscoe's attempt to paint Mrs Ramsay's portrait, the text investigates the ethical questions embedded in the difficult task of representing another individual.

Jessica Berman, in her ground-breaking article "Ethical Folds: Ethics, Aesthetics, Woolf," argues convincingly for an ethics which, developed through Woolf's modernist aesthetic practice, combines radical alterity with intimacy. Following Irigaray, Berman locates intimacy in care, eros and love, all of which manifest themselves in the caress or embrace. As Berman observes, Irigaray's ethical philosophy privileges the physical proximity of the loving touch; for Irigaray, "sensory apprehensions" through touch, but also the sound of the voice, are an integral part of our wish to "com[e] closer to the other" (*SW* 12). Berman is right in claiming an intersection between Irigaray's and Woolf's thought in their respective affirmation of the touch as an essential medium of intimacy and recognition. In *To the Lighthouse*, the touch is crucial also in stirring up a desire for intimacy as oneness: Lily's longing to be "like waters poured into one jar, inextricably the same, one with [the other]" arises as, sitting on the floor, she rests her head on Mrs Ramsay's lap, "her arms round Mrs. Ramsay's knees, close as she could get" (57).

Woolf's focus on intimacy as sensual and embodied relations between separate subjects, Berman holds, is part of a feminist aesthetic which deviates from the formalist and, she argues, disembodied tenets of Roger Fry and Clive Bell.[1] The question of Woolf's complex relation to the formalist theories of Bloomsbury has been much debated, especially in discussions of *To the Lighthouse* and Lily Briscoe's experimentation with Post-Impressionist painting techniques.

Woolf and Fry engaged in continuous discussions about art at the time she was composing *To the Lighthouse*, and the novel was published in the same year the Hogarth Press published Fry's *Cézanne: A Study of His Development* (1927). In her study of Woolf's attempts to translate aspects of Post-Impressionist painting into writing, C. J. Mares stresses Woolf's indebtedness to Fry's aesthetic theory as well as her "efforts to protect the novel from the dangers of excessive formalism" (327). Mares' stance is a widely accepted one; in her aesthetic experiments of the 1920s, critics tend to agree, Woolf embraced certain aspects of formalism and remained critical of others. Much attention has been given to the various distinctions between the media of painting and writing claimed by Fry on the one hand and Woolf on the other, and to their respective attempts to cross disciplinary boundaries and find a common language for the visual and the verbal.[2]

How, then, can we account for Woolf's original adaptation of Fry's formalist principles and her novel's visual, Post-Impressionist experiments in light of its sensory, and sensual, ethics of intimacy? Irigaray notably excludes the visual from her ethically productive category of the sensory: "To turn our eyes towards the heart of the intimate risks undoing its touch – dividing, distinguishing, cutting off and thus isolating. Our eyes are not capable of seeing, nor even contemplating, intimacy" (*SW* 20). For Irigaray, "A logic that favours sight precludes coexistence and communication with the other as other," since the visual "favours the object" (126, 128); the act of looking is a "perception from a distance that allows a grasping of this object" and therefore "prevents an economy of intersubjectivity. . . . Here touch would be the necessary medium" (128). I want to suggest, in this chapter, that Woolf's notion of intimate relations in *To the Lighthouse* emerged directly out of her engagement with Fry's formalist theory, and that her novel both validates and prompts interrogation of Irigaray's philosophy in favouring sight rather than touch as the primary medium of its intimate ethics.[3] Through her critical and selective appropriation of Post-Impressionist strategies for writing, I propose, Woolf locates the desire for intimacy, in the radical sense of a return to pre-subjective oneness, mainly in the visual. If, as Jane Goldman and other critics have claimed, Woolf re-embodies Fry's formalism in emphasising the importance of sensory experience for artistic creation,[4] my argument here is that in *To the Lighthouse*, visual observation emerges as sensual, non-possessive and non-objectifying. In integrating sight with other aspects of the sensory, Lily's and Woolf's respective aesthetic experiments put into practice a central aspect of Fry's aesthetic theory and, in so doing, complicate Irigaray's notion of the visual as necessarily distancing and objectifying. As we shall see next, the novel's ethics stems from Woolf's productive use of Fry's distinction between literary and painterly qualities.

A Formalist Literary Ethics: Fry, Woolf, Irigaray

In his essay collections *Vision and Design* (1920) and *Transformations* (1926), Fry posits his famous division between aesthetic emotions aroused through a "disinterested intensity of contemplation," that is, responses to the formal qualities of a work of art, and the "sensations of ordinary life" (*VD* 21, 169). Sensory experience, he claims, belongs to the latter; "our response to sensations" must be distinguished from "our response to works of art. . . . The esthetic emotion, then, is not an emotion about sensations" (*T* 3, 3–4, 5).[5] Throughout his essays, Fry associates the "sensations of ordinary life" with what he terms photographic, illustrational or naturalistic modes of representation, all of which, he argues, are inherently literary rather than painterly. While conceding, in *Transformations*, that literature may well have painterly characteristics and vice versa, he nonetheless maintains that "we must regard illustration as more closely akin in its essence to literature than it is to plastic art" (16).

The two Post-Impressionist exhibitions in 1910 and 1912 came about as a critical response to what Fry describes as a literary bias among English painters: "the English have cultivated almost exclusively the illustrational aspects of painting in defiance of the great plastic tradition of European art" (26). Fry called the painters represented at these exhibitions *Post*-Impressionist because he detected in their work a break with "a deep-rooted conviction . . . that the aim of painting is the descriptive imitation of natural forms" (*VD* 167). The Impressionist painter, Fry holds, is a "pure visualist" whose effort to "directly record . . . visual experience" (*T* 200) lacks "design and formal co-ordination, . . . architectural framework or structural coherence" (*VD* 7). In "Retrospect" (1920), the last essay in *Vision and Design,* Fry reflects on his role as an art critic: "I have never been a pure Impressionist, a mere recording instrument of certain sensations. I have always had some kind of aesthetic" (*VD* 199).[6] Fry thus closes *Vision and Design* by confirming his distinction between representational, "literary," or Impressionist painting concerned with subjective impressions and the sensations of life and the privileged focus on form which he terms "aesthetic." This distinction is maintained in *Transformations*, where art dominated by literary or Impressionist features is considered "psychological" and contrasted with "plastic" or structural elements which, for Fry, are impersonal and genuinely painterly. In the opening essay "Some Questions in Esthetics," Fry ponders different ways in which the respective media of painting and writing can be alternatively psychological and plastic. Literature, he claims, is "a medium which admits the mixture of aesthetic [plastic] and non-aesthetic [psychological] treatment to an almost unlimited extent" (*T* 7), but he never views this "mixture" in terms of integration, influence or productive interplay; while a formalist and an Impressionist approach may coexist in a literary work, they remain separate and distinct.[7]

Woolf, on her part, explores the ethical implications of Fry's aesthetic theory. I shall argue in this chapter that in *To the Lighthouse*, Woolf not only claims Fry's "mixture" of vision and design for the art of fiction; she locates the novel's ethics precisely in the interplay of the psychological or subjective and the impersonal or formal features of her writing. In this, her selective appropriation of Fry's ideas inspires an ethics which can be illuminated via recourse to Irigaray's philosophy. By defining visual observation as potentially ethical, Woolf relies on Fry's painterly distinction between vision and design, but unlike Fry, she explores the possibility of their complete integration. Like Fry, however, she connects a literary and representational fidelity to visual impressions with the subjective expression of sensations. Throughout *To the Lighthouse*, Impressionist textual features such as fluid colours and a lack of shape open up a space for intimacy, that is, for a potential and momentary dissolution of the boundaries separating self and other. The impressionistic, personal and psychological, however, also serve to mark the integrity of subjective perspectives. The novel's emphasis on form and design, on the other hand, signals the importance of detachment, of calling into question the first-person perspective, the worldview of the gazing eye or 'I.' In this sense, Woolf's use of a formalist aesthetic can be considered an ethical commitment. Formalist textual devices are associated in the novel not only with the ethical limits of knowing and the fundamental unknowability of the other but also with a desire to apprehend another's worldview and share it, as if self and other were one. Focused on the intimacy of shared perception, which suspends the autonomous, knowing self, the novelistic universe of *To the Lighthouse* affirms a multiplicity of irreducible viewpoints. Woolf, then, diverges from Fry in demonstrating not only the aesthetic but also the ethical possibilities of the Post-Impressionist combination of vision and design.

Before elucidating this claim further, it is worth reviewing Fry's statement, in "An Essay in Aesthetics," on art as independent and exempt from moral obligations:

> Art, then, is an expression and a stimulus of [the] imaginative life, which is separated from actual life by the absence of responsive action. Now this responsive action implies in actual life moral responsibility. In art we have no

such moral responsibility – it presents a life freed from the binding necessities of our actual existence. (*VD* 15)

The freedom of aesthetic response from moral responsibility resides here in the dissociation of the "restful contemplation of the work of art as a whole" from the "merely sensual pleasures" which, according to Fry, belong to "our actual existence" (22, 16, 15; see 16–22). While Woolf, in her many reflections on writing and fiction, alternatively reiterated and problematised Fry's art-life distinction, she never believed in a complete dissociation of the aesthetic from the sensual and ethical responses of life. Even so, she did not fundamentally disagree with Fry who, after all, claimed the literary to be close to the "binding necessities of our actual existence." She differs from Fry, however, in asserting the possibility that the conditions of "life" may in fact be addressed through the formal qualities of an artwork. In her review of E. M. Forster's *Aspects of the Novel* (1927), Woolf questions Forster's critical assessment of Henry James in that work. The essay paraphrases Forster's argument for "life" or "the humane as opposed to the aesthetic view" of fiction. In Woolf's words, Forster "maintains that the novel is 'sogged with humanity'; that 'human beings have their great chance in the novel,'" hence his "notably harsh judgement" of James, who "created patterns which, though beautiful in themselves, are hostile to humanity." Woolf responds to Forster's claims with a question: "What is this 'life' that keeps on cropping up so mysteriously in books about fiction? Why is it absent in a pattern and present in a tea party?" ("Is Fiction an Art?" *E* 4: 461).[8] This challenge to Fry's and Forster's respective separation of life or the humane from a formalist aesthetic would be worked into *To the Lighthouse* as an integration of the ethical into the novel's formal features.[9] As a central part of this integrative process, I propose, Woolf held Fry's connection of sensual perception and visual impressions in life to be inextricable from aesthetic design or pattern.

In her essay "Pictures" (1925), Woolf echoes Fry in contrasting "the partial and incomplete writers" in whose work visual observation serves description as an end in itself with Proust's writing, in which "the eye . . . has come to the help of the other senses, combined with them" (*E* 4: 243, 44). For Woolf, however, the Impressionist ideal of sight combined with other aspects of the sensory need not be distinguished from a formalist aesthetic. This stance is strikingly apparent in Woolf's analysis of Fry's life and work. In her 1940 biography of Fry, Woolf reflects on his treatment of art and life as separate categories: "But, it is tempting to ask, were they distinct? It seems as if the aesthetic theory were brought to bear upon the problems of private life" (*RF* 214).[10] Fully aware that Fry distinguishes between aesthetic responses to form and sensory responses in life, Woolf purposefully, it seems, effaces this distinction in her interpretation of Fry's aesthetic theory. In Woolf's account, Fry considers sensation to play a vital role in aesthetic contemplation: "So [intellectual] curiosity is stimulated. And then sensation is roused. For he assumes that we all have sensations; all that is necessary is to let ourselves trust to them." Sensation in Woolf's definition encompasses Fry's aesthetic emotion as well as his notion of a life-like, Impressionist treatment of the visual as sensory. Both, Woolf suggests, are specifically literary: "Undoubtedly he wakes the eye; and then begins what is in its way as exciting as the analysis by a master novelist of the human passions – the analysis of our sensations" (227). Fry himself "seems to have [had] an inexhaustible capacity for sensation," his biographer reflects, remembering how his analysis of these sensations would "miraculously stimulat[e]" her own "desire for seeing" (228).

Woolf, then, was convinced that the ethical and sensual/visual dimensions of life, both dismissed by Fry as incompatible with an aesthetic privileging of form and design, could be integrated into his formalist theory. As we have seen, this conviction is suggested in two essays written in the years of the composition and publication of *To the Lighthouse* and confirmed retrospectively in her biography of Fry. Woolf's integration of Fry's "vision" and "design" is central to the ethics developed in the novel, an ethics which affirms the personal and subjective, but also demands that the first-person perspective be called into question. In *Roger Fry: A Biography*, Woolf associates his formalist project with continuous self-analysis and a perpetual suspension of the personal viewpoint. Considerable attention is given to Fry's own failure to attempt self-examination. "Only one subject seemed to escape his insatiable curiosity," she writes, "and that was himself. Analysis seemed to stop short there" (289). "But the central figure remained vague," she continues, "'. . . I don't pretend to know much on the subject. It so rarely interests me,' he wrote when asked to explain himself" (290). For Woolf, as we saw in the previous chapter, the need to explain, or give an introspective account of oneself, is an ethical imperative to critically examine the "central figure" of the 'I' and apprehend other points of view. Fry's "lack of interest in . . . that central figure which was so increasingly interested in everything outside itself," she reflects, "had its drawbacks, for if he ignored himself, he sometimes ignored other people also. . . . Absorbed in some idea, set upon some cause, he ignored feelings, he overrode objections. Everybody he assumed must share his views" (290, 290–91).

Yet, Fry's biographer records, his friends all speak of "his considerateness, of his humanity, and of his profound humility" (292). In stark contrast to the egocentric 'I' imposing his worldview on others, Woolf emphasises another side of Fry, most tellingly, perhaps, through a selected extract from Fry's account of a friend and lover's tragic suicide: "Il faut que l'on se résigne à ne pas croire même dans sa propre personnalité. . . . La vie n'est qu'une longue (sic) apprentissage dans l'art de se ficher complètement de son égo" (252). In selectively presenting Fry's own words on this "art" of life – "life is but a long apprenticeship in the art of not giving a damn about one's ego" (translation mine) – Woolf again suggests that Fry's distinction between art and life was not as absolute as he claimed in his criticism. She also, however, suggests that for Fry, the process of learning to renounce the first-person perspective was as important in art as in life. Later in the text Woolf explicitly links this learning process to Fry's method as a formalist art critic. When reflecting, in "Retrospect," on the development of his formalist theory, Fry himself emphasised the importance of practice, experiment, and of constantly calling his ideas into question: "My aesthetic has been a purely practical one, a tentative expedient. . . . I have always looked on my system with a certain suspicion. I have recognised that if it ever formed too solid a crust it might stop the inlets of fresh experience" (*VD* 199). Woolf puts it more strongly, "He detested fixed attitudes" (*RF* 291), and stresses this point as she quotes Fry's saying that "There is great danger in a strong personal rhythm . . . unless [the artist] constantly strains it by the effort to make it take in new and refractory material it becomes stereotyped" (228, Woolf's insertion). Through his focus on process and practice, Woolf suggests, Fry resisted the "imprisonment in egotism" which might follow the excess of "a strong personal rhythm"; "It was thus . . . by experiments, by revisions and perpetual reorientations that he avoided with astonishing success the fate that attends so many artists, both in paint and life – repetition. . . . he broke the rhythm before it got quite fixed" (296).

In writing *To the Lighthouse*, Woolf implicitly acknowledged the importance of Fry's "perpetual reorientations" for her own creative practice. Towards the novel's closure, Lily reflects: "There it was – her picture . . . its attempt at something. It would be hung in the attics, she thought; it would be destroyed. But what did that matter?" (*TL* 225). As critics such as Jane Fisher and Thomas G. Matro have noted, Woolf's focus on Lily's aesthetic experiments draws attention to the process of creation, whether in painting or writing. In Fisher's words, the novel "emphasizes process over goal, the psychological moment of perception and creation over the completed aesthetic object" (101), and for Matro, the significance of Lily's painting "is not what it captures but what it attempts. . . . Lily is grasping for the very act of perceiving, the creating 'vision' before it is influenced by the 'phrases' or already made 'visions' . . . before it develops a picture in the mind or on canvas" (219). Like Lily's artwork, Matro suggests, Woolf's novel insists on "the act of making, on invention itself in whatever mode" (223). Building on these observations, I propose that Lily's and Woolf's respective focus on the creative act reveals a shared commitment to a Post-Impressionist aesthetic which, for both, enables a resistance to "fixed attitudes" (*RF* 291). Inspired by Fry, Woolf developed in *To the Lighthouse* an experimental, formalist poetics aimed at countering the "imprisonment in egotism" which she, like Fry, considered problematic. For Woolf, however, unlimited egotism was an ethical problem, and she addressed it primarily through her novel's form and design. In her emphasis on the creative process, Woolf developed a notion of writing as practice and constant reinvention, and Irigaray's theory of poetic representation offers a compelling way to elucidate this complex aspect of her work.

For Irigaray, absolute subjective autonomy is asserted through the "already existing language" of "a world that is already there" (*SW* 15), and the worldview of the transcendental self operates within what Irigaray calls the Same, that is, a closed world in which other viewpoints cannot be apprehended. Such language, she writes, "programs the speaker" and "encloses the subject in a dwelling from which they cannot or do not want to leave" (*WL* 34, 34–35). The autonomous subject thus speaks in "a language foreign to dialogue"; the unlimited first-person perspective is maintained in "an already existing circle of discourse" (*SW* 14, 16). In order to perceive and affirm the integrity of other worlds, Irigaray holds, this circle must be broken. We must "open the house of language in which we dwell" and, in so doing, momentarily give up our worldview or, in Irigaray's terms, "brea[k] out of our everyday dwelling" (15, 10). How, then, can the circular discourse reducing the other to the Same be suspended? Can words achieve it, she asks, "even if they try to unite within them poetry and thought, thought and poetry?" (12). The answer is affirmative: words may enable ethical recognition insofar as they "do not designate the world and things from a single perspective" (14). In this, Irigaray theorises a communicational language which is "different, and necessarily poetic: a language that creates" (*WL* 12). Crucially, poetic representation for Irigaray is an "experience of speaking," a "practice of saying" (*WL* xi; *SW* 15), and when "the language-house finds itself questioned, even abandoned" in the moment of poetic articulation, the subject "accepts being unsheltered" in a "radical disappropriation" (*WL* 45). Speaking on the threshold of one's dwelling is an experimental, tentative process, a "search for words that correspond to this reciprocal abandon" (*SW* 6).

In *To the Lighthouse*, Woolf delineates a conception of experimental, poetic writing which, like Irigaray's act or "practice of saying," interrupts the habitual perspective of the autonomous 'I.' Like Irigaray, Woolf was sensitive to the capacity of language to form linguistic and social habits. During the dinner at the end of "The Window," Mrs Ramsay is compared to the chairman of a meeting who, in order to "obtain unity . . . when there is a strife of tongues," suggests "that every one shall speak in French." While different tongues stand here for separate worldviews, speaking French or "the same language" functions as a social code which "imposes some order, some uniformity" (*TL* 98). The idea of language as a fixed code, order or "uniformity" is elaborated in Lily's reflections on the lawn in the novel's last section "The Lighthouse," where she doubts her creative capacity:

> What was the good of doing it then, and she heard some voice saying she couldn't paint, saying she couldn't create, as if she were caught up in one of those habitual currents which after a certain time experience forms in the mind, so that one repeats words without being aware any longer who originally spoke them. (173)

Charles Tansley's words ten years earlier – "Women can't write, women can't paint" (94) – are now absorbed into an "already existing circle of discourse" (*SW* 16). Caught up in the "habitual currents" of this circle, Lily automatically repeats a language which, as Irigaray puts it, is "already there."

Lily's repetition of Charles Tansley's words is contrasted in the novel with poetic language, which has the capacity to defamiliarise words and suspend the viewpoint of the speaking subject. Hearing her husband recite a poem after dinner, Mrs Ramsay experiences "relief and pleasure" as the words, "like music . . . see[m] to be spoken by her own voice," yet "outside her self." Detached from the conscious perspectives in the room, the words of the poem reach Mrs Ramsay "floating like flowers on water . . . cut off from them all, as if no one had said them" (*TL* 120). If Lily is no longer conscious of who originally spoke the words "women can't paint," it is because they uphold a discourse which she is bound to repeat in her own voice. Mrs Ramsay's free-floating poetry, on the other hand, is impersonal because it is "cut off" (120) from the personal voice in the moment it is spoken. Reading poetry is for Mrs Ramsay a tentative, passive, half-conscious experience: "like a person in a light sleep" (131), she "read and turned the page, swinging herself, zigzagging this way and that, from one line to another as from one branch to another, . . . and so reading she was ascending, she felt, on to the top, on to the summit. How satisfying! How restful!" (129, 131). We have already seen, in Chapter 2, the significance of *jouissance* for Woolf's poetic revolt against the ubiquitous ideal of unlimited subjective autonomy. In what follows,

I shall read Woolf's specifically Post-Impressionist aesthetic experiments in *To the Lighthouse* as committed not only to suspending the self and questioning the "fixed attitudes" which Roger Fry supposedly detested (*RF* 291) but also, and vitally, to the defamiliarising, reparative practice of affirming the irreducibility of separate perspectives and worldviews.

Beyond Solipsism: Post-Impressionism, "Time Passes" and the Suspension of the 'I'

If Woolf in her biography of Fry associated Post-Impressionism with a concern to break the rhythm of the first-person perspective "before it got quite fixed" (*RF* 296), in *To the Lighthouse*, I have suggested, she developed an aesthetic aimed at disrupting the fixity of Lily's "habitual currents" of thought, or Irigaray's circular discourse of the "already there." For Irigaray, the process of "breaking out of our everyday dwelling" (*SW* 10) is necessary for an individual to begin approaching another as other. The questioning of the habitual, Irigaray holds, is motivated by a desire for the other, that is, a desire to overcome what she terms "a solitary destiny" – the solipsism of the transcendental self (17). Seen "from a unique standpoint," the world is "closing up, even in advance, in a circle" (ix); the "horizon of a unique totality" is "fixed and frozen" (xv), a "sort of prison cell," an "enclosed and saturated world" (24). As for Levinas, the other for Irigaray becomes reduced to an object of knowledge when part of an individual's totality. In order to break out of the solipsism of the Same, "to be involved in a being with the other that does not amount to a sharing of the same in the Same," we must "accept in our nearness what remains incomprehensible to our mind, still unknown and not representable" (17, 92).

According to Irigaray, then, solipsism as a philosophical and intersubjective problem may be addressed and potentially overcome through the process of questioning the knowing subject and defamiliarising the known. On this point, her philosophy converges in striking and perhaps surprising ways with Fry's theory of Post-Impressionism. As Ann Banfield has demonstrated, Fry's aesthetic project was developed in dialogue with Bertrand Russell's epistemology. Like Russell, Banfield argues, Fry responded to Leslie Stephen's epistemological concern with solipsism and the limits of the knowing consciousness. Stephen's "'problem' of knowledge" was a critique of philosophical idealism and, in particular, its assumption "that reality is knowable and knowledge modeled on perception" (Banfield 22, 44). The objects of the external world, Stephen claimed, cannot be known through the sensual impressions of the perceiving subject: "we cannot get outside our own consciousness" (Stephen, "What is Materialism?" qtd. in Banfield 22). Stephen's subject, then, is a solipsistic consciousness confined, through the crisis or problem of knowledge, to its own processes of thought and perception. In response to Stephen's "intellectual effort to escape the prison of solipsism" (47), Russell reconfigured the epistemological problem through shifting the focus from the perceiving subject to the world of objects. As Banfield astutely notes, Russell's epistemology problematises Stephen's suspension of knowledge in "externalizing perception from the subject." Logic, Russell assumes, will prove that "Whatever exists is perceptible, but not necessarily perceived by anyone" (48).[11] In imagining an object world existing independently of the perceiving subject, Banfield maintains, Russell calls into question the "omniscient, omnipresent observer . . . and not just the object of his observations"; "a knowledge of the unobserved is a non-psychological knowledge whose subject matter is irreducible to any subject's mental state" (49, 48).

In Banfield's illuminating account, Russell's suspension of the perceiving subject inspired Fry's aesthetic theory of vision and design. In 1910, the year Fry became acquainted with the Bloomsbury group and arranged the first Post-Impressionist Exhibition, an intellectual exchange was initiated between the Bloomsbury members representing the visual arts and those influenced by the logical epistemology developed earlier at Cambridge by Russell and G. E. Moore.[12] In this exchange, Banfield writes, "philosophy developed eyes, and art, including that of the novel, gained eyeless principles" (247). If "Impressionism is all eye" (274), then Fry's emphasis on design or *Post*-Impressionism marks his indebtedness to Russell's "eyeless" logic. Throughout his essay collections, Fry connects Impressionism with the subjective and psychological expression of the visual impressions and sensory perceptions registered by the painter's eye or 'I.' Or, as Banfield observes, Post-Impressionism brings together the sensory-visual and the eyeless-logical, vision and design. However, as we have seen, Fry also conceived of Impressionism as the dead-end or impasse of a representational and imitative painterly tradition. In Banfield's genealogy, a Cambridge tradition of "'revolt' against Idealism" (4) can be traced from Stephen to Russell and Fry and, ultimately, Woolf.[13] Impressionism by this account operates in accordance with the idealist assumption that the external world can be known through the visual and sensory perception of the 'I,' and so does realism in literature (247). If, for Fry, Impressionism is inherently "literary," his use of the word does indeed connote a specific literary mode; in Fry's terms, we recall, Impressionist representation is descriptive, illustrational and naturalistic.[14] Banfield here makes a convincing case for Woolf's and Fry's respective dissatisfaction with realism in writing and Impressionism in painting. Fry's emphasis on the lack of aesthetic form in Impressionist art, she maintains, emerged in dialogue with Russell's privileging of logic and "eyeless" structure. In this sense, Post-Impressionist form and design enable a defamiliarisation of the objects perceived: "Objects familiar because seen, heard, sensed, observed, tucked cosily into the observer's viewpoint, lose their familiarity once rendered unseen, unheard, unobserved, revealed to have a sensible existence independent of an observer" (1). Like Russell's epistemology, Fry's aesthetic was fundamentally concerned with "making the familiar strange" (257).

In Woolf's literary engagement with Post-Impressionist tenets and artistic practices, the epistemological significance of form and design pertains not only to subject-object relations; the process of suspending the viewpoint of the perceiving subject and defamiliarising the perceived is equally central to her conception of human relations. For Woolf, however, the questioning of the observing subject is ethical as well as epistemological, informed as it is by an imperative to suspend the perspective of the 'I.' In line with her father's critique of philosophical idealism, Woolf interrogates the realist (and Impressionist) assumption that reality is knowable through perception. As we saw in the previous chapters, she highlights in *Jacob's Room* and *Mrs Dalloway* an ethically problematic ideal of unlimited subjective autonomy underlying the realist convention of narrative omniscience. In *To the Lighthouse*, however, she suspends the viewpoint of the observing, omniscient subject in her attempt to represent a reality unobserved, without recourse to the mediation of a perceiving eye or 'I.' Through her poetic experiments in the middle section "Time Passes," Woolf follows Russell and Fry in exploring the potential of fiction to convey a world existing independently of human perspectives. She thereby problematises the solipsism of the philosopher trapped in the "prison cell," to quote Irigaray, of his consciousness or "unique standpoint" (*SW* 24, 9). In this way, Woolf turns Russell's and Fry's epistemological and aesthetic responses to Stephen's problem of knowledge into an ethical concern.

Woolf's ethical interrogation of philosophical solipsism begins in the novel's first section, thus foreshadowing the more aesthetically radical "Time Passes." As Banfield observes, Woolf's father's critique of idealism is reproduced through Mr Ramsay's problem of "Subject and object and the nature of reality" (*TL* 28). In "The Window," the philosopher's voice reiterates a concern with "the dark of human ignorance, how we know nothing and the sea eats away the ground we stand on" (50). The "nature of reality" cannot be known, and, as Woolf shows, Mr Ramsay is trapped in his own thoughts; these are reiterated with slight variation throughout the section. The metaphor of the island eaten away by the sea, the inscrutable nature of reality, the obsession with fame – in repeating these "themes" of Mr Ramsay's mind, Woolf emphasises the repetitive tendencies of the consciousness obsessed with Stephen's philosophical problem of knowledge. No wonder Mr Ramsay fails to reach the letter R in the alphabet of progressive thought. The circularity Woolf associates with Mr Ramsay's consciousness is also related to solipsism and the "imprisonment in egotism" (*RF* 296) to which she objects in her biography of Fry. Isolated and excluded from the community of the house and its inhabitants, Mr Ramsay is solitary also in Irigaray's sense of the term. Described variously as "egotistical," narrow-minded and "absorbed in himself" with "astonishing lack of consideration for other people's feelings," he imposes his 'I,' his "enclosed and saturated world," on the many worlds or dwellings around him (*TL* 44, 52, 37; *SW* 24).

Like Irigaray, Woolf associates a habitual, familiar way of seeing the world with the repetition and "danger" of "a strong personal rhythm" (*RF* 228). In "The Window," rhythm is depicted as upholding the familiar, unquestioned reality of the observing 'I.' Mrs Ramsay is "soothed" when hearing "some habitual sound, some regular mechanical sound . . . something rhythmical" and, later, "relieved to find that . . . domesticity triumphed; custom crooned its soothing rhythm" (*TL* 36). A similar rhythm marks the first section formally: the focalising perspective alternates in a regular, rhythmical movement between the characters' individual voices or worldviews. This rhythm is broken in "Time Passes," where the house is no longer inhabited and its decay unobserved by the characters in sections 1 and 3. On 20 July 1926, Woolf notes in her diary that her new novel is to have three parts, and reflects that "It might contain all characters boiled down; & childhood; & then this impersonal thing, which I'm dared to do by my friends, the flight of time, & the consequent break of unity in my design" (*D* 3: 36). If the design of sections 1 and 3 is held together by the rhythm of shifting focalisation, Woolf disrupts this formal unity in writing the "impersonal thing" which is "Time Passes." The formal break or interruption posited by her novel's middle section, in which the focalising perspective remains unidentified, achieves a suspension of the personal voices composing "The Window" and "The Lighthouse." These voices are silenced in "Time Passes," where the characters' life stories are literally parenthesised and reported indirectly, seen from other perspectives: "[Prue Ramsay, leaning on her father's arm, was given in marriage that May. What, people said, could have been more fitting? And, they added, how beautiful she looked!]" (*TL* 143). The problem preoccupying Mr Ramsay – "the dark of human ignorance, how we know nothing" – is similarly bracketed, as it were, insofar as the "profusion of darkness" in the night opening the section effaces the presence of individual observers: "Not only was furniture confounded; there was scarcely anything left of body or mind by which one could say 'This is he' or 'This is she'" (137). The darkness of the night, for Mr Ramsay metaphoric of an unknowable external reality, is no longer a philosophical problem, but a world existing independently of the philosopher's solipsistic consciousness. The philosopher concerned with the problem of knowledge, no longer the specific character of Mr Ramsay, is reduced to a general, impersonal figure: "the mystic, the visionary, walked the beach, stirred a puddle, looked at a stone, and asked themselves 'What am I?' What is this?'" (143).

While "Time Passes" is "eyeless" in suspending the perceptions of human and personal observers, Woolf turns the tables by giving eyes to the unobserved non-human world. Through her modernist personification of nature – spring is a "virgin . . . wide-eyed and watchful and entirely careless of what was done and thought by the beholders," and the winds or "airs" are asking about the traces of human life in the empty house: "Will you fade? Will you perish?" (143, 141) – Woolf forcefully conveys the irreducibility of a world which exceeds human consciousness. In so doing, she achieves a reversal of subject-object relations which has ethical as well as epistemological significance.[15] For Woolf, as for Irigaray, the suspension of the all-knowing 'I' before an inscrutable non-human reality is a precondition for ethical encounters between subjects. If, as Banfield claims, Woolf follows her father, Russell and Fry in questioning the idealist assumption that reality is knowable through the sensory-visual impressions of the eye/'I,' it is because, for her, an idealist reliance on the perceiving eye is ethically problematic. In Irigaray's ethical theory, "Two dimensions allow us to open the structure of [our] world . . . relations with nature as an autonomous living world and relations with the other"; like the irreducible other, nature is a space which must "be subjected by, or to, none" (*SW* 66). Out of "respect for non-human existence, for oneself, and for the other considered in his or her difference," Irigaray writes, the transcendental subject's freedom "must, at every moment, limit its expansion in order to respect other existing beings and . . . find ways of forming with them a world always in becoming" (xx).[16] Woolf anticipates Irigaray's philosophy in "Time Passes," where she depicts nature as resisting appropriation by human thought. The Romantic "mirror" of "cliffs, sea, cloud and sky brought purposely together to assemble outwardly . . . the vision within" is broken as nature is revealed to exist independently of "the minds of men" (*TL* 144), and for the visionary philosopher or poet walking the beach, "no image with semblance of serving and divine promptitude comes readily to hand bringing the night to order and making the world reflect the compass of the soul" (140).[17]

Woolf thus achieves the effacement of the solitary, thinking 'I' through the structure or design of her writing; the "Time Passes" section is a "break of unity in [her] design" because its internal logic of focalising perspectives disrupts the character-centred focalisation pattern of sections 1 and 3. The friends who according to Woolf's diary dared her to write "this impersonal thing" were presumably the Post-Impressionist painters and art critics of the Bloomsbury circle. Whereas Woolf's fictional exploration of painterly ideas and techniques was inspired primarily by her exchanges with Roger Fry and Vanessa Bell, the sisters were both influenced by Fry's theory of vision and design, as was Vanessa's husband Clive Bell.[18] Indeed, sections of "Time Passes" stylistically emulate a particular feature Fry identified with Post-Impressionist painting: plastic colour. In *Transformations*, Fry describes what he sees as a gradual development in the history of painting "towards a view of colour as an inherent part of the expressive quality of form" (*T* 214). This "process of the gradual identification of colour with plastic and spatial design," Fry writes, marks a shift from decorative or ornamental uses of colour to an understanding of colour as functional, that is, capable of conveying form and structure (216; see 213, 222). While, in Fry's view, the Impressionists "increased in some directions the plastic expressiveness of colour," their painting lacked "clear and logical articulation of volumes within the picture space." It was with Cézanne that colour became "an integral part of plastic expression" (218). Fry writes similarly about M. Lévy, a "devoted student of Cézanne," that for this painter "colour is given a much weightier task" than that of "a decorative or melodic accompaniment" (220). "Weightier" in this context has an at least partly literal meaning. The structural function Fry ascribes to Post-Impressionist colour is reflected in its material texture; the colours in a painting by Cézanne or Matisse are thick, dense and layered and, as such, visibly structured. Banfield notes a verbal version of Post-Impressionist colour in Woolf's fiction which, she argues, demonstrates Woolf's indebtedness to Fry: "Color achieves a stone-like denseness in Woolf's descriptions. . . . So convinced is Woolf of Fry's plastic color that in her descriptions the more color deepens to Cézannesque intensity, the heavier and more structured it becomes" (280). I propose here that in her descriptions of colour in "Time Passes," Woolf imitates plastic structure and solidity to suggest the materiality of an external world which cannot be reduced to an object of human thought and perception.

We have seen how, on the level of form and design, the experimental aesthetic of "Time Passes" resists "bringing the night to order and making the world reflect the compass of the soul" (*TL* 140). The darkness of the night is treated in this section neither as a Romantic reflection of interiority nor as a metaphor of the problem preoccupying Mr Ramsay: "the dark of human ignorance, how we know nothing" (50). Like the "wide-eyed and watchful" spring, the night, "flowing down in purple; his head crowned; his sceptre jewelled," is personified as the observer of the unseeing sleepers, all of which are enveloped by his mantle: "the curtains of dark wrapped themselves over the house, over Mrs. Beckwith, Mr. Carmichael, and Lily Briscoe so that they lay with several folds of blackness on their eyes" (155). By drawing attention to the texture and many folds of the purple mantle and the black "curtains of dark," Woolf connects the night, unseen and existing independently of the sleepers, with the compact density of Post-Impressionist colour. And like Fry's plastic colour, the "folds of blackness" covering the sleepers' eyes like layers of black paint serve a functional, or performative, rather than decorative purpose. Resembling a painting in which human eyes are literally concealed under multiple folds or layers of colour, the passage both radically effaces human perspectives and foregrounds the opacity and inscrutability of the night; through the image of the folded mantle, the night comes to stand for an unheard as well as unseen non-human reality. An earlier passage prefigures the image above: "Nothing it seemed could . . . disturb the swaying mantle of silence which, week after week, in the empty room, wove into itself the falling cries of birds, ships hooting, the drone and hum of the fields, a dog's bark, a man's shout, and folded them round the house in silence" (141–42). Woven metaphorically into the texture of the mantle, the sounds reaching the empty house form a curiously material presence-as-silence: each sound is all the more real for being silent, for existing independently of human ears which would receive it as sound. In thus appropriating the painterly device of plastic colour, Woolf claims for writing the aesthetic attempt to convey non-human reality, something Fry thought could be done primarily through painting (which is wordless and therefore, it has been argued, capable of representing a world beyond human relations and psychology).[19] Woolf, that is, contests Fry's (early) notion of literature as necessarily mimetic and based on uncritical observation.[20] Like Fry though, Woolf questions, on the one hand, the realist or representational assumption that reality is knowable and can be adequately described by an omniscient subject and, on the other, the dominance of subjective perception in Impressionist art.

In "Time Passes," then, Woolf evokes the material density and thickness of Post-Impressionist colour in order to ascribe solidity to the darkness of the night and the sporadic sounds, both of which would appear evanescent and immaterial to a thinking and perceiving consciousness – or to an Impressionist artist. Described impressionistically as objects of a focalising character's thought and sensory perception, the night and the sounds would in all likelihood have been treated by Woolf as fleeting and transient, a thin veil rather than a mantle in many folds.[21] Jesse Matz defines literary Impressionism as commonly understood: "pictorial descriptions of shifting light and colour, subjective accounts of sensuous experience, transmission of immediate and evanescent feelings." Impressionist modernist writing, Matz explains, drew at least partly on Louis Leroy's definition of the "impression," in his review of Monet's *Impression: Soleil Levant*, as "transient, insubstantial, passive sensation" (*Literary Impressionism* 12). In Matz's account, painterly as well as literary Impressionism is characterised by "an interest in subjective perception" which entailed both a "shift" in focus "from object to subject" and a subsequent "emphasis on point of view" (45).[22] In other words, Matz's definition of Impressionist representation converges largely with Fry's.[23]

While Matz explores Woolf's writing through the paradigms of literary Impressionism, critics concerned with the painterly influences on her modernist experiments frequently position her work in between Impressionism and Post-Impressionism.[24] Others argue that her use of Post-Impressionist aesthetic devices evinces a dissatisfaction with the conceptual and aesthetic assumptions of Impressionism. Jane Goldman thus made a crucial contribution to the field of modernist studies by observing that Woolf's privileging of Post-Impressionist strategies over an Impressionist focus on subjective perception furthered her political commitment.[25] I would argue that her Post-Impressionist aesthetic also gave rise to the ethics of *To the Lighthouse* and "Time Passes" in particular, where Woolf gives objects Post-Impressionist structure and solidity in order to distance her poetics from the practice of recording fleeting subjective impressions. If Impressionism marked a representational "shift from object to subject" (Matz 45), Woolf's writing turns focus back on the object and away from the perceiving 'I'; objects in "Time Passes" acquire an unfamiliar materiality and form when no longer apprehended impressionistically through what Matz terms "transient, insubstantial, passive sensation." In *Transformations*, Fry writes further about M. Lévy's use of plastic colour: "It is characteristic that the oppositions of tone are never made with a view to elucidate the situation by a clear definition of the objects; the picture is built up of coloured planes rather than of objects" (221).

A painting by M. Lévy, Fry suggests here, asks the observer to give up a habitual practice of discerning the shape of familiar objects presenting themselves to the eye. In this respect, the following passage from "Time Passes" functions like a Post-Impressionist painting:

> The autumn trees, ravaged as they are, take on the flash of tattered flags kindling in the gloom of cool cathedral caves where gold letters on marble pages describe death in battle and how bones bleach and burn far away in Indian sands. The autumn trees gleam in the yellow moonlight, in the light of harvest moons. (*TL* 139)

This is not a literal or impressionistic depiction of the autumn trees. In a process of displacement, the shape and colour of the trees are suggested through a series of images, all of which evoke the spatial, structural and material properties of plastic colour and, in so doing, refer elsewhere than to the objects and spaces described. Through the flash and solid texture of "tattered flags," the architectural space of the cathedral caves is superimposed on the image of the trees so that, in the process, the trees gleam with the same autumnal intensity as the yellow light of the harvest moons. This layering of images is not only a verbal achievement of what Fry termed the "identification of colour with plastic and spatial design" (*T* 216); Woolf's appropriation of this painterly device serves to displace her reader's focus so that each object refers to another object in another space. The reader is asked to visualise the shape and colour not only of the actual trees but also of the flags and the letters written on marble in the cathedral caves. Woolf's poetic juxtaposition of images thus achieves a three-dimensional spatial effect similar to that created by "coloured planes" in painting. Through this textual strategy, the novel highlights the structure, materiality and shape of solid things, all of which resist literal description because they are not present as recognisable (and therefore reducible) objects for the observing poet or philosopher's autonomous 'I'/eye.

Defamiliarising the Seen: Depicting Mrs Ramsay's Integrity

If Woolf in "Time Passes" explores the capacity of words to express the material density and spatial design characterising plastic colour, she achieves a radical defamiliarisation of objects which forms a necessary and integral part of the distinctive ethics developed in *To the Lighthouse*; her suspension of subjective perception in this section informs in central ways the novel's conception of ethical human relations. A key device in this respect is her imagery – strikingly similar to Irigaray's – of inaccessible buildings evoking another subject's irreducibility as well as the fundamental unknowability of another mind. We have seen how the architectural space of the cathedral denotes the structure and form of objects which exist independently of a perceiving 'I' or eye. The same image shapes Lily's idea of Mrs Ramsay's inscrutable mind. "But into what sanctuary had one penetrated?" Lily asks herself as she imagines

> how in the chambers of the mind and heart of the woman who was, physically, touching her, were stood, like the treasures in the tombs of kings, tablets bearing sacred inscriptions, which if one could spell them out would teach one everything, but they would never be offered openly, never made public. (*TL* 57)

The cathedral image here creates the same multidimensional spatial effect as does the vision of the autumn trees in "Time Passes." While the sanctuary conjured up by Lily is a metaphor of Mrs Ramsay's inner life, this imagined space refers not metaphorically to Mrs Ramsay's specific character or subjectivity, but metonymically to another space within it: the tombs. These chambers, in turn, metonymically contain the tablets with inscriptions whose literal meaning is not offered for Lily or the reader to decipher. Configured as a series of enclosed spaces, each "sealed" as it were by its own metonymic logic, Mrs Ramsay's interiority eludes the reader as an object of thought. This is one passage in which the novel's ethics is expressed through a formalist aesthetic. In giving each image the structure and shape of an architectural space, Woolf achieves in words something like the "clear and logical articulation of volumes within the picture space" which Fry identified with "plastic and spatial design" in Post-Impressionist painting (*T* 218, 216).[26] Through her verbal creation of spatial effect, Woolf contests Fry's definition of "that spaceless, moral world which belongs characteristically to the novel" (17). Reflecting on the possible convergence of "dramatic and plastic experiences" in a picture, Fry concludes that the observer is "compelled to focus the two elements separately." How, he asks, "can we keep the attention equally fixed on the spaceless world of psychological entities and relations and upon the apprehension of spatial relations?" (23). I believe Woolf offers an answer to Fry's question by shifting its focus from the art of painting to the art of writing. In her painterly cathedral image, a literary Post-Impressionist rendering of spatial relations becomes a vehicle for raising complex psychological and ethical questions.

Indeed, each of Woolf's formalist, metonymical cathedral images functions like Irigaray's "dwelling." In Irigaray's ethical philosophy, a subject's dwelling stands for a project and a worldview which cannot be fully known and, therefore, resists appropriation by another 'I': "Always already defined, the other has to become absolute in order to remain irreducible to our grasp" (*SW* 27). Another subject, that is, does not "belong to my world," but is "irreducible to any object, pre-given or constructed by our plan. The other does not for all that lack objectivity, but this is in great part determined by their own subjectivity" (86). This is the ethics conveyed by Woolf's cathedral images; like each enclosed space, Mrs Ramsay's subjectivity is an irreducible "dwelling" which cannot be accessed through metaphor or literal description. Erich Auerbach famously observed that in *To the Lighthouse*, Woolf "achieves the intended effect by representing herself to be someone who doubts, wonders, hesitates, as though the truth about her characters were not better known to her than it is to them or to the reader" (472). The novel's author, he notes further, "certainly does not speak like one who has a knowledge of his characters – in this case, of Mrs. Ramsay – and who, out of this knowledge, can describe their personality and momentary state of mind objectively and with certainty" (469). But might not the "intended effect," which Auerbach does not define, be precisely Mrs Ramsay's opacity? What the author of *Mimesis* seems to miss is that, for Woolf, a writer's display of absolute, supposedly objective knowledge of their characters would be ethically problematic.[27] Mrs Ramsay resists knowing description to the same extent as the autumn trees in "Time Passes"; in both instances, the closed "sanctuary" of the cathedral space refers metonymically to another space or object, each of which refers beyond itself so as to never be defined by an observing 'I'/eye. Like Woolf, Irigaray connects the fundamental unknowability of each subject with an irreducible non-human world. The following passage from *Sharing the World* illuminates Woolf's related portrayal of the autumn trees and Mrs Ramsay's subjectivity:

> The transcendence of the other with regard to me is simultaneously that of the plant, in part that of an animal but also that of a human being. It is complex and asks me to stop my journey in order to let the other be. . . . The sole a priori starting point from which I can approach the other is respect, that is, a going-towards that will as well be a withdrawing-before and -around the other in order to let this other exist and be. (87)

Insofar as Lily's "sanctuary" is metaphoric of Mrs Ramsay's interiority, it enables a "going-towards" the subjectivity of another, while the metonymic function of the image may well be said to achieve something like "a withdrawing-before and -around the other in order to let this other exist and be." This version of the cathedral image indicates that Mrs Ramsay's interiority is as indefinable as the shape of the unobserved autumn trees. In the same way, Mr Ramsay becomes aware of his wife's "remoteness" as he "look[s] into the hedge," observing its dense structural pattern, "its intricacy, its darkness" (*TL* 71).

For Irigaray, to recognise the other's irreducibility is to defamiliarise the individual before me, to suspend a habitual way of seeing him or her as a familiar part of my world in the Same (*SW* 76). The moment I realise that another subject's singularity is "still unfamiliar, . . . incomprehensible to [my] mind, still unknown and not representable" (92), I enter into an ethical relation with this other. Such an encounter calls me to momentarily leave my dwelling and to accept that, when I return, my world, outlook or horizon has changed. This opening of my dwelling "undoes the weaving of the relations that structured the world for me, especially their bonds of subordination. For a moment, the totality of the world is kept in suspense to welcome the other." In other words, my recognition of another subject's alluring, unfamiliar singularity leads to a defamiliarisation of my habitual perspective: "Through the meeting with the other, what seemed to me close has become partly strange because I distanced myself from my world in order to open myself to the world of the other" (89). Irigaray's ethics of defamiliarisation, in which a habitual way of seeing is suspended, offers a compelling way to approach the ethical complexity of Lily's and Woolf's respective aesthetic projects. Only in section 3, where Lily returns to the familiar world of section 1 but finds it strange and "unreal" (*TL* 160), can she complete her portrait of Mrs Ramsay. Woolf eventually decided to have Lily finish the painting she began in section 1: the one in which Mrs Ramsay, reading to James, figures as a "triangular purple shape" (58). This decision is significant because it links Lily's concern with Mrs Ramsay's irreducibility in "The Window" to the completion of her abstract painting in "The Lighthouse."

Back on the same lawn with her easel, Lily is overwhelmed by a sense of "extraordinary unreality" which is both "frightening" and "exciting" (161). Unable to "shake herself free from the sense that everything this morning was happening for the first time," she reflects how "coming back from a journey, or after an illness, before habits had spun themselves across the surface, one felt that same unreality, which was so startling; felt something emerge. Life was most vivid then" (210, 208). With this vertiginous sense of seeing the world anew, Lily invokes the image which incited her, ten years earlier, to attempt her experiments with colour and abstract form: "Mrs. Ramsay, she thought, stepping back and screwing up her eyes. (It must have altered the design a good deal when she was sitting on the step with James. There must have been a shadow.)"

(175). The design of her painting is equally in the foreground as the younger Lily looks at "the mass, at the line, at the colour, at Mrs Ramsay sitting in the window with James" (22). Mass, line and colour – these are three of the five devices Fry identified as "emotional elements of designs," devices which serve to arouse what Fry called aesthetic emotion in a viewer receptive to the formal as opposed to the representational qualities of an artwork (*VD* 23; see 23–25). However, while Fry dissociated aesthetic responsiveness from the moral obligations of life, Lily's Post-Impressionist aesthetic explores the ethical dimensions of her attempt to depict another individual.

Observing Mrs Ramsay and James together with William Bankes, Lily becomes aware of having "seen a thing they had not been meant to see"; they have, she reflects, "encroached upon a privacy" (*TL* 23). Lily's abstracting gaze focuses not on the figure of the mother reading to her child, but on the relations between mass, line and colour in her composition, and through this abstraction emerges a concern to preserve the privacy of the scene. Mrs Ramsay, she realises, is "different... from the perfect shape which one saw there. But why different, and how different?" (55). These questions are followed, a few pages later, by another: "did [Mrs Ramsay] lock up within her some secret which certainly Lily Briscoe believed people must have for the world to go on at all?" (57). Instead of seeking access to the secret of Mrs Ramsay's interiority, Lily imagines her subjectivity as a series of metonymically sealed spaces or, as Irigaray puts it, a singularity which is "still unknown and not representable" (*SW* 92). Lily's cathedral images become a geometrical shape on her canvas; rather than answering the question "why different, and how different?" she takes the abstract shape to stand for and preserve this difference. Her formalist reflections on Mrs Ramsay's inscrutability are followed by an exchange on painting with William Bankes, a conversation in which the problem of representational "likeness" is bound up with questions of respect:

> What did she wish to indicate by the triangular purple shape, "just there?" he asked.
>
> It was Mrs. Ramsay reading to James, she said. She knew his objection – that no one could tell it for a human shape. But she had made no attempt at likeness, she said. . . . Mr. Bankes was interested. Mother and child then – objects of universal veneration, and in this case the mother was famous for her beauty – might be reduced, he pondered, to a purple shadow without irreverence.
>
> But the picture was not of them, she said. Or, not in his sense. There were other senses, too, in which one might reverence them. By a shadow here and a light there, for instance. Her tribute took that form. (58–59)

Lily here reverses the assumptions underpinning William Bankes's aesthetic bias. Mrs Ramsay, the passage suggests, would be somehow "reduced" if presented, habitually, as a mother with her child. In portraying her as a "triangular purple shape," Lily defamiliarises her model, thereby paying a "tribute" to her integrity.

It is ultimately Woolf who makes this connection between the non-representational and the ethical. Lily's purple shape, the reader notes, is similar to the "wedge-shaped core of darkness" (69) which in Mrs Ramsay's own imagery stands for the integrity of a self "invisible to others":

> When life sank down for a moment, the range of experience seemed limitless. And to everybody there was always this sense of unlimited resources, she supposed; one after another, she, Lily, Augustus Carmichael, must feel, our apparitions, the things you know us by, are simply childish. Beneath it is all dark, it is all spreading, it is unfathomably deep; but now and then we rise to the surface and that is what you see us by. Her horizon seemed to her limitless. (69)

In this passage, Mrs Ramsay describes her own "range of experience" as limitless; she also, however, attributes a "sense of unlimited resources" to others. In a vocabulary close to Irigaray's, Woolf points here to a discrepancy between the reductive "things [others] know us by," preconceptions which determine the way we see and are seen by one another, and the limitless expansion of each perspective or worldview. Through the formalist image of the abstract shape, these passages articulate an ethics in which 'I' am asked to realise that each individual is as complex as 'I' take myself to be. That is, Woolf makes the abstract shape stand for, on the one hand, Lily's recognition of Mrs Ramsay's unrepresentable complexity and, on the other, Mrs Ramsay's subjective awareness of her own "unlimited resources." In so doing, she affirms and seeks to protect not only the irreducibility of the individuals 'I' encounter but also the boundless "horizon" of each self.

Lily's and Woolf's respective privileging of abstract form, then, engenders a novelistic design which presents a multiplicity of unbounded subjective perspectives. "As soon as I recognize the otherness of the other as irreducible to me or to my own," Irigaray writes, "the world itself becomes irreducible to a single world: there are always at least two worlds" (*SW* x). The moment 'I' apprehend the existence of multiple worlds alongside with my own, my solipsistic, enclosed dwelling must open up and re-form (76). A shared world is thus "another space" which "no longer obeys a single focus. I am no longer, in some way, the centre of the world or the centre of a unique world" (100). In *To the Lighthouse*, a pattern of constantly shifting focalising perspectives achieves something like a shared world as imagined by Irigaray. With the exception of "Time Passes," the novel is composed of numerous individual viewpoints. As Auerbach observes, "The essential characteristic of the technique represented by Virginia Woolf is that we are given not merely one person whose consciousness (that is, the impressions it receives) is rendered, but many persons, with frequent shifts from one to the other" (473).[28] The shift from one point of view to another is often marked out with a paragraph or chapter break, which has the effect of underlining the integrity and separateness of each worldview. Towards the end of Chapter 3 in "The Window," the chapter's focaliser Mrs Ramsay becomes aware of Lily's presence:

> the sight of the girl standing on the edge of the lawn painting reminded her; she was supposed to be keeping her head as much in the same position as possible for Lily's picture. Lily's picture! Mrs. Ramsay smiled. With her little Chinese eyes and her puckered-up face she would never marry; one could not take her painting very seriously; but she was an independent little creature, Mrs. Ramsay liked her for it, and so remembering her promise, she bent her head. (21)

The opening of Chapter 4 depicts the same scene but seen from Lily's perspective. Lily, the object of Mrs Ramsay's preconceptions – "she would never marry; one could not take her painting very seriously" – is now the subjective observer, and Mrs Ramsay in the window becomes the focus of her experiments with mass, line and colour. The device of the chapter break exemplifies beautifully Woolf's novelistic universe, which is never the product of a unique viewpoint, but emerges in the intersection of many horizons. In this, she compels her reader to realise that, as Irigaray writes, "the world itself [is] irreducible to a single world: there are always at least two worlds" (*SW* x).[29]

Seeing Together: Vision, Design and the Intimacy of Shared Perception

For Woolf as for Irigaray, then, to recognise another individual's complex world is to affirm that this world is unfamiliar and irreducible to one's own outlook or horizon. However, as Berman observes, they also see mutual recognition as the outcome of relations in which respect for another subject's radical alterity emerges through a longing for intimacy. Both aspects coincide in Lily's non-representational painting of Mrs Ramsay, but not only, or even primarily, as a result of the erotic or loving touch; Lily, whose abstract shape comes to stand for her model's unknowability, also desires intimacy in the double sense of fusing with Mrs Ramsay and seeing the world from her perspective. Realising that Mrs Ramsay "lock[s] up within her" a secret which can and must not be revealed (*TL* 57), Lily reflects that "it was not knowledge but unity that she desired, not inscriptions on tablets... but intimacy itself, which is knowledge." She thereby dislodges a common notion of intimacy as the outcome of a process of familiarisation, and questions the definition of the intimate as "closely connected by friendship or personal knowledge; characterized by familiarity (with a person or thing); very familiar" ("intimate, *adj.* and *n.*" def. A.3.a). As Berman and Martha C. Nussbaum both note, Lily's preoccupation with knowing another mind is treated by Woolf as an epistemological as well as an ethical problem. According to Nussbaum, Woolf substitutes epistemological knowledge for "a knowledge that does not entail possession"; Lily ultimately accepts her status as "a human being, finite in body and mind, partial and incomplete, separate from other humans of necessity and always" (743). Nussbaum, however, considers Lily's erotically charged desire for unity or oneness – "What device for becoming, like waters poured into one jar, inextricably the same, one with the object one adored?" (*TL* 57) – as a wish "to possess, to grab hold [of]... the other's thoughts and feelings" (Nussbaum 741; see 741–43). I agree with Nussbaum that Woolf conceptualised in *To the Lighthouse* an alternative way of knowing which is non-objectifying and respectful of alterity. In my reading, however, this new mode of knowledge emerges not in opposition to, but as an integral part of the quest for intimacy as unity which inspires Lily's aesthetic project.

Indeed, Irigaray's account of intimacy and alterity in *Sharing the World* enables an understanding of the ethics embedded in Lily's radical notion of intimacy. A shared world for Irigaray is a space, "always in becoming" (xx), in which each individual apprehends the many transcendental worlds or perspectives composing it. This space constitutes a threshold between separate worlds, all of which are suspended as the threshold "marks the limits of the world of each one," while also creating an opening "in which both I and the other risk losing ourselves" (1). Such thresholds emerge from two individuals' mutual desire to inhabit the other's perspective in "some conjunction between being-within and being-with" (70); sharing the world means seeking "access to another way of looking at, another way of perceiving the world" (105). The "wish for the other" is thus a longing for "an intimacy that I have not yet experienced," a desire, that is, for "a familiarity more familiar than that of the world already known" (97; see 97–98). Like Lily's longing to become "inextricably the same, one with" Mrs Ramsay,[30] the desire theorised by Irigaray "asks us to overcome all dichotomies: body/spirit, outward movement/inward movement, substance/becoming, unity/duality, etc." (98). Crucially, this intimate overcoming of differences is experienced as a momentary dissolution of the boundaries separating 'I' and 'you':

> Their being-with and their being-within, for a moment, harmonize the one with the other, at a bodily and spiritual level. This does not last and is partly illusory. But, for a time, the exile of each one in a world in which the other cannot dwell seems to be overcome. For a time, the invisible covering that divides each one from the other seems to vanish. The one and the other seem to be returned to this natural site where they were in communion with one another through the same air, the same breath, the same energy, uniting them through a sharing of the surrounding world. At least this would be their quest. (70)

For Irigaray, this ephemeral state of oneness is the end of a quest which must be cultivated and remain unfulfilled; insofar as attraction is awakened "by the difference between two worlds, by the mystery that the one represents for the other" (*WL* 151), desire and attraction are the forces inspiring the construction of a "common dwelling" or shared world (*SW* 71; see 71–73). In other words, ethical relations according to Irigaray cultivate a mode of intimacy which is respectful of difference: "nearness here is also always remoteness. Even when sitting at my side or present in front of me, the other remains distant, strange to me – the other does not dwell in my world" (99).

For Woolf, too, a desire for intimacy with another is a desire to share this other's perceptions, emotions and worldview. In this sense, Lily unity corresponds to what Mrs Ramsay calls "that community of feeling with other people which emotion gives as if the walls of partition had become so thin that practically (the feeling was one of relief and happiness) it was all one stream, and chairs, tables, maps, were hers, were theirs, it did not matter whose" (*TL* 123). In such moments of "feeling with" another, Woolf suggests here, 'I' let go of my unique viewpoint and realise that 'my' objects are not only mine; they are also perceived by the various others whose perspective I momentarily share. However, unlike Irigaray, Woolf associates intimacy with visual perception; her novel's ethics emerges primarily in the dynamics of the gaze. In Irigaray's philosophy, as we have seen, the act of looking is "dividing, distinguishing, cutting off and thus isolating," whereas intimacy "will remain invisible, irreducible to appropriation, and thus strange to the logic of Western discourse, to the logos" (*SW* 20). For

Irigaray, then, sight must perpetuate the autonomous subject's self-assertion and mastery. Woolf, on the other hand, explores through her textual experiments with painterly techniques a mode of looking which entails a loss of mastery in a pleasurable suspension of the first-person point of view.

In her most painterly novel *To the Lighthouse*, Woolf conceives of visual observation as a means for the coherent 'I' to call its worldview into question so as to apprehend or, at best, share the perspective of another. Throughout the novel, the act of looking together with another achieves an expansion of the individual viewpoint so that two perspectives briefly fuse into one. As Lily observes the sea together with William Bankes, their seeing in common becomes a feeling in common: "They both felt a common hilarity, excited by the moving waves; and then by the swift cutting race of a sailing boat . . . both of them looked at the dunes far away, and instead of merriment felt come over them some sadness" (25). A different kind of unity arises between Mrs Ramsay and Augustus Carmichael as their two pairs of eyes focus on a common object – the fruit plate on the dinner table: "to her pleasure (for it brought them into sympathy momentarily) [Mrs Ramsay] saw that Augustus too feasted his eyes on the same plate of fruits, plunged in, broke off a bloom here, a tassel there, and returned, after feasting, to his hive. That was his way of looking, different from hers. But looking together united them" (105–06). The image of the bee and the hive points back to Lily's earlier reflection on the problem of knowing Mrs Ramsay:

> How then, she had asked herself, did one know one thing or another thing about people, sealed as they were? Only like a bee . . . one haunted the dome-shaped hive, ranged the wastes of the air over the countries of the world alone, and then haunted the hives with their murmurs and their stirrings; the hives which were people. (57–58)

The "dome-shaped hive" is a version of Woolf's cathedral space and Irigaray's dwelling, both of which stand for the integrity of subjective viewpoints which cannot be appropriated or represented by a knowing 'I.' If each individual is a hive, as the metaphor suggests, then the flight of the bee figures the aspiration to leave one's dwelling in order to approach the dwelling of another. In the dinner scene, this aspiration is expressed in the act of looking; Augustus Carmichael reaches out of his hive in the moment he rests his eyes on the fruit plate. The sympathy which briefly unites him and Mrs Ramsay is not, however, a fusion of their perspectives – "his way of looking" is "different from hers" – but precisely a mutual recognition of this difference.

A further dimension to the novel's ethics of looking is articulated in Lily's decision to let William Bankes see her painting:

> She braced herself to stand the awful trial of someone looking at her picture. One must, she said, one must. And if it must be seen, Mr. Bankes was less alarming than another. But that any other eyes should see the residue of her thirty-three years, the deposit of each day's living, mixed with something more secret than she had ever spoken or shown in the course of all those days was an agony. At the same time it was immensely exciting. (58)

They discuss her picture and the aesthetic implications of the abstract purple shape, after which Lily reflects: "But it had been seen; it had been taken from her. This man had shared with her something profoundly intimate" (60). One way to understand this apparent contradiction – something has been "taken from her," yet something has been shared – would be to consider Lily's painting as a specifically Post-Impressionist project. What Lily lets William Bankes see, the passage suggests, is not merely the colours and shapes on the canvas, but the process in which the painter works her limitless "range of experience," to use Mrs Ramsay's phrase, into each brush stroke. The showing of her canvas is a moment of exposure in which she offers secrets of her inner life for William Bankes to see. In this sense, he takes something from her in looking. Lily's gesture is also, however, an invitation to see with her eyes, as it were, in a "profoundly intimate" moment of shared perception. Through Lily's painterly approach, Woolf stages Fry's idea of artistic creation as a process of expressing and sharing perceptions and emotions. Although Fry distinguished between art and life, between aesthetic emotion and the "sensations of ordinary life" (*VD* 169), between the plastic and the psychological, Woolf was right in asking, provocatively, in her biography of Fry: "But . . . were they distinct?" (*RF* 214). As we saw at the outset of this chapter, Woolf did not consider the Impressionist's subjective recording of visual impressions and sensory experience to be incompatible with a formalist aesthetic; Fry's biographer conspicuously conflates his respective categories of aesthetic emotion and life-like sensations. Woolf's interpretation should not be seen as a distortion of his formalist theory, however, but a perceptive indication that Fry's distinctions may in fact be less clear-cut than his rhetoric tends to suggest.

In his essay "The French Post-Impressionists," originally published as "The French Group" in the *Catalogue of the Second Post-Impressionist Exhibition* (Grafton Galleries, 1912), Fry describes a "new movement in art" in which the imitative representation of objects was "completely subordinated to the direct expression of feeling" (*VD* 166). By "feeling" Fry intends the kind of emotion defined, in "An Essay in Aesthetics," by its intrinsic value: "we must . . . give up the attempt to judge the work of art by its reaction to life, and consider it as an expression of emotions regarded as ends in themselves." Dissociated from their capacity as affective responses in life, sense perceptions and emotions become heightened and, as such, they enter the realm of the aesthetic (*VD* 20–21). It is difficult, however, not to note the proximity of Fry's aesthetic emotions to the emotions in life from which they originate. This closeness is particularly apparent as Fry supports his theory with a passage from Tolstoy's *What is Art?* where Tolstoy considers the aesthetic implications of a boy narrating how he was pursued by a bear. Fry agrees with Tolstoy's claim that "if [the boy] describes his state first of heedlessness, then of sudden alarm and terror as the bear appears, and finally of relief when he gets away, and describes this so that his hearers share his emotions, then his description is a work of art" (*VD* 20). In "Retrospect," Fry maintains again Tolstoy's influence on his aesthetic theory. Tolstoy, he writes approvingly, "saw that the essence of art was that it was a means of communication between human beings. He conceived it to be *par excellence* the language of emotion." As Fry seeks to integrate this conviction into his formalist paradigm, he undermines entirely his earlier distinction between aesthetic emotion and emotion in life: "I conceived [in 'An Essay in Aesthetics'] the form of the work of art to be its most essential quality, but I believed this form to be the direct outcome of an apprehension of some emotion of actual life by the artist" (*VD* 205–06).[31]

The communicative aspirations embedded in Fry's formalism are in the end remarkably similar to Lily's notion of her canvas as "the deposit of each day's living." "One must keep on looking," she reflects, "without for a second relaxing the intensity of emotion" (*TL* 218). Like Fry's artist, for whom aesthetic form is "the direct outcome of an apprehension of some emotion of actual life," Lily invites the observer of her painting to share the perceptions and emotions accumulated in the triangular purple shape. While Fry never speaks of intimacy, he does speak of a "special tie" with the artist, a "relation of sympathy" felt by the viewer of an artwork who, in the moment of observation, experiences the emotions expressed there by the artist. In contemplating the formal relations in a painting, Fry holds, "We feel that [the artist] has expressed something which was latent in us all this time, but which we never realised, that he has revealed us to ourselves in revealing himself. And this recognition is, I believe, an essential part of the aesthetic judgement proper" (*VD* 21). It is not clear, in this passage, who feels and communicates this "something" to whom. His critical attitude to psychoanalysis notwithstanding,[32] Fry seems to imply that in the creation and reception of an artwork, a transmission of feelings between artist and observer occurs independently of their conscious selves, and that the moment of aesthetic judgement is a becoming conscious of this process.[33] It is in this sense that Lily becomes aware, after looking at her painting together with William Bankes, that "This man had shared with her something profoundly intimate" (*TL* 60).

We could ask here whether Woolf's idea of aesthetic transmission as an intimate sharing of interiority does not ultimately create a recognisable Bloomsbury ethics, one that both affirms and exceeds G. E. Moore's transposition of the ethical into the region of aesthetics and eros. Modelled on Lily's exchange with William Bankes, the Post-Impressionist aesthetic of *To the Lighthouse* may well embrace Moore's notion that an ethically good life begins with the passionate contemplation of an artwork and the sharing of aesthetic experience with one's intimates. However, if Woolf thus follows Moore in cultivating the aesthetically receptive self (rather than moral rules of conduct), she diverges from his belief in what Tom Regan has termed "the virtue of Egoism over Altruism as a means of producing good" (246); intimacy, for Woolf as for Irigaray, is the creative instant of sharing (thoughts, perceptions, emotions) where care for the self becomes care for the other because the two cannot, in that moment, be told apart. In her intriguing chapter on Woolf's recurring, enigmatic rendering of erotic love in quotation marks, as the state of being "in love," Rachel Bowlby comments on Lily Briscoe's reconception of love as her aesthetic vision merges with that of William Bankes:

> For him to gaze as Lily saw him gazing at Mrs. Ramsay was a rapture. . . . It was love, she thought, pretending to move her canvas, distilled and filtered; love that never attempted to clutch its object; but, like the love which mathematicians bear their symbols, or poets their phrases, was meant to spread over the world and become part of the human gain. (*TL* 53)

As Bowlby notes, this bringing together of love and an impersonal aesthetic "hints at a violence in the attempted 'clutch' of love's object" (187). I would go further and suggest that while, as Berman observes, Lily's respect for Mrs Ramsay's alterity cannot be distinguished from her love for the model of her painting (*Modernist Commitments* 57), Woolf's Post-Impressionist ethics resists violence in situating intimacy beyond the object attachments structuring the realm of eros.

As we have seen, Irigaray's recent writings locate intimacy in the wish to experience the inner life another and, for both Fry and Woolf, an intimate sharing of interiority may be achieved through the creation and sharing of an artwork. That is, Woolf's thought follows Fry's but differs from Irigaray's in connecting intimacy with the act of looking and with the visual dimension of the creative process. Whereas Irigaray's category of "sensory apprehensions," the "medium par excellence of interiority," includes the touch and the sound of the voice but excludes the visual (*SW* 12, 128), Fry connects the sensations and emotions of life with the recording and transmission of visual impressions. Painting according to Fry must convey the vision or sensory impressions of the painter's 'I' as well as form or design, which would achieve a defamiliarisation of the objects perceived. If *To the Lighthouse* connects design with the questioning of the all-knowing 'I' and the recognition of each individual's irreducibility, vision is what enables brief moments of intimacy where self and other, as Irigaray puts it, "become just one" in "some conjunction between being-within and being-with" (*SW* 70). I shall end this chapter by returning to Woolf's ethical appropriation of Fry's plastic colour, a device in which formless, Impressionist vision and Post-Impressionist design converge. An "inherent part of the expressive quality of form," Fry writes, Post-Impressionist colour is a combination of line, shade and colour "into a single indissoluble whole" (*T* 214). In Fry's definition, plastic colour contains but is not reducible to "pure colour," which is a medium of vision and sensations (*VD* 58). Fry connects pure colour dissociated from form and design with fourteenth-century paintings in which "the *rôle* of colour was mainly decorative" (*T* 213), but a similar treatment of colour is also ascribed, provocatively, to the work of the Impressionists. Initially interested in "the more scientific evaluation of colour which the Impressionists practised," Fry reflects in "Retrospect" that he nonetheless "came to feel more and more the absence in their work of structural design" (*VD* 201).

In Woolf's novel, the combination of shape and shapelessness characteristic of plastic colour operates as a vehicle for *jouissance*, a state in which the boundaries separating 'I' and 'you' dissolve. This state is a crucial component in the novel's ethics of shared emotion; the moment of rapture is configured as an intimate union attained by two individuals seeing together. During the September evening in "The Window," Lily observes the garden she is painting, and then walks towards the sea with William Bankes:

> for it was bright enough, the grass still a soft deep green, the house starred in its greenery with purple passion flowers, and rooks dropping cool cries from the high blue. . . . So off they strolled down the garden in the usual direction, past the tennis lawn, past the pampas grass, to that break in the thick hedge, guarded by

red-hot pokers like brasiers of clear burning coal, between which the blue waters of the bay looked bluer than ever. (24)

The intense blue of the water, we read, "gave to their bodies even some sort of physical relief. First, the pulse of colour flooded the bay with blue, and the heart expanded with it and the body swam" (24–25). As they look at the sea together, each wave is felt as a "pulse of colour" in which, the image suggests, the water and the perceiving subject become one. The metaphors of fluidity – the heart expanding with the accumulating wave and the body swimming as the wave breaks – evoke a primary oneness with the world presenting itself to the senses. Together, Lily and William Bankes thus experience an intimate return to a formative state where self and other are not yet perceived as separate entities.[34] Equally receptive to the "pulse of colour," the two attain a momentary unity in which, as Irigaray puts it, "the exile of each one in a world in which the other cannot dwell seems to be overcome" (*SW* 70).

Lily's painting becomes the very device which enables this radical intimacy. As she fills her canvas with Post-Impressionist colours and her mind becomes "like a fountain spurting over that glaring, hideously difficult white space," Lily loses consciousness of "her name and her personality and her appearance" (*TL* 174). Her habitual perspective suspended, Lily, "painting steadily, felt as if a door had opened, and one went in and stood gazing silently about in a high cathedral-like place, very dark, very solemn" (186). The cathedral space, this metaphor of Mrs Ramsay's inscrutability, momentarily opens up as Lily stands on the threshold, to use Irigaray's image, between two dwellings. For Woolf, then, plastic colour as exemplified in Lily's painting opens up a relational space where intimacy and alterity may converge. Grounded in the Impressionist fluidity of what Fry terms pure colour, Post-Impressionist colour thereby enables an individual's experience of becoming one with another. Unlike pure colour, however, plastic colour is an inextricable combination of colour and form. For the Impressionist or "pure visualist," Fry holds, "drawing presents, as compared with painting, a peculiar difficulty (*T* 200). The drawn line does not directly record any visual experience. It describes a contour, and that contour is presented to the eye as the boundary of one area of tone seen against another area of different tone and colour." Only with Cézanne did colour "ceas[e] to play any separate *rôle* from drawing"; in Cézanne's work, colour is "an integral part of plastic expression" (218). As Banfield puts it, "Fry baptized 'plastic colour' the resolution of the ancient debate between colorists and draughtsmen . . . the 'combination of lines and colours'" (276).[35] If the Impressionists' colours are formless and their work lacks "structural design" (*VD* 201), plastic colour is structural because it expresses line and contour.

In *To the Lighthouse*, the plastic integration of colour and structural form comes to stand for relations in which intimacy between two individuals converges with irrevocable separateness. In this sense, Lily's painting becomes a metaphor of the perceiving self: "Beautiful and bright it should be on the surface, feathery and evanescent, one colour melting into another like the colours on a butterfly's wing; but beneath the fabric must be clamped together with bolts of iron" (*TL* 186). The "bolts of iron" connote structure and solidity, lines and contours, all of which, for Woolf, delineate subjective integrity and a gathering together of the 'I'. This is how Mrs Ramsay "use[s] the branches of the elm-trees outside to help her to stabilise her position" (122); as she observes the solid shape of the branches, Mrs Ramsay regains her position, perspective or worldview. For Woolf as for Irigaray, to open up one's dwelling is not to abandon it; both stress the importance of affirming whatever defines one's singular point of view. In the boat on the way to the lighthouse with his father and sister, sixteen-year-old James recalls how, ten years earlier, he saw the lighthouse "as a silvery, misty-looking tower with a yellow eye" (202). Thus remembering his childhood, "Turning back among the many leaves which the past had folded in him, peering into the heart of that forest where light and shade so chequer each other that all shape is distorted," he then seeks "an image to cool and detach and round off his feeling in a concrete shape" (200). The clear-cut shape and intense colours of the lighthouse call him back to his present self: "He could see the white-washed rocks; the tower, stark and straight; he could see that it was barred with black and white; he could see windows in it" (202). However, the 'I'-shaped tower is metaphoric of James's autonomous 'I' only insofar as this image is superimposed on the earlier image of the misty-looking tower. The two are "folded" onto each other like the leaves in James's forest metaphor, much like layered plastic colour is grounded in Impressionist colours with their play of light and shade.[36]

As Mrs Ramsay gazes out at the sea, the lighthouse appears, as it does to James, "distant, austere, in the midst" (17). The same view, she notes, would be seen differently by Mr Paunceforte, a fictional Impressionist painter whose colours are not "solid" and whose pictures are "green and grey, with lemon-coloured sailing boats" (18, 17). Looking at "the mass, at the line, at the colour, at Mrs. Ramsay" (22), Lily at her easel reflects similarly how Paunceforte would have made colour "thinned and faded, the shapes etherealised." Lily herself sees "the colour burning on a framework of steel; the light of a butterfly's wing lying upon the arches of a cathedral" (54). She keeps looking "till the colour of the wall and the jacmanna beyond burned into her eyes. . . . The jacmanna was bright violet, the wall staring white." It would not, she decides, have been "honest to tamper with the bright violet and the staring white . . . fashionable though it was, since Mr. Pauncefortes's visit, to see everything pale, elegant, semi-transparent. Then beneath the colour there was the shape" (22–23, 23). An emphasis on shape and contrast structures Lily's painting as well as James's image of the lighthouse. Lily's wall is "staring white," and James's rocks are "white-washed"; Lily focuses on the sharp contrast of the white against the bright violet of the jacmanna whereas James's lighthouse is black and white; the lighthouse is "stark and straight," and Lily's painting is to have a structural "framework of steel." Suggestive of shape, form and design, this framework is, significantly, likened to "the arches of a cathedral," an image which throughout the novel expresses Lily's respect for her model's subjective complexity. In equating James's and Lily's respective images of the lighthouse and the cathedral space, metaphors of James's individuality and Mrs Ramsay's integrity, Woolf uses a Post-Impressionist integration of shape and colour to articulate her notion of ethical relations. As James's straight tower is conditional on an earlier, hazier image, so Lily's cathedral image materialises on her canvas as a combination of framework and colour, which expresses both her respect for and her desire to be one with Mrs Ramsay. The novel's ethics is thus located precisely in Woolf's integration of colour and form, in between intimate union and the marked separateness of different perspectives.

Observing the party gathered around the dinner table in "The Window," Mrs Ramsay initially contemplates a scene "robbed of colour," where "Nothing seemed to have merged. They all sat separate" (91). After this reflection follows an account of the many different, conflicting viewpoints asserted by the diners, each sharply distinguished from the others by abrupt shifts in focalisation. The painterly metaphor of a picture which is all form and no colour describes a company of separate individuals with irreconcilable worldviews; if colour in the novel is associated with a desire for intimacy as oneness, form without colour connotes the assertion of the 'I.' Against the relational implications of colourless form, Woolf imagines the impression as a way to mutual recognition. Standing next to William Bankes on the lawn, Lily suddenly perceives how

> the load of her accumulated impressions of him tilted up, and down poured in a ponderous avalanche all she felt about him. That was one sensation. Then rose up in a fume the essence of his being. That was another. She felt herself transfixed by the intensity of her perception; it was his severity; his goodness. I respect you (she addressed him silently) in every atom. (28–29)

Lily then proceeds to analysing this shower of impressions, asking herself: "How did one judge people, think of them? How did one add up this and that and conclude that it was liking one felt, or disliking?" (29). That is, after the overwhelming experience of receiving sensory impressions of the individual next to her, the Post-Impressionist artist Lily begins to interrogate the ways we habitually see and frequently judge one another. Such receptiveness to impressions of others, Woolf suggests, may even lead an individual to suspend his or her habitual viewpoint, as Mrs Ramsay becomes aware during the dinner:

> It could not last she knew, but at the moment her eyes were so clear that they seemed to go round the table unveiling each of these people, and their thoughts and their feelings, without effort like a light stealing under water. . . . for whereas in active life she would be netting and separating one thing from another; she would be saying she liked the Waverly novels or had not read them; she would be urging herself forward; now she said nothing. For the moment she hung suspended. (116)

Via the Impressionist image of the light stealing through the nets in the water, the passage depicts a moment of suspension, in which Mrs Ramsay abandons the idea of her self as strictly autonomous. A spirit of communality arises at the table as each of the diners experiences a similar suspension of the individual self:

> Now all candles were lit, and the faces on both sides of the table were brought nearer by the candle-light, and composed, as they had not been in the twilight, into a party round a table, for the night was now shut off by panes of glass. . . . Some change at once went through them all, as if this had really happened, and they were all conscious of making a party together in a hollow, on an island, . . . when solidity suddenly vanished, and such vast spaces lay between them; and now the same effect was got by the many candles in the sparely furnished room. (106)

The Impressionist fluidity achieved here by the candles connotes a blurring of the boundaries separating different selves, but in this instant of dislocation, a process of re-formation is initiated where the image of the island does not stand for the solitary 'I' oblivious to other worldviews. Like the party looking together out of the window into the night, the island becomes a metaphor of a group of individuals in which each is acutely receptive to the irreducible presence of others. Through the Post-Impressionist aesthetic of *To the Lighthouse*, then, Woolf conceptualised the fusion of separate perspectives into a common outlook on a world that, for a moment, may be shared.

4

Chalk Marks: Violence and Vulnerability in *The Waves*

How are we to understand Woolf's much cited diary note that *The Waves*, her most "abstract poetic" book, was to be about "A mind thinking" (*D* 3: 185, 229)? If the monologues of Bernard, Jinny, Louis, Neville, Rhoda and Susan emerged from a vision about a novel form capable of depicting the workings of a single mind, this mind eventually branched out into six, each separated from the others by thin membranes. As Susan Gorsky once put it, "a startling intimacy" unites the six perspectives through shared phrases and images, an aesthetic achievement which "breaks down the usual barriers . . . of the individual mind" (44, 50). This intimacy is curiously at odds with a persistent critical tradition in which Woolf's aesthetically innovational monologues are thought to render the human mind as essentially closed in upon itself. Since the year of its publication, *The Waves* has been considered the high point in Woolf's experimental writing and her most radical break with novelistic conventions. Among the reviews appearing in 1931, several praise the novel for its formal complexity, its densely poetic language and impressive representation of psychic processes.[1] When Winifred Holtby wrote that Woolf "has explored further and further into the regions of human experience lying outside our bright, busy world of deliberate speech and action," she lingered on the novel's "orchestral-soliloquy form" (5–6, 6). Like Holtby, Edith Shackleton and Gerard Bullet distinguish between thought and action. In a review significantly entitled "Virginia Woolf Soliloquises," Bullet takes Woolf's focus on interiority to create a lyric, poetic imagery which "does not, for the most part, relate to the physical world from which it is borrowed" (8).

The title of Bullet's piece draws attention to an assumption underlying many of the first reviews of *The Waves*: because the novel fundamentally challenges realist conventions in its formally complex account of six individual characters' inner life, Woolf the novelist speaks in solitude like an actress alone on stage to a rather small audience. This idea has been furthered by critics maintaining that the novel's concern with interiority and the vagueness of its spatial and temporal setting reflect the author's alienation. Gerald Sykes was among the first to hold that *The Waves* could only have been conceived by a writer more interested in stylistic experiments for their own sake than in the "real" world of society and politics (11),[2] and even Alex Zwerdling, whose landmark study *Virginia Woolf and the Real World* set out as late as 1986 to contest an ingrained notion of Woolf as "out of touch with the life of her time" (9), omits the novel from his argument. For Zwerdling, Woolf is detached from socio-political reality when she looks inwards instead of outwards, and he sees *The Waves* as the high point in her poetic exploration of individual psychic life (9–10). In contrast to the historical and political relevance of *The Years* and *Three Guineas*, he claims, *The Waves* lacks "a realistic base" (12). Indeed, for about five decades, *The Waves* was widely held to have little to say about the political climate in the years of its composition, and at the centre of these debates is a problematic association of the novel's soliloquy form with an escapist retreat into interiority.

But to return to my initial question – the very notion of Woolf's soliloquy as a mere channel for her characters' mind/s needs interrogation. "Soliloquy" was Woolf's own term for what has often been read as a form of interior monologue,[3] and it remains a key strategy in her combination of novelistic conventions with those of drama and poetry. As a dramatic concept, the soliloquy denotes the *staging* of a thinking mind articulated in words, a voiced performance addressed to an audience. This should alert us to the limitations of the critical view of Woolf's soliloquy as the transparent expression of a solipsistic consciousness, whether her own or, say, Rhoda's.[4] My point is not to contest the possibility that the soliloquy form of *The Waves* may well have been designed to represent "A mind thinking"; on the contrary, I venture that Woolf's writing of interiority through the soliloquy as an aesthetic device is an ethical as well as a political act. As a lyric, poetic engagement with intimacy and self-reflection on the one hand, and a dramatic performance of vocal expression and the dynamics of the address on the other, Woolf's introspective monologues become the very locus of a non-violent ethics and an anti-nationalist politics.

I align myself here with the many scholars, from Jane Marcus to Jessica Berman, who have argued convincingly for almost three decades that *The Waves* delivers a critique of nationalism, imperialism and the fascist movements spreading in Europe. Since the publication of Marcus's ground-breaking 1991 essay "Britannia Rules *The Waves*," a feminist, pacifist and non-conformist textual politics has been detected in the novel.[5] From this perspective, Woolf's poetic experimentalism articulates a timely response to a worrying political climate; Mussolini's fascist party ruled Italy from 1922, and the emergence of fascism in Britain was contemporaneous with her writing of *The Waves*. My engagement with this text builds on Marcus's insight that *The Waves* is "a cultural icon of the 1930s," "part of the discourse about ... fascism, war, and imperialism in which it participated" ("Britannia" 77). However, the pioneering critical trajectory initiated by Marcus has been notably reluctant to include Woolf's poetic soliloquy form in its politicised readings due, perhaps, to an underlying poststructuralist alignment of introspective lyricism and a Western fantasy of self-possessed individualism epitomised by the fascist's aggressive 'I.' Thus in Marcus's largely unchallenged account, *The Waves* "exhaust[s]" the soliloquy form by parodying the Romantic poet's introspection and its sustainment of British imperialism ("Britannia" 83–84). In this chapter, I follow a more recent, new formalist attention to the political affordances – "the potential uses or actions latent in materials and designs" – of literary forms as advocated by Caroline Levine (6), arguing that Woolf radically expands the affordance of the soliloquy beyond solipsistic escapism and literary-political violence.

In what way, then, does Woolf's idiosyncratic deployment of the soliloquy make *The Waves* a text of the 1930s, a time that demanded socio-political commitment from writers and artists? I propose that a careful reading of the novel alongside a later text, *Three Guineas* (1938), might reveal how some of the key questions of violence, pacifism and poetic representation articulated there were already problematised in *The Waves*. Nearly a decade before the publication of *Three Guineas*, Woolf was, in writing *The Waves*, spelling out by aesthetic means the convictions informing her pacifist opposition to militarism and violence. Given the composition history of these books, it is remarkable that *The Waves*, as Woolf's last experimental novel of its kind, is so seldom read together with her later, more overtly political writings. It was in 1931, while she was still working on *The Waves*, that Woolf gave her speech on "Professions for Women," which she imagined as the beginning of a sequel to *A Room of One's Own*. The previous year, she wrote her Introductory Letter for Margaret Llewelyn Davies's collection *Life as We Have Known It* (1931), reflecting on her impressions from her work for the Women's Co-operative Guild. Regarding the political agenda of the WCG, Woolf was particularly compelled by their uncompromising pacifism.[6] In light of this context, reading *The Waves* with *Three Guineas* can make us see the extent to which Woolf's most abstract novel expresses her belief in the capacity of art to resist conformist thinking and promote critical thought. Moreover, the politics of the novel arguably proceeds precisely through its introspective lyricism as crystallised in Woolf's use of the poetic-dramatic soliloquy. In order to elucidate these connections, I will briefly shift my focus to her polemical pre-war text.

An aspect of *Three Guineas* which has not been substantially explored is Woolf's reliance in that work on what she calls psychology – "that understanding of human beings and their motives" (*TG* 158) – to explain the aggressive desire to acquire and possess which, she holds, causes violence and war.[7] She analysed this desire closely in *A Room of One's Own*, and her continued emphasis in *Three Guineas* on the psychology of violence motivates the pacifism through which she responded to the impending event of another war. In *Three Guineas*, Woolf locates the origins of nationalism, imperialism and fascism, which is both nationalist and imperialist, in patriarchal family structures, thereby drawing attention to the interconnectedness of public and private spaces in the years between the two world wars. This has frequently been pointed out.[8] Connections between the intensely political *Three Guineas* and the abstract, poetic *The Waves* have been noted, although less frequently, and only in recent years have critics observed that *The Waves* engages political questions around violence and aggression.[9] I shall suggest, in this chapter, that it is the effort to imagine violence in psychological terms which gives *The Waves* a decisive role in the pacifism eventually articulated in *Three Guineas*.

It is no doubt because they differ so widely in their mode of expression that *The Waves* and *Three Guineas*, which show Woolf at her most poetic and her most prosaic, are not usually considered together. "[S]ober prose," a term used in *Three Guineas* to describe the transactions involved in the founding of a college for women, is considered the medium for communicating financial, historical and political facts and events throughout Woolf's work. It is also an accurate description of Woolf's own language in this polemic, which is more ostensibly based on such facts than any of her other writings.[10] In 1938, under the very real threat of a Nazi invasion, Woolf has her narrator imagine, as she observes Westminster and the Houses of Parliament, the reproach of the elderly man she is writing to: "It is a place to stand on by the hour, dreaming. But not now. Now we are pressed for time. Now we are here to consider facts." In response to his question – how can another war be prevented? – she renounces the possibilities of writing letters to newspapers and joining a society. Rather than taking immediate measures through such acts, Woolf's narrator argues that any sustained effort to prevent war must proceed through an understanding of the psychological connections between possessiveness, aggression, nationalism and violence. Aware that her addressee will object that there is no time to think, she insists nonetheless: "Let us never cease from thinking – what is this 'civilization' in which we find ourselves?" (190, 240, 244).[11]

Thinking and dreaming rather than acting – these terms are strongly evocative of the poetic writing composing *The Waves*, a kind of writing for which there is no longer time. The narrator of *Three Guineas* is too pressed for time in 1938 to write poetically because, as Woolf remarks in *A Room of One's Own* (73–74), the poetic mode requires detachment from the world of facts and politics. And the 1930s, in which writers were expected to take a stance in urgent political questions, were not the times for novels such as *The Waves*. Indeed, in the years of planning and writing *The Waves*, Woolf's diary demonstrates a heightened interest in interiority. "Every day," she writes in 1926, "I have meant to record a state of mind" (*D* 3: 111), and the entries of that year frequently include subheadings such as "Art & Thought," "My own Brain" and "A State of Mind" (102, 103, 110). Her diary notes also describe the novel almost exclusively as abstract, and there are few references, in the years of its composition, to social and political questions. How, then, can we read *The Waves* as a forceful political statement delivered through, not despite, its aesthetics of interiority? A reassessment of the introspective poetics in this novel can be achieved, I propose, through close attention to *Three Guineas* and its radical revision of the established dichotomy between thought and action.

The narrator of *Three Guineas* articulates Woolf's conviction that art may be a vehicle for explaining as well as opposing war insofar as it remains disinterested (*TG* 107), which is not the same as apolitical. Disinterested writing as defined in this text assumes an anti-nationalist stance through its "weapon of independent opinion" (237). A weapon in the pacifist opposition to fascism, violence and war, Woolf holds, critical thought entails an absolute refusal to participate in patriotic action. Throughout *Three Guineas*, the narrator's focus on psychic processes from reflective thinking to dreaming is connected with literature which does not serve immediate political ends but, instead, sets out to analyse the psychological motives which structure societies in war and peace. Even in 1940, during Germany's intense bombings of London, Woolf persists in her belief that we must fight the aggressive will to conquer and dominate "with the mind" ("Thoughts on Peace in an Air Raid," *E* 6: 242).[12] Two years earlier, when the question of how to prevent war was still a matter for discussion, Woolf has the narrator of *Three Guineas* call for "some more active method of expressing our belief . . . that war is inhuman" than practical measures such as signing manifestos and joining societies (166; see 277). Successful resistance to war does not, for Woolf, proceed through such counteracts, but through detached, introspective analysis of patriotism. In this sense, "to be passive is to be active" (329).¹³ A genuinely original aspect of Woolf's political radicalism in *Three Guineas*, then, one that has yet to be fully appreciated, is her dismantling of the simplistic divisions between active and passive, political and apolitical, thought and action, looking inwards and looking out, which have informed the field of Woolf criticism since the 1930s.

The opposite of disinterested thought is what Woolf calls "unreal loyalties," that is, uncritical submission to the nationalist, militaristic and imperialist doctrines which found their most extreme expression in fascism.¹⁴ In order to analyse and eventually detach oneself from such loyalties, Woolf's narrator insists, one must "rid [one]self of pride and nationality in the first place; also of religious pride, college pride, school pride, family pride." In this account, a new war is inevitable because of unreal loyalties and positions in England as well as Germany,¹⁵ and war amounts to a meaningless protection of artificial boundaries between nations whose leaders are "childishly intent upon scoring the floor of the earth with chalk marks" (*TG* 271, 322, 308). The word "unreal" does not suggest that Woolf took these discursive chalk marks lightly; according to the logic of *Three Guineas*, they structure relations between individuals as well as nations. As the image of the child drawing implies, the aggressive defence of national boundaries originates, in Woolf's analysis, in the process of self-formation, and the autonomous self is depicted throughout her work as a precarious entity.

If such fortification of self and nation was unreal for Woolf, it is because she was acutely aware of the fragility of these constructs; of the ways in which chalk marks tend to be violently drawn because they are so easily effaced. Andrew John Miller points out that *Three Guineas* problematises a pervasive crisis of political, personal and national sovereignty represented in modernist writing between the two world wars. The massive redrawing of national borders after the First World War caused a concern with unstable boundaries in Britain as well as "a heightened anxiety regarding both internal and external threats to the homeland," and this crisis led Woolf and other modernist writers to question national sovereignty along with national identities (viii, xxi). Miller's insights can be usefully extended to Woolf's analysis of the autonomous self. I have argued, in the previous chapters, that her fiction of the inter-war period highlights the ethical and political consequences of asserting at all cost one's 'I,' thereby alerting readers in her own time and ours to an ideal of unlimited subjective autonomy which continues to cause ethical as well as political forms of violence. This line of thought informs a section left out of the published version of *Three Guineas*, where Woolf connects patriarchy, nationalism and fascism with the superiority complex of the hyper-masculine male denounced throughout the text: "He has become an egomaniac; always writing about I; an egotist on such a scale that to assuage the pangs of his egotism he must keep a whole sex devoted to his service. The recreation of heroes. Women's place is in the home" (*Three Guineas* typescript, qtd. in Zwerdling, *Real World* 263).[16]

Against the reactionary politics emerging from the impulse to "always writ[e] about I," Woolf conceptualises an ethics and poetics of intimacy, which is also a form of political intervention. She closes *Three Guineas* by imagining a way of being with others that takes into account a primary unity which she describes as more real than the defensive constructs of the sovereign self and nation. Before ending her letter, the narrator reflects:

> Even here, even now your letter tempts us . . . to listen not to the bark of the guns and the bray of the gramophones but to the voices of the poets, answering each other, assuring us of a unity that rubs out divisions as if they were chalk marks only; to discuss with you the capacity of the human spirit to overflow boundaries and make unity out of multiplicity. But that would be to dream . . . the dream of peace, the dream of freedom. But, with the sound of the guns in your ears you have not asked us to dream. You have not asked us what peace is; you have asked us how to prevent war. Let us then leave it to the poets to tell us what the dream is. (365–66)

In 1938, peace is a dream, an impossible pacifist vision detached from reality, and so is poetry. And yet, even when writing the sober prose of *Three Guineas* Woolf saw poetic writing, introspection and psychological reflection, all of which were modes of dreaming at the time, as a sustainable answer to the question of how to prevent war. Precisely because there is no time for dreaming, Woolf holds, because an aggressive protection of national interests has taken Europe to the brink of another war, literary efforts to interrogate the relationship between violence and intimacy remain more important than ever. To dream in this context is not to ignore historical facts and events, but to analyse them from a perspective detached from nationalist allegiances.[17] When writing the passage above, she still conceived of poetry as a forceful vehicle for disinterested analysis because of its capacity to imagine divisions between individuals as well as nations as chalk marks. She shows how poetic contemplation is necessary for any attempt to explain and oppose war, and, crucially, she considers it the role of the poet to define the dream of peace. As Zwerdling has observed, Woolf's pacifism is rooted in an "ideal of harmony and fellow feeling across artificial human boundaries" (277; see 281). The ethical manifestations of this ideal in her experimental modernist texts deserve close attention, as does her statement in *Three Guineas* that poetic writing is essential for the sustainment of peaceful relations.

The question of intimacy brings us back to *The Waves*. In what follows, I examine how the novel's poetic and introspective aesthetic promotes critical thought, exposes the psychological aspects of violence and imagines a non-violent way of being with others. The text remains Woolf's most thorough engagement with self-formation and the formation of self-other relations, but these processes also form the basis of ethical as well as political reflection. Intersubjective relations are depicted in terms of boundaries which are upheld, transgressed and dissolved, and psychological parallels are established between the defensive borders separating the self from the other and outside, and the redrawing of borders between nations which is the result of war. Woolf exposes in *The Waves* the fragility of the constructs of self and nation, and suggests that an awareness of this fragility may form the basis for non-violent relations in which clear-cut divisions between 'I' and 'you' become difficult to sustain. As we shall see, the novel's pacifist stance is founded on the idea of intimacy, the overflow of boundaries emerging in *Three Guineas* as the poet's awareness of a "unity that rubs out divisions as if they were chalk marks only" (*TG* 163).

Woolf's negotiation of private and public boundaries in *The Waves* remains ever-relevant, and post-Levinasian theory opens up a fresh perspective on the novel's ethico-political dynamics. In this chapter, I read Woolf's novel alongside works by contemporary thinkers which consider intimacy, vulnerability and exposure in the interconnected realms of ethics and politics. At the heart of this dialogue is Judith Butler's concern with the fragility of subjective as well as national boundaries in present-day United States, which resonates in more than one way with Woolf's response to an increasingly nationalist and militaristic climate in Europe throughout the 1920s and 1930s. In *Precarious Life* and the more recent *Frames of War*, Butler elaborates a non-violent ethics grounded in "a primary vulnerability to others, one that one cannot will away without ceasing to be human" (*PL* xiv). Because an exposure to and dependency on others precedes the subject's formation as autonomous, she argues, each individual is tied to others, and these ties complicate any notion of 'I' as irrevocably separate from 'you'. Moreover, recognition of this precariousness – that we are not and cannot be ontologically autonomous individuals – entails a Levinasian obligation to preserve the life of those others, not all of whom we know, love or care for, but with whom we live in unwilled, intimate proximity (*FW* 14, 30–31). For Butler, to always assert and defend the boundaries of self and nation is to disavow this obligation, and such refusal causes violence at once ethical and political. While the US nationalism justifying its recent wars operates through a pervasive idea of the subject as invulnerable, a fantasy which enables the moral sanctioning of outwards aggression and concomitant disavowal of primary vulnerability at work in (neo-)imperialist wars (*FW* 47–48), the experience of vulnerability does not have to lead to violence: "If national sovereignty is challenged, that does not mean it must be shored up at all costs" (*PL* xii). From this perspective, acknowledging one's continuous exposure to others before taking measures to protect subjective and national sovereignty is a stance against violence, and ethical relations between individuals constitute the foundation on which a non-violent politics must be based. I will engage these aspects of Butler's thought to shed new light on the ethical and pacifist dimensions of *The Waves*.

If Woolf made the intimate suspension of subjective boundaries central to her critique of violence, she developed in *The Waves* an ethics of intimacy, sensitivity and exposure which counters the aggressive discourses of inter-war nationalisms. In this respect, my reading of the novel owes much to Julia Kristeva's *The Sense and Non-Sense of Revolt* and *Intimate Revolt*. These works describe a European culture of doubt and critique in philosophy, psychoanalysis, art and literature which opposes conformist thinking and nationalism as well as fascism and totalitarianism (*SNR* 19, 5). In this culture, the momentary dissolution of the subject's unity creates as a form of intimacy which is "indispensable to the faculty of representation and questioning" (*IR* 7). Kristeva's association of intimacy with revolt is strikingly relevant to Woolf's figuration of poetry and independent thought in her image of chalk marks. Indeed, Kristeva's idea of a certain kind of social critique delivered through poetic writing makes possible an understanding of *The Waves* as performing the mode of critical thinking advocated in *Three Guineas*. Kristeva famously privileges the individual, singular subject, and the introspective individual is the agent of the critique she theorises. Her notion of the writer in revolt, the subject-in-process whose unity is constantly called into question through the act of writing, resonates strongly with how *The Waves* depicts the thinking mind and the individual voice as effective channels for opposing nationalism as well as fascism.

"A Mind Thinking": Woolf's Soliloquy and the Dissolution of Boundaries

Insofar as Woolf's critique of conformism in *The Waves* proceeds through her exploration of individual psychic life, the soliloquy becomes a poetic strategy for representing singularity and individual thought. While each soliloquy can be read as an interior monologue, this does not mean that the novel lacks realistic grounding. On the contrary, Woolf makes use of the dramatic monologue to raise ethical and political questions around individuality, vulnerability and violence. Her soliloquies emulate the theatrical dynamics of address, in which an actor speaks on stage to an audience. In this, they combine novelistic, dramatic and poetic strategies: "Why not invent a new kind of play. . . . prose yet poetry; a novel & a play" (*D* 3: 128). The novel is framed as a narrative addressed to the reader through Bernard's last soliloquy, which begins: "Now to sum up. . . . Now to explain to you the meaning of my life" (*W* 183). With these words, Bernard, the writer, begins a Butlerian account of himself. His account is incomplete and subject to continuous disruption, and from this incompleteness emerges an ethics of alterity as well as intimacy.

In Butler's theory, an individual becomes accountable in the presence of another; because the account implies an exposure to another subject, the process of telling becomes a self-questioning – it "involves putting oneself at risk." "My efforts to give an account of myself founder in part because I *address* my account, and in addressing my account I am exposed to you" (*GAO* 23, 38). Bernard's last soliloquy engages the same problem. His story is addressed to a 'you,' an anonymous interlocutor or the reader of *The Waves*, whose presence calls his coherent 'I' into question. Bernard himself conceives of his life as a gift, something complete and self-contained to be given away through his narrative. The moment he addresses his interlocutor, however, he realises that this notion of his life as a coherent whole is illusive:

> The illusion is upon me that something adheres for a moment, has roundness, weight, depth, is completed. This, for the moment, seems to be my life. If it were possible, I would hand it to you entire. I would break it off as one breaks off a bunch of grapes. . . . But unfortunately, what I see (this globe, full of figures) you do not see. You see me, sitting at a table opposite you, a rather heavy, elderly man, grey at the temples. (*W* 183)

Feeling his interlocutor's eyes on him, Bernard sees the globe containing everything he thinks, knows and remembers vanish, and he is acutely aware of being reduced to an object under the other's gaze. His story unfolds from the unsettling experience of this encounter.[18]

In thus staging an ethics of the address, Woolf brings the question of subjective autonomy into the realm of politics. Throughout his narrative, Bernard describes the formation of his self as a hardening process: "A shell forms upon the soft soul, nacreous, shiny." This shell is constructed as a defence against others, whose presence threatens to disintegrate the self (196; see 222). At the end of his story, Bernard is again reminded of his interlocutor's presence, of "the pressure of the eye": "Oh, but there is your face. I catch your eye. I, who had been thinking myself so vast, a temple, a church, a whole universe . . . am now nothing but what you see. . . . That is the blow you have dealt me." In response to shocks such as this one, Bernard becomes conscious of having sought perpetually to construct his shell anew: "'Fight!' 'Fight!' I repeated. It is the effort and the struggle, it is the perpetual warfare, it is the shattering and piecing together – this is the daily battle, defeat or victory" (226, 224–25, 207). These lines connect the process of self-formation with aggression and warfare at the same time as they depict the self as a frail entity, and throughout *The Waves*, Woolf speaks of the shattering and recovery of the autonomous self in terms such as fight, triumph, hostility and enmity. Written in a time when national sovereignty was commonly held to be in a state of crisis, Bernard's account is no doubt foregrounding Woolf's later equation of intersubjective and political modes of violence. That is, his use of a vocabulary of warfare to describe the self suggests that "the public and the private worlds are inseparably connected" (*TG* 162). The novel thus problematises the fragility of national borders in the inter-war years by interrogating the defensive assertion of individual autonomy.

For Woolf, such interrogation is a matter of representation; Bernard's account stages an ethical questioning of narrative coherence which is also performed by the novel as a whole. His interlocutor's gaze has disintegrated his self as well as his attempt to relate a completed narrative. As he speaks, Bernard understands that his life has been "imperfect, an unfinished phrase," and that he has never been able to "keep coherency" (*W* 218). His story functions like Butler's account in that it has a performative dimension; the act of telling is a process in which his autonomous 'I' is called into question. In this way, Woolf's dramatic soliloquy becomes a site for performative self-reflection and self-questioning. To give an account of oneself, for Butler, is to produce a disruptive mode of communication which draws attention to the limits and dangers of articulability (*GAO* 57–58). While full articulability upholds subjective and linguistic autonomy, an ethically valid account "mocks the posture of narrative control": "There are clearly times when I cannot tell the story in a straight line, and I lose my thread" (81, 68).

In *The Waves*, Bernard loses his thread in precisely this way. His eloquent narrative is interrupted by a recollection of an earlier moment, a day when he found himself unable to write poetry: "This self now as I leant over the gate looking down over fields rolling in waves of colour beneath me made no answer. He threw up no opposition. He attempted no phrase. His fist did not form. I waited. I listened. Nothing came, nothing" (*W* 218; see 217–18). Bernard's language undergoes a transformation in this passage from the rich imagery and elaborate structure of the first sentence to the short, syntactically plain sentences which follow. As he describes his self through the distance of the third person, the speaking Bernard is dissociated from the 'I'; he slips out of the shell which enabled the coherence of his narrative. Like Butler's account, Bernard's story is about his formation as an individual, and the break in his narrative causes his experience of being "A man without a self." This is also an experience of a kind of death (219; see 218). Unlike the writer in *A Room of One's Own* whose autonomous 'I' casts a shadow across the pages of his book (130–31), Bernard walks "unshadowed" in this selfless state, and "without shelter of phrases" (*W* 220).

With the undoing of his phrases, Bernard's self undergoes a decentering, which is "only the death of a certain kind of subject . . . the death of a fantasy of impossible mastery" (*GAO* 65). Bernard realises that the shell he has tried to form cannot protect him against the persistence of an earlier way of relating to the world around him. The selflessness he describes, in which his 'I' "attempted no phrase. His fist did not form," is a state of passivity and defencelessness: "immeasurably receptive . . . so my being seems" (*W* 218, 223–24). The introspective self-narration enacted through Bernard's monologue resonates with contemporary theories of vulnerability and bodily exposure such as Butler's. With the disintegration of my story, Butler writes, I "relive an abandonment and dependency that is overwhelming" (*GAO* 68). This abandonment is a physical dependence on caretakers; because the helpless infant depends on others for its life support, it is formed as a human being through a primary passivity (70, 77). To refuse to admit that this passivity continues to form us, Butler argues, is to disavow the precariousness of human life. My life is implicated in the lives of those on whom I depend, an entanglement which produces "an indistinguishability between the other and myself at the heart of who I am." This originary disposition, then, is "a scene . . . to which we return" (75, 81).

Butler's notion of precariousness has remarkable affinities with Woolf's. At the end of a dinner with his interlocutor, Bernard becomes aware that his life cannot be told as a self-sufficient entity because it is implicated in the lives of others. He recalls here the scene of his formation as a separate self, a scene from early childhood to which he attributes his heightened bodily sensitivity in the moment of speaking: "ever since old Mrs. Constable lifted her sponge and pouring warm water over me covered me with flesh I have been sensitive, percipient." Once abandoned to and physically dependent on the care of his nurse, Bernard has never become the strictly autonomous 'I' which he likens to an impenetrable shell. Addressing his interlocutor, he realises that he has never been entirely distinct from his five friends, all of whom developed into separate individuals as children:

> And now I ask, "Who am I?" I have been talking of Bernard, Neville, Jinny, Susan, Rhoda and Louis. Am I all of them? Am I one and distinct? I do not know. . . . I cannot find any obstacle separating us. There is no division between me and them. As I talked I felt "I am you." This difference we make so much of, this identity we so feverishly cherish, was overcome. (*W* 222)

Bernard's story makes possible his return to the scene in which the boundary between self and other is yet to be established: "Here on my brow is the blow I got when Percival fell. Here on the nape of my neck is the kiss Jinny gave Louis. My eyes fill with Susan's tears. I see far away, quivering like a gold thread, the pillar Rhoda saw, and feel the rush of the wind of her flight when she leapt." Like Butler's subject in constant formation, Bernard relives continuously moments of exposure to overwhelming sensory impressions, intensely corporeal moments in which he cannot tell his self apart from other embodied selves. This intimacy is what Woolf would later, in *Three Guineas*, call a poetic unity and an overflow of boundaries. My reading of Bernard's final soliloquy thus differs markedly from a dominant idea that his "summing up seems to be the means to self-completion, to filling in the notorious crack in the structure of his identity. He seems intent on capturing his friends for his own use, rewriting them to construct his own [self-sufficient] life story" (Berman, *Modernist Fiction* 153).[19]

Indeed, the relived moment of embodied oneness with others changes Bernard's story when he resumes his telling. As he tries anew to "sum up," Bernard realises that his narrative encompasses his continuous bodily exposure to and affinity with other embodied individuals. What he offers his interlocutor at this moment is not a fragmented story, but one that is more complete than that which he began to narrate. The passage describing how he still feels what his friends once felt is not a linear, orderly story, but a piece of poetry in which simultaneity replaces sequence. These lines express his sense of merging with others by conflating poetically his moment of speaking and past moments in his friends' lives: "My eyes fill with Susan's tears." Bernard's insight that he is crying because Susan once cried reshapes his self as well as his narrative, both of which emerge, through the process of telling, as non-static entities. As Butler writes, "We're undone by each other. And if we're not, we're missing something" (*PL* 23). She also insists that there is a constructive and affirmative dimension to being undone: "our 'incoherence' establishes the way in which we are constituted in relationality" (*GAO* 64). This aspect of Butler's thought is not only highly relevant to the monologue which closes *The Waves*; it also has implications for Woolf's use of the soliloquy form throughout the novel. As the novel's artist figure, Bernard is the character who most persistently interrogates the relationship between self-formation and narrative, and, as we shall see, this interrogation forms the basis of Woolf's aesthetic experiments in *The Waves*.

Waves and Torrents: The Aesthetic Politics of Rhythm

The ethical dimension of Bernard's soliloquy can be linked directly to the politics of Woolf's aesthetic practice, if this politics is understood as a resistance to the conformist mind-set enabling inter-war nationalism. The centrality of intimacy to this politics becomes apparent if we read *The Waves* alongside Kristeva's work, and in particular her idea of an intimate poetics which is also a form of revolt. Using Kristeva's terminology, we could say that Bernard's gradual awareness that he is composed as an individual by his relations to others makes him a subject-in-process.[20] His final monologue might well be one outcome of Woolf's early plan to write a novel about "A mind thinking" (*D* 3: 229), in which case his narrative can be seen as the introspective, lyrical representation constituting intimate revolt. For Kristeva, we recall, poetic language is the channel through which the subject in formation becomes a critically thinking individual. Intimacy in this context is "where we end up when we question apparent meanings and values" (*IR* 43). It is "similar to the life of the mind, that is, the activity of the thinking ego," but "obtains a depth far beyond that of the thinking ego thinking of itself": "It was this interiority that the Greeks called 'soul' (*psukhê*), defined by its proximity with the organic body as well as by preverbal sensations" (44, 51, 44). This is how Bernard, in the process of putting his life story into words, relives the intense bodily sensations which precede and sustain his formation as a singular subject.[21]

Kristeva's emphasis on the constructive dimension of the pre-subjective semiotic provides a way to understand Woolf's conviction, articulated in *Three Guineas*, that the "chalk marks" separating individuals are secondary, something superimposed on an originary unity which "rubs out divisions" and causes boundaries to overflow (*TG* 365). The semiotic is defined by Kristeva as the opposite of unity; it is that which disrupts the unity of the symbolic subject. It is, however, also that which produces the subject in new form in a continuous "renewal of the psychical space" (*SNR* 28). Woolf, too, was interested in the disruptive capacity of that which exceeds boundaries, but she also created a mode of radical intimacy enabled by overflow and excess, a relational dynamic which attains its fullest expression in *The Waves*. On this point, I diverge from classic Kristevan readings of Woolf such as Minow-Pinkney's, which casts *The Waves* as a text privileging the semiotic, and hence refusing "to be 'embedded' and 'committed' in the socio-temporal, symbolic order" (165). This common focus on a politics of subversion and refusal in Woolf's writing makes it difficult to account for her interest in intersubjective, ethical and political relations within the symbolic. I find it more compelling to explore how the novel enacts aesthetically Woolf's pacifist claim, in *Three Guineas*, that a poetic awareness of "the capacity of the human spirit to overflow boundaries" (365) is what makes critical thought possible. Through the reflective soliloquy as a formal device, Woolf places the poetic writing of individuality against extreme forms of authoritarian nationalism, which are fundamentally concerned with defending the boundaries defining the national community, demand uncritical commitment to the ideals of this community and enforce a silencing of the dissenting individual voice. In what follows, I suggest that through the form and style of *The Waves*, Woolf foregrounds the fragility of the subject as well as the vitally constructive bodily experience of sharing the inner life of another. Intimacy emerges thereby as a precondition for political dissent and non-violent relations, as well as the foundation for Woolf's belief in the capacity of art to protect individuality and critical thought in a time when fascist movements were gaining ground in Europe.

If we are now in a position to see Woolf's most experimental novel as partaking in the twentieth-century avant-garde culture of revolt in which non-conformist thinking proceeds through the act of artistic creation, Kristeva herself has followed a now obsolete tradition of reading Woolf's fiction as apolitical. In *About Chinese Women* (1986), she famously relates Woolf's suicide to the woman writer's failure to identify with the symbolic social order. Like Sylvia Plath, who "fled [words and meanings] to the refuge of lights, rhythms, sounds," Woolf, Kristeva writes, "sank wordlessly into the river. . . . Haunted by voices, by waves, by lights, in love with colours – blue, green" (40, 39). Elsewhere, Kristeva considers rhythm, colour and voice to be central features of poetic language, in which semiotic energies destabilise and renew the symbolic (*RPL* 26–28).[22] If we consider Woolf's poetic prose alongside Kristeva's more recent work, we can begin to appreciate her aesthetic use of visual, rhythmic and vocalic devices as a forceful political strategy. While Woolf's depiction of light and colour in *To the Lighthouse* furthers an ethics of intimacy and recognition, her experimental rendering of voices, waves and rhythm in *The Waves* reveals not the author's retreat into the semiotic but an effective way of promoting non-conformism and non-violence. By exploring the poetic and sensory implications of the voice, rhythm and the movement of waves, Woolf imagines an embodied relationality which unsettles the boundaries dividing individuals as well as nations.

"I am writing [*The Waves*] to a rhythm and not to a plot," Woolf reflected in August 1930: "though the rhythmical is more natural to me than the narrative, it is completely opposed to the tradition of fiction" (*L* 4: 204). As she turned away from realist narrative towards the poetic, she saw rhythm as central to a more capacious novel form that would "give the moment whole; whatever it includes. Say that the moment is a combination of thought; sensation; the voice of the sea" (*D* 3: 209).[23] This lyrical mode, which aptly describes *The Waves*, is closely bound up with the novel's ethics. As AnnKatrin Jonsson and Tamlyn Monson have both observed, Woolf's use of rhythm in *The Waves* raises ethical questions around subjectivity and representation. Various rhythms structure *The Waves*, and most pervasive is perhaps that of waves accumulating and breaking. In Jonsson's reading through Levinas and Paul Ricoeur, *The Waves* depicts a constant wavering or oscillation between autonomous, self-contained subjectivity and subjectivity as exposed to the other and outside (100–01, 106). Monson approaches the rhythm of what Bernard calls "the shattering and piecing together" (*W* 207) via Levinas's ethical theory and Kristeva's notion of the subject-in-process:

> the central metaphors of the novel suggest a cyclical model of subjectivity – a process of self-constitution and dissolution represented by the image of a wave rising and then crashing, only to be drawn back into the sea where it rises once more.... The image of the wave rising associates identity with agency, will and force, while the crashing of the wave ... represents a disintegration of totality and agency – a passivity in opposition to the certainty, desire, and will associated with identity. This state is, in turn, characterised by an awareness of the inadequacy and violence of language. (173–74)

In Monson's fine analysis, the novel highlights "the inherent violence of representation in all its forms" (174). But if Monson is right in observing that Woolf's image of the breaking wave conveys the shock of subjective and linguistic disintegration, does it necessarily follow that the novel exposes all forms of representation as violent? What if Woolf's own aesthetic practice forms a non-violent poetics, a literary practice of revolt as defined by Kristeva?

What is needed, I think, in order to reassess the novel as an intervention where ethics and politics converge, is close attention to Woolf's writing via Kristeva's more recent notion of the intimate. Such attention would reveal that Woolf does more in *The Waves* than depict the transgression of representational language by that which exceeds and destabilises the autonomous self: Levinas's Other and Kristeva's semiotic. There is, then, a constructive and reparative dimension to Woolf's figuration of subjectivity beyond the endless cycles of disruption and re-formation which Kristevan critics like Monson, Minow-Pinkney and Chloë Taylor describe.[24] Indeed, Woolf's own ambition, when writing the novel, to "give the moment whole" stresses the unifying rather than fragmenting force of poetic language. My point is that Woolf's writing in *The Waves* formulates an ethics of intimacy which complements the Levinasian ethics of recognition observed by Monson,[25] and that this ethics is conveyed through poetic devices such as rhythm. The recurring return to a state in which 'I' cannot be separated from 'you,' foregrounded in Bernard's final soliloquy, is distributed across the text in a rhythmic pattern of breaking waves. Woolf herself noted about her dramatic monologues that "The thing is to keep them running homogeneously in & out, in the rhythm of waves" (*D* 3: 312). As we shall see, the novel's wave-like rhythm also forms an integral part of a pacifist politics because it reshapes individuality in terms of intimacy.

In contrast to the movement of waves rising and breaking, Woolf depicts the onward flow of the torrent, which emerges as the rhythm of habitual thought and action as well as militarism. "How swift life runs from January to December!" Bernard reflects. "We are all swept on by the torrent of things grown so familiar that they cast no shade; we make no comparisons . . . and in this unconsciousness attain the utmost freedom from friction." The same image structures an earlier passage focalised through Bernard's character, in which a group of boys "like a torrent jumping rocks, brutally assaulting old trees, pours with splendid abandonment headlong over precipices. On they roll; on they gallop; after hounds, after footballs. . . . All divisions are merged – they act like one man." In their games of hunting and conquest, the boys move forwards like a powerful current hurling itself against obstacles. The rhythm of this passage conveys the flow of the torrent; the commas in the first sentence mark the encounters with obstacles – the rocks, trees and precipices – all of which are eliminated as the sentence flows on, and the two semicolons give the second sentence its sense of persistent onward movement. The image of the torrent in these passages suggests a link between, on the one hand, the familiar and habitual aspects of everyday life and, on the other, the school boys' ceremonial group activities, in which the individuality of the participants is effaced. Both of these are related explicitly to militarism and war by Bernard as he looks back on his life: "We are not always aware by any means; we breathe, eat, sleep automatically. We exist not only separately but in undifferentiated blobs of matter. With one scoop a whole brakeful of boys is swept up and goes cricketing, footballing. An army marches across Europe" (*W* 166, 67–68, 189).

These three passages lay the ground for Woolf's claim, in *Three Guineas*, that the British education of boys is a training in patriotism and, as such, a preparation for militarism and war. They also raise the questions of individuality and group identity discussed in *Three Guineas*, where the letter form is distinguished from societies in the broadest sense: "a society is a conglomeration of people joined together for certain aims; while you, who write in your own person with your own hand are single." Woolf contrasts, provocatively, the letter as a dyadic exchange between an 'I' and a 'you' with the formation of people into societies, which, she argues, "releases what is most selfish and violent, least rational and humane in the individuals themselves" (306, 307–08). Her analysis of societies as essentially prone to aggression resonates with theories of group psychology that were widely debated in the inter-war years. Freud's *Group Psychology and the Analysis of the Ego*, which similarly associates individual psychology with civilisational achievement and group psychology with regression, offers a particularly compelling intertext for *Three Guineas*, although Woolf claimed not to have read Freud before 1939.[26]

Woolf goes even further than Freud in her polemical description of societies as conspiracies which "inflate [in men] a monstrous male, loud of voice, hard of fist, childishly intent upon scoring the floor of the earth with chalk marks" (*TG* 308).[27] As Zwerdling (*Real World* 271–301) and Froula (*Bloomsbury Avant-Garde* 1–32) have observed, the barbarity of the Great War had unsettled the Bloomsbury artists' and thinkers' humanist belief in an international civilisation based on rational thought, and Woolf's image of childlike, monstrous political leaders taking the world to the brink of a second war conveys such fear of regression. Woolf does not, in this polemic, attribute the description of societies as nationalistic and aggressive conspiracies to the fascist state only, but suggests that there is something about the organisation of individuals into societies in Italy, Germany or Britain, whether in schools or on a national political level, which makes fascism possible.[28] From this perspective, societies define themselves through an aggressive protection of the boundaries which constitute them, the boundaries of ideals, doctrines as well as the geographical borders of the nation-state. Woolf thus highlights the interwar conundrum that membership in a society requires a blind acceptance of its ideals and, thereby, a surrendering of individuality, an "intolerable unanimity" (308). Unanimity is Woolf's term for the opposite of Kristevan singularity and individual, critical thought; it is also the outcome of fascist indoctrination. Like Freud, she sees a pervasive conformist tendency in the constitution of any society, and this insight is central to her controversial insistence on the fine line separating patriarchal and nationalistic social structures in Britain from their fascist counterparts.[29]

In *The Waves*, the dynamic in which group thinking absorbs individual thinking is imagined in terms of rhythm and movement. Bernard's reflections as he approaches London with the morning train foreground the analysis of aggression and conformism in *Three Guineas*:

> But we roar on. We are about to explode in the flanks of the city like a shell. . . . I am become part of this speed, this missile hurled at the city. I am numbed to tolerance and acquiescence. My dear sir, I could say, why do you fidget, taking down your suitcase and pressing into it the cap that you have worn all night? Nothing we can do will avail. Over us all broods a splendid unanimity. We are enlarged and solemnised and brushed into uniformity . . . because we have only one desire – to arrive at the station. I do not want the train to stop with a thud. (*W* 83)

The metaphor of the train effectively suggests Woolf's idea of a society as "a conglomeration of people joined together for certain aims" (*TG* 306). The passage describes a group of individuals being passively rushed on towards one goal – the station – where individual effort – the man fidgeting – will not change the set course. Woolf's imagery blurs any distinction between public and private, warfare and day-to-day life; the morning train is a missile and a shell, and the pressing of a cap into a suitcase is a gesture of resistance. In this, the passage stages what Miller refers to as a principle of total war emerging in the 1920s and '30s, that is, "the collapse of traditional efforts to delimit the territorial scope of war in ways that maintain a distinction between combat zone and the realm of civilian life" (xi). The constellation of passive individuals in the train is also a metaphor of aggressive social formations prone to violence and attack, and the everyday register suggests that aggression is a likely outcome of habitual, unreflected thought and action, what Bernard calls being "swept on by the torrent of things grown . . . familiar" and acting like one person

(166–68). As Berman astutely points out, "*The Waves* undermines action as directed progress. Woolf's work runs determinedly counter to the onward rush of fascism" (*Modernist Fiction* 156).[30]

In *Three Guineas*, unanimity has a circular, repetitive rhythm, the rhythm of "a gramophone whose needle has stuck" and the song: "Here we go round the mulberry tree. . . . Three hundred millions spent upon war" (238). Similar imagery appears in *The Waves*, where the wheel, the ring and the circle depict Louis's desire to impose his worldview on others and make them think like him.[31] Attending a school ceremony, Louis reflects: "I become a figure in the procession, a spoke in the huge wheel that turning, at last erects me" (25). The rhythm of the wheel is also performed aesthetically in the novel through the recurrence of circular images and Louis's phrase: "I will reduce you to order" (70–71). This repetition posits a harmony, a central rhythm, to use Louis's terms (70), of the novel as a whole. Lyndsey Stonebridge argues in a reading of *Between the Acts* that Woolf no longer conceived of rhythm, in 1941, as enabling a subversion of autonomous subjectivity and repressive social structures, but as serving fascist ideology and aesthetics: "If, in her earlier work, rhythm was used to expose the 'lie' of a unitary subjectivity, by the end of the 1930s, Woolf's concern lies . . . with the ideological and social effects of rhythmic perfection upon the community as a whole" (94; see 82). While Stonebridge's observation is important, it seems fair to say that Woolf had already begun to interrogate the politically regressive implications of rhythm while writing *The Waves*. Among Woolf's novels, *The Waves* explores with particular intensity the "opposing affordances" of rhythm as a literary form: "on the one hand [rhythms] can produce communal solidarity and bodily pleasure; on the other, they can operate as powerful means of control and subjugation. . . . Rhythmic form has the potential to do serious political work" (Levine 49).

The rhythms of aggression, violence and self-contained subjectivity – the turning of the wheel and the flow of the torrent – are countered and disrupted in the novel by another: the movement of waves rising and breaking. In response to the threat to individual, critical thought posed by extreme nationalisms, *The Waves* invents a less static notion of the thinking and acting individual than the category of the coherent 'I.' Indeed, the rhythm in which the soliloquies follow one another affirms a singularity that is different from subjective autonomy. Each soliloquy unfolds like a wave succeeding and succeeded by others, and each shift in focalisation emulates the breaking of one wave and the accumulation of another. These clashes of different perspectives remind the reader of the multiple viewpoints, the six individual voices composing *The Waves*, in such a way that the wave-like rhythm of the soliloquy form highlights the friction absent from the unanimity conveyed by the figures of the torrent and the wheel.

In Woolf's 1938 polemic, unanimity is also described as a merging of individual identities (*TG* 308), a phrasing which recalls the school boys in *The Waves* as they rush on: "All divisions are merged" (67). How, then, can we distinguish between the unanimity enabling violent action and the unity, the overflow of boundaries which, according to *Three Guineas*, makes non-violent relations possible? This is one of the most challenging political questions prompted by *The Waves*. In Berman's reading, the novel problematises oceanic feeling, that is, the dissolution of boundaries and "potential for plenitude in a group" central to fascist aesthetics (*Modernist Fiction* 140). She also suggests that the text's oceanic imagery of effaced distinctions ultimately challenges fascist ideology in "a feminist narrative that swirls water against fascist boots" (141). Berman's insight about the radically different connotations ascribed to fluid boundaries in *The Waves* is a crucial one; if Woolf elaborated in this novel the key aspects of her pacifist stance in *Three Guineas*, an important part of this process was to spell out a distinction between unthinking unanimity and intimacy.

Even if Woolf began to read Freud after completing *Three Guineas*, a counterpart to this distinction can be found in *Group Psychology*. While Freud saw the "contagion of feelings and ideas" uniting the members of a group as hampering the capacity for critical, non-conformist thought (103), he also explored a different relational mode – identification. Identification for Freud is not sufficiently known as a process: like Woolf's overflowing boundaries, it precedes erotic object-ties insofar as it expresses a primary desire to be rather than have someone else. This is a state to which an individual can return by sharing the emotions and inner life of another (133–37). However, Freud only hinted at the ethical potential of identification; in a footnote, he considers the possibility that identification may limit an individual's aggression towards others, and calls for further research in this area (140).[32] It was only much later, in the late twentieth and early twenty-first centuries, that the correlation between ethics, non-violence and intimacy would be more fully theorised and considered as a question of representation. In this respect, the work of Kristeva and Butler, both of whom exemplify this later development in psychoanalytic thought, allows us to see Woolf's literary treatment of intimacy in a new light.

"Our Senses Have Widened": Sensitivity and Non-Violence

As a novel firmly situated in the political reality of the inter-war years, *The Waves* also grapples with the ethical implications of suspended subjectivity. In the first of two restaurant scenes where the characters come together for dinner, two kinds of closeness – the conformist effacement of individuality and the intimate return to the pre-subjective – are juxtaposed. As the friends reflect on their formation as distinct beings, they gradually become aware of a deep unity which unsettles their sense of being separate. For Louis, individuality is effaced in this moment: "We have tried to accentuate differences. From the desire to be separate we have laid stress upon . . . what is particular to us. But there is a chain whirling round, round, in a steel-blue circle beneath" (*W* 103). In contrast, Bernard visualises the "communion" which, he reflects, they are all "drawn into." Contemplating the red carnation on the table, he realises that the flower is perceived from separate viewpoints and, as such, it stands for relations based on individuality and difference: "A single flower as we sat here waiting, but now a seven-sided flower, many-petalled . . . a whole flower to which every eye brings its own contribution" (95).

Bernard's vision of an object which comes into sharper focus when seen by many eyes, from multiple perspectives, recalls the intense receptivity to sensory impressions associated with the act of looking together in *To the Lighthouse*. In that novel, as we have seen, the observation of a common object by separate individuals enables simultaneously a blurring of intersubjective boundaries and a recognition of differences. If intimacy emerges in *To the Lighthouse* as the pre-subjective, heightened sensitivity attained in the moment of joint seeing, a similar intimacy is described in the first dinner scene in *The Waves*:

> "Look," said Rhoda; "listen. Look how the light becomes richer, second by second, and bloom and ripeness lie everywhere; and our eyes, as they range round this room with all its tables, seem to push through curtains of colour, red, orange, umber and queer ambiguous tints, which yield like veils and close behind them, and one thing melts into another."
>
> "Yes," said Jinny, "our senses have widened." (101)

As Rhoda observes the room seen through more than one pair of eyes, the colours gain intensity and become, eventually, part of a fluid world without distinct objects. Colour is central to Woolf's poetic language in this passage, which stages a Kristevan return to pre-verbal sensations. Jinny's "response" affirms Rhoda's notion of acute receptivity as a ground for exchange between singular beings rather than a solipsistic immersion in one's own sensations. This way of perceiving is contrasted with a different one as Louis's soliloquy follows Jinny's: "The roar of London . . . is round us. Motorcars, vans, omnibuses pass and repass continuously. All are merged in one turning wheel of single sound. All separate sounds . . . are churned into one sound, steel blue, circular" (101). In a narrowing rather than a widening of the senses, Louis's hearing registers only one sound into which the disparate sounds composing it are absorbed.

Ultimately, the novel's poetic exploration of sense perception forms the basis of its non-violent ethics. While Louis's forging of a steel-blue circle reduces others to objects of his imagination by effacing their individuality, the novel depicts the unsettling of the self by the presence of another singular being in terms of Rhoda's and Jinny's heightened sensitivity. This is a state of exposure which Louis himself likens to nakedness: "You are all protected. I am naked," he says repeatedly in response to his continuous failure to "reduce these dazzling, these dancing apparitions to one line capable of linking all in one" (72, 168). Overwhelmed by impressions whose impact he cannot explain or control, Louis is unable to force others to adopt his worldview: "It breaks . . . the thread I try to spin; your laughter breaks it, your indifference. . . . 'This is the meaning,' I say. . . . Believe –,' and then am twitched asunder. Over broken tiles and splinters of glass I pick my way" (167– 68). The image of the broken glass suggests the shattering of a figurative mirror in which Louis saw himself as whole and self-contained.[33] And as Bernard, the writer, seeks a set of phrases capable of accounting for the unsettling presence of another 'I' – "There is no panacea (let me note) against the shock of meeting" (161) – so Woolf developed in *The Waves* a vocabulary for the shattering of the self: a blow, a stab, the smashing of something whole, the shock of a wave breaking (66, 224–25).

All these images link violence and sensitivity to the disruption of the first-person perspective, that is, the painful ways in which "we're undone by each other" (*PL* 23). To be undone is to be forced into a state of total passivity, as Bernard becomes aware in a visit to the hairdresser:

> I leant my head back and was swathed in a sheet. Looking-glasses confronted me in which I could see my pinioned body and people passing; stopping, looking, and going on indifferent. The hairdresser began to move his scissors to and fro. I felt myself powerless to stop the oscillations of the cold steel. So we are cut and laid in swaths, I said. (*W* 215)

His paralysing incapacity to act is depicted here as an intensely physical experience; with his arms tied and the metal of the hairdresser's scissors against his head, Bernard is literally given over into the hands of another. The "oscillations of the cold steel" suggest the menace of potential violence against which he is powerless and incapable of protecting himself. The image of his arms pinioned by the sheet is also metaphoric of the reduction of his 'I' in the moment he sees himself simultaneously as a reflection in the mirror and as an object of the indifferent gaze of the passers-by. This passage dramatises the kind of exposure theorised by Butler, whereby "The body implies mortality, vulnerability, agency: the skin and the flesh expose us to the gaze of others, but also to touch, and to violence, and bodies put us at risk of becoming the agency and instrument of all these as well" (*PL* 26). In *Frames of War*, Butler underlines the political necessity of a "new bodily ontology" articulated around an apprehension of the physical body's inherent vulnerability as a transnationally and transhistorically shared predicament (2, 33):

> war seeks to deny the ongoing and irrefutable ways in which we are all subject to one another, vulnerable to destruction by the other, and in need of protection through multilateral and global agreements based on the recognition of a shared precariousness. . . . The subject that I am is bound to the subject I am not [so] that we each have the power to destroy and to be destroyed, and that we are bound to one another in this power and this precariousness. In this sense, we are all precarious lives. (43)

Madelyn Detloff has claimed that Woolf, in *Three Guineas* and her Second World War writings, develops a Butlerian "postnationalist response to threat" ("Tis Not my Nature to Join in Hating, But in Loving" 54), a non-violent political imperative grounded in an ethical recognition of the human body's fragility (58–59). I believe that we should look for the source of this response in the introspective aesthetic of *The Waves*.

Indeed, deep resonances can be traced between *The Waves* and Butler's recent works in how these texts imagine different ways of handling the unsettling experience of being under the threat of violence, an experience bound up with the loss of subjective autonomy. For Butler, to "shore up the first-person point of view" is to assume a defensive position in order to respond with violence if need be (*PL* 6; see 6–7). On the other hand, to acknowledge our corporeal vulnerability as a formational condition which we cannot will away is an ethical stance and a way of resisting violence (*PL* 29; *FW*). Woolf similarly delineates two responses to what Louis calls nakedness and what Bernard experiences as a paralysing passivity. The first is a recentring of the autonomous 'I.' As he signs documents, "I, and again I, and again I," Louis becomes, as Bernard observes, "stone-carved, sculpturesque" (*W* 87), thereby protecting himself from this exposure. Bernard himself develops a "hard shell" as a way of overcoming his unsettling sensitivity as a child going to school for the first time: "I must . . . interpose something hard between myself and . . . staring faces, indifferent faces, or I shall cry" (222, 21).

Another, more painful response to vulnerability is problematised through Rhoda's character. Rhoda, for whom social encounters are "intermittent shocks, sudden as the springs of a tiger" (47), remains exposed and acutely sensitive. In her soliloquies, the images of the wave breaking and the door opening describe an overpowering confrontation with the faces of others:

> But I am not composed enough, standing on tiptoe on the verge of fire, still scorched by the hot breath, afraid of the door opening and the leap of the tiger. . . . I am to be cast up and down among these men and women . . . like a cork on a rough sea. Like a ribbon of weed I am flung far every time the door opens. The wave breaks. I am the foam that sweeps and fills the uttermost rims of the rocks with whiteness. (80)

No gathering together of the self is possible in this state of complete disintegration. Rhoda not merely perceives her self as helplessly thrown about on rising and breaking waves; she *is* the waves she visualises, indistinguishable from the water and the foam. Unable to develop a shell-like identity, Rhoda cannot, like Bernard, identify with her reflection in the mirror: "That is my face . . . in the looking-glass behind Susan's shoulder – that face is my face. But I will duck behind her to hide it, for I am not here. I have no face" (30–31). Rhoda's incapacity to adopt a first-person point of view entails an absolute passivity which makes violent action directed towards others impossible. As her suicide illustrates, though, a permanent as opposed to a momentary passivity also makes survival unsustainable. And despite her persistent efforts to assume a stable subject position, Rhoda remains unable to raise her voice: "[Jinny and Susan] say, Yes; they say, No; they bring they fists down with a bang on the table. But I doubt; I tremble, . . . afraid . . . to make even one sentence" (79–80).

Throughout *The Waves*, the movement of the fist hitting something hard depicts the gathering together of autonomous subjectivity, but also the figurative blows which reduce others to objects of the imagination. As Bernard describes the loss of his autonomous self, he speaks of this self as a person incapable of verbal as well as physical forms of fighting: "He threw up no opposition. He attempted no phrase. His fist did not form" (218). If *The Waves* is one of the central texts in which Woolf articulates her critique of all forms of violence, then how can we account for Rhoda's total passivity in the context of Woolf's pacifism? If committing acts of violence is impossible for Rhoda, she is also incapable of any oppositional practice through what Woolf terms "the weapon of independent opinion" (*TG* 237). Yet, Rhoda's disintegration proves crucial to Woolf's defence of critical thinking as a way of opposing war. That is to say, the novel delineates an ethically viable mode of individuality which acknowledges and encompasses Rhoda's extreme sensitivity and resists Louis's circle of conformist thought.

It is ultimately in Woolf's aesthetic patterning of her novel, in the poetic repetition and resonance of key images and metaphors, that its ethics of sensitivity emerges. This is how nakedness appears as a recurring metaphor of vulnerability; Rhoda's conviction that "I am the youngest, the most naked of you all" echoes Louis's reflection – "You are all protected. I am naked" – a few pages earlier (*W* 79, 72). The shared metaphor suggests that the unsettling exposure they both experience is a common predicament. Similarly, in linking the theme of Louis's "infinitely young and unprotected soul" (168) to Bernard's struggle to suppress his tears during his first trip to school, Woolf relates their vulnerability to the relationality of childhood in a way that defies the common association of lyrical expression with solipsism. When Bernard speaks of being "utterly unprepared for impacts of life" (195), he could be referring to the first soliloquies in the novel:

> "I see a ring," said Bernard, "hanging above me. It quivers and hangs in a loop of light."
>
> "I see a slab of pale yellow," said Susan, "spreading away until it meets a purple stripe."
>
> "I hear a sound," said Rhoda, "cheep, chirp; cheep, chirp; going up and down." . . .
>
> "Suddenly a bee booms in my ear," said Neville. "It is here; it is past."
>
> "I burn, I shiver," said Jinny, "out of this sun, into this shadow." (5, 7)

These lines describe the shower of impressions received by the bodies of individuals in formation. While each short "speech" expresses a separate viewpoint, the characters do not yet speak as autonomous subjects with a clear perception of distinct objects. Rather than the realist bird's-eye perspective literalised as the birds in the interludes "*perc[h] in the upper branches of some tree, and loo[k] down on upon leaves and spires beneath, and the country*" (82), the passage depicts a set of close-ups which convey the child's overwhelming exposure to intensely physical sensations. It stages, in other words, the primary vulnerability which continues to form us, "a passivity that is prior to the subject" (*GAO* 77).

Insofar as *The Waves* interrogates the consolidation of subjectivity, it also exposes the violence inherent in this development. In the first soliloquies, the close-up perspective is all the more significant because it is juxtaposed to the metaphor of formation in the first interlude, where the sea is initially "indistinguishable from the sky." Gradually, the birds in the garden begin to tentatively sing separate melodies – "*One bird chirped high up; there was a pause; another chirped lower down*" (*W* 3) – while the imagery in the opening interlude suggests the formational process described in Bernard's recollection of the early childhood scenes:

> In the beginning, there was the nursery, with windows opening on to a garden, and beyond that the sea. I saw something brighten – no doubt the brass handle of a cupboard. Then Mrs. Constable raised the sponge above her head, squeezed it, and out shot, right, left, all down the spine, arrows of sensation. And so, as long as we draw breath, for the rest of time, if we knock against a chair, a table, or a woman, we are pierced with arrows of sensation. . . . But we were all different. . . . We suffered terribly as we became separate bodies. (184–86)

On one level, the passage delineates a sequence: the primary state in which the perceiving self is not yet distinct from a world of objects (only retrospectively does Bernard realise that the bright something is a brass handle) is succeeded chronologically by his bodily awakening, which causes his awareness of being an individual irrevocably separate from others. Throughout the novel, the formation of an autonomous 'I' entails a gradual loss of early sensitivity which is forcefully dramatised through the birds in the interludes. Insensitive and acting out of pure instinct, the birds become a metaphor for unthinking aggression and violence: "*their heads turned this way; that way; aware, awake; intensely conscious of one thing, one object in particular. . . . Then one of them . . . spiked the soft, monstrous body of the defenceless worm, pecked again and again*" (54–55).[34] In a later interlude, the one followed by Bernard's account of the train as a missile, the attack is performed through the synchronised action of many birds: "*They spied a snail and tapped the shell against a stone*" (82). This imagery merges ominously into the human world of the soliloquies in Bernard's notion of a "hard shell which cases the soul, which . . . shuts one in, hence the fierceness, and the tap, tap, tap of the remorseless beaks of the young" (222).

If the soul is the receptive mind exposed and unprotected like a snail without shell (*W* 196), then the figurative shell is a metaphor of the 'I' which, insensitive and "hard as a nut," is prone to inflict ethical as well as physical and political violence on others (*AROO* 130). However, in problematising vulnerability as a persistent condition, Woolf imagines an alternative to the seemingly inevitable chronology in which becoming an individual is to grow insensitive. While the novel conveys the violence of which an autonomous 'I' is capable, it also draws attention to a sensitivity integral to our continuous formation as subjects. This is how Bernard undermines the chronology he delineates: "And so, as long as we draw breath, for the rest of time . . . we are pierced with arrows of sensation" (*W* 184). The birds' cruelty, then, foregrounds the characters' humanity; the attacks in the interludes stand in contrast to the relations portrayed in the soliloquies, a contrast which highlights a vulnerability to others which "one cannot will away without ceasing to be human" (*PL* xiv).[35]

The experience and recognition of this common fragility, Butler argues, enables "the possibility of making different kinds of ties" (*PL* 40). In *The Waves*, the relational and ethical potential of acute sensitivity is vividly depicted in the first restaurant scene. As the characters gather around the dinner table, they remember their time together as children. In this moment of recollection, their soliloquies recall those composing the novel's first pages: "'Old Mrs. Constable lifted her sponge and warmth poured over us,' said Bernard. . . . 'The breath of the wind was like a tiger panting,' said Rhoda" (*W* 93). These intensely corporeal phrases put the memory of the formational scene into words, thereby enabling an intimate return to this scene. In this way, Woolf's portrayal of seven characters dining together challenges a tradition of reading *The Waves* as a text about the solitary "interior monologue of the isolated character" (Zwerdling, *Real World* 10). What needs attention is the many ways in which her dramatic monologues raise ethical questions about being together with others. As more than one character experience the gradual dissolution of the boundaries separating them, the soliloquies assume a notably dialogic mode, as in the following transition between Neville's and Rhoda's voices:

> Let Rhoda speak . . . Rhoda whom I interrupted when she rocked her petals in a brown basin, asking for the pocket knife that Bernard had stolen. Love is not a whirlpool to her. She is not giddy when she looks down. She looks far away over our heads. . . . "Yes, between your shoulders, over your heads, to a landscape," said Rhoda. (*W* 104)

Neville's attempt to depict Rhoda's interiority becomes something different in this passage from an objectifying incorporation of her viewpoint into his own. Rather than an assertion of his own suitability as the teller of her story, the attempt to imagine her thoughts and perceptions is part of Neville's wish to hear

Rhoda speak for herself, and his recognition of Rhoda's subjective integrity is affirmed on a structural level as her soliloquy follows his.

The act of representing the interiority of another is problematised in the novel, and especially through Bernard's character, as involving an ethics particular to the writing of fiction. Monson is one critic who has commented on Neville's reflection that "We are all phrases in Bernard's story, things he writes down in his notebook under A or under B. He tells our stories with extraordinary understanding, except what we most feel" (51). In Monson's Levinasian reading, any attempt to depict another individual inevitably reduces them to an object of knowledge, so that "Neville reveals the violence exercised by Bernard's phrases upon his friends" (179). I read Woolf's treatment of Bernard's storytelling as far more ambivalent. Indeed, Bernard's efforts to tell his friends' stories do not only exemplify objectification; they are equally central to Woolf's articulation of a non-violent form of representation. Her belief in the potential of words to counter aggression becomes particularly apparent in the staging of anger, tenderness and physical closeness in the episode where Susan runs away after having seen Jinny kiss Louis:

> I saw them, Jinny and Louis, kissing. Now I will wrap my agony inside my pocket-handkerchief. It shall be screwed tight into a ball. I will go to the beech wood alone . . . I will take my anguish and lay it upon the roots under the beech trees. . . . "Susan has passed us," said Bernard. "She has passed the tool-house door with her handkerchief screwed into a ball. . . . I shall follow her, Neville. I shall go gently behind her, to be at hand, with my curiosity, to comfort her when she bursts out in a rage and thinks, 'I am alone.'" (8–9)

As he follows Susan into the forest, Bernard makes up a narrative which echoes her own so closely that the reader must wonder if the passage really depicts two separate minds: "Susan has spread her anguish out. Her pocket-handkerchief is laid on the roots of the beech trees and she sobs, sitting crumpled where she has fallen" (9).

Woolf is clearly concerned here with something other than the ethical violence which representation can inflict. Bernard's storyteller's curiosity, his desire to understand every aspect of Susan's anger, is indistinguishable from his compassion and wish to comfort her. As he reaches Susan and sits down next to her, Bernard's third-person narrative turns into words addressed to a 'you':

> I followed you, and saw you put down your handkerchief, screwed up, with its rage, with its hate, knotted in it. But soon that will cease. Our bodies are close now. You hear me breathe. You see the beetle too carrying off a leaf on its back. It

> runs this way, then that way, so that even your desire while you watch the beetle, to possess one single thing (it is Louis now) must waver, like the light in and out of the beech leaves; and then words, moving darkly, in the depths of your mind will break up this knot of hardness. (9–10)

Susan's "response" confirms Bernard's reading of her anger as a desire to possess an object: "I love ... and I hate. I desire one thing only.... I see the beetle ... It is black, I see; it is green," while her eyes' sharp focus on the beetle recalls the birds in the interludes: "intensely conscious of one thing, one object in particular.... they fixed their gaze." "But," Bernard objects, "when we sit together, close ... we melt into each other with phrases. We are edged with mist" (10, 54–55, 10).[36] For Berman, Bernard's notion of a dissolution of intersubjective boundaries through language exemplifies the oceanic feeling central to the fascist aesthetic practice which *The Waves* ultimately opposes (*Modernist Fiction* 139–40). This assumption makes it difficult to account for the idea, developed in this passage, that words can undo knots of anger, possessiveness and absolute subjective autonomy, all of which are connected, in Woolf's imagery, with hardness.[37] The phrases Bernard describes here would counter, not endorse fascism with its aggressive rhetoric and celebration of violence; rather than fascist "plenitude in a group" (Berman, *Modernist Fiction* 140), his misty edges suggest an intimate one-to-one encounter in which two individuals momentarily lose their sense of being separate. When Butler speaks of an "unwilled physical proximity with others" (*PL* 26), she refers to the vulnerability felt by a subject in the bodily presence of another, a vulnerability which, if recognised as a shared human condition, may lay the ground for a non-violent ethics with political repercussions (*FW* 43). As Bernard sits next to Susan, their physical closeness does not lead to ethical violence, but to a way of being together attuned to the enduring inseparability of 'I' and 'you.'

While their voices remain distinct, aesthetic devices such as the precise echo of Susan's metaphor in Bernard's voice complicate any notion of the corporeal state depicted by this metaphor as confinable to a single body. Throughout the novel, the characters' selves emerge as at once clear-cut and fluid notably through Woolf's use of the dramatic monologue. Each soliloquy forms a unit by establishing the identity of a new speaker, yet the monologues are not independent, autonomous entities. They refer outside of themselves insofar as they continue and depend on others, and the characters' sharing of the same phrases, images and metaphors has an effect of unity across divisions.[38] The structural interdependence of the monologues creates a mode of individuality which is radically different from autonomous subjectivity; the dialogic dimension of the soliloquies is significant precisely because it undermines their status as autonomous entities. Woolf's monologues, then, are written in a poetic language capable of undoing the knots of hardness, anger and possessiveness which uphold and reinforce subjective autonomy. In this sense, *The Waves* affirms through its aesthetic achievement an ethics of intimacy in which the boundary separating 'I' and 'you' is yet to be established. Indeed, Woolf's reinvention of the soliloquy form compels us to reflect on the ways in which, as Butler puts it, "our lives are profoundly implicated in the lives of others" (*PL* 7).

Relational Monologues: Intimacy and the Singularity of the Voice

We have seen how Woolf's soliloquies envision intimate and non-violent relations. As poetic strategies exposing each individual's originary dependence on others, the six characters' apparently solipsistic monologues articulate a complex form of self-expression in which intimacy fundamentally reshapes individuality. Recalling the aesthetic devices which enable the Kristevan avant-garde practice of intimate revolt – colour, rhythm and voice – I will now attend to Woolf's dramatisation of speaking voices as another strategy through which *The Waves* resists conformist thinking, aggression and violence. Vocal expression remains a central concern throughout the novel, and human speech is likened repeatedly to the song of birds, the "chanting" of a chorus and the singing of distinct melodies. Given that Woolf described the novel as a "playpoem" composed of soliloquies and interludes (*D* 3: 203; see 312, 285), it is remarkable that the theatrical aspects of the novel have received so little sustained critical comment.[39] Because the monologues following the indicatory "said X" read as contemplative introspection rather than speech in its ordinary sense, they have often been treated by critics as thought rather than as spoken statements to be performed on stage and addressed to an audience.[40] If *The Waves* playfully combines novelistic and poetic conventions with elements of drama, the soliloquies deserve to be considered precisely as speech delivered by six voices. I shall conclude this chapter with a reading of the characters' utterances as vocal and acoustic, where I consider the novel alongside an unrivalled work by Adriana Cavarero: *For More than One Voice: Toward a Philosophy of Vocal Expression* (2005).

Cavarero's book is a ground-breaking philosophical study of vocality and intimacy as ethically and politically charged. Drawing on the theories of Kristeva as well as Levinas, Cavarero argues that the manifest uniqueness of the voice signals the speaker's singularity; since a specific human voice is different from all other voices, two human beings communicate their uniqueness to one another through the act of speaking. Cavarero uses the term "unique" to describe the human being whose voice is recognised as singular before it can be attributed to a subject.[41] In its privileging of voiceless thought over the act of speaking, she holds, Western philosophy has failed to consider the physicality of the voice as a central feature of speech (46). She distinguishes, then, between vocal expression, which is by definition embodied and relational, and thought, which upholds the ontological solitude of subjective autonomy. For Cavarero, thinking performs "the soliloquy of an *I* whose disembodied ear concentrates on its own mute voice," while speaking is a corporeal "interlocution with others and requires a reciprocity of speech and listening" (46; see 174–75).

Insofar as Woolf's soliloquies dramatise introspection as a mode of intimacy, they resist equations, such as Cavarero's, of thought and autonomous subjectivity. While Woolf initially meant *The Waves* to be about "A mind thinking" (D 3: 229), her channelling of this single consciousness into six separate yet indistinguishable minds complicates any notion of thought as the monologue of an isolated 'I.' If the soliloquies in *The Waves* are to be considered as thought, they demonstrate that thinking can be intensely physical and is by no means inherently disembodied. I would nonetheless like to suggest that Woolf's soliloquies emulate speaking as defined by Cavarero, and that the novel's vocal dimension is central to its non-violent ethics. Writing the novel as a "playpoem," Woolf did more than liken her characters' utterances to speech on stage in the form of dramatic soliloquies. While, for Cavarero, the terms "monologue" and "soliloquy" refer to the egocentric 'I' of Western philosophy, Woolf's monologues stage a mode of spoken self-expression which is also a form of address. Configured as speech to be delivered to an audience, they perform what Cavarero calls a communication of embodied singularity.

The soliloquies composing *The Waves* resemble vocal expression in numerous ways; the novel differs notably from Woolf's other experimental inter-war fiction in that its language imitates the rhythm of speech. With the occasional exception of Bernard, the writer, the characters tend to express themselves in sentences which are shorter and more emphatic than the intricate combinations of subclauses in *Mrs Dalloway* or *To the Lighthouse*. Furthermore, Woolf's monologues suggest the physicality Cavarero connects with vocal expression in that they enable a communication of embodied perception. The characters continue to express the acute sensitivity they experienced as children: "'I burn, I shiver,' said Jinny"; "The stones of a necklace lie cold on my throat. My feet feel the pinch of shoes" (*W* 7, 75). The many metaphors evoking intensely physical states, such as Susan's handkerchief and Rhoda's leaping tiger – "I am afraid of the shock of sensation that leaps upon me" (97) – are also phrases which denote uniqueness by positing the six speakers as distinct from one another. The singularity of Woolf's speakers has ethical and political significance; throughout the novel, the singular, embodied voices of the soliloquies are contrasted with the "chorus," a term used to describe conformist thinking and a suppression of the individual voice.[42]

In the course of telling the story of his life, Bernard reflects: "I am so made that, while I hear one or two distinct melodies, such as Louis sings, or Neville, I am also drawn irresistibly to sound of the chorus chanting its old, chanting its almost wordless, almost senseless song . . . which we hear now booming round us" (189). If Bernard's remark might not immediately appear as a comment on the attraction of fascism, it attains a political dimension when considered in relation to the novel's figuration of different kinds of singing. Elsewhere in Bernard's retrospective narrative, the characters are likened to birds singing with "rapt egotism" and breaking the shells of snails (190). This idea refers back to the interlude in which each bird sings "*stridently, with passion, with vehemence, as if to let the song burst out of it, no matter if it shattered the song of another bird with harsh discord*" (81). The image of the bird singing its own melody without listening to the tunes sung by other birds suggests the autonomous subject's aggressive assertion of their voice, and the vehemence of the birds' singing is followed by the synchronised attack in which separate songs become subsumed into a "they" acting like one. In a different interlude, the formation of birds singing together reads as a metaphor of precisely the kind of group formation which Woolf connects with violence and fascism in *Three Guineas*: "The birds, whose breast were specked canary and rose, now sang a strain or two together, wildly, like skaters rollicking arm-in-arm" (20). Images similar to that of the birds flaunting their flamboyant breasts recur throughout *Three Guineas* as descriptions of the medals and ornaments worn by members of the patriarchal establishment as well as the fascist dictator; the "monstrous male, loud of voice, hard of fist" is portrayed as "daubed red and gold, decorated . . . with feathers" (*TG* 179–80, 308). And the birds' unmitigated violence in *The Waves* becomes, again, part of the human world of the soliloquies as the group of school boys aggressively rushing forwards is likened to a chorus in which "All divisions are merged – they act like one man" (*W* 67–68).

In contrast to the effacement of differences suggested by the chorus metaphor, Woolf conceptualises intimate relations between singular beings. The blurring of intersubjective boundaries in dyadic encounters is associated in the novel with the singing of multiple distinct melodies, each of which responds to rather than seeks to shatter other tunes. A compelling parallel can be drawn here to Cavarero's focus on vocal expression through, as her title declares, *more than one voice*; the act of speaking and listening is relational, she claims, because this communication of uniqueness enables a perpetual rediscovery of the Kristevan semiotic. Cavarero theorises the vocal as a link to "the fusal relationship between mother and child" which "frustrate[s] the category of the individual" (11, 131). She follows Kristeva also by privileging poetic representation, in which the voice plays a crucial subversive role.[43] Significantly with regard to Woolf and *The Waves*, Cavarero does not locate the vocal mother-infant bond beyond and outside of language. Rather, this vocalic dialogue is the necessary origin of all communication. Dialogue is defined not as an exchange of semantic meanings, but as "a cadence of demand and response" which expresses a mutual dependence (170; see 169–71).[44] The infant's dependence on others is thus a precondition for later communication between singular persons: "The uniqueness of the vocalic is inaugurated on a scene where, unlike what happens on the scene of the 'subject,' there are no dreams of autonomy" (171–72).

While Woolf's experimental inter-war fiction unsettles the autonomy of the coherent 'I,' it does not reject but transforms individuality. Her notion of individuality corresponds to Cavarero's uniqueness in that it acknowledges the bodily exposure to others which makes possible intimate and non-violent relations. Reading *The Waves* with Cavarero illuminates the novel's association of intimacy with the vocal: "The human voice has a disarming quality – (we are not single, we are one)" (*W* 50). This vocality appears in Woolf's use of shared metaphors and a rhetoric of dialogue and address to create soliloquies which form separate yet interdependent statements. The relational force of these aesthetic features becomes apparent if we assume that the characters actually speak, if we suppose that Bernard, for instance, seeks to undo Susan's "knot of hardness" by talking to her: "when we sit together, close . . . we melt into each other with phrases" (10). Similarly, the moment of intimacy in the first dinner scene emerges through the characters' vocalisation of their childhood memories. The boundaries separating them become indistinct as they relive the sensory impressions they articulate in spoken words: "'Old Mrs. Constable lifted her sponge and warmth poured over us'. . . . 'The breath of the wind was like a tiger panting'" (93).

What Cavarero's theory of embodied speech can make us to see is that these acutely physical phrases enable intimate relations because they are vocal utterances spoken by singular beings. Later, Bernard recalls that in the moment of "return[ing] from that immersion," from the overwhelming feeling that "I am you" (214, 222), he can no longer perceive his self as a hard shell or respond to the call of the chorus:

> The sound of the chorus came across the water and I felt leap up that old impulse, which has moved me all my life, to be thrown up and down on the roar of other people's voices, singing the same song; to be tossed up and down on the roar of almost senseless merriment, sentiment, triumph, desire. But not now. No! I could not collect myself; I could not distinguish myself. . . . I could not recover myself from that endless throwing away, dissipation, flooding forth without willing it and rushing soundlessly away out there under the arches of the bridge, round some clump of trees or an island, out where the sea-birds sit on stakes, over the roughened water to become waves in the sea. (214)

Woolf describes here a passivity which makes conformist thinking and violent action impossible. The passage highlights the difference between, on the one hand, being an 'I' supported and elated by the conformist thought and action of a group and, on the other, momentarily giving up one's autonomous perspective in an overflow of boundaries, as Woolf puts it in *Three Guineas*. These states are figured metaphorically by the respective images of being tossed up and down on waves and of the self aimlessly drifting towards the sea to eventually merge with the waves. The one kind of passivity causes the "disastrous unanimity" associated in *The Waves* as well as *Three Guineas* with patriotism, fascism, violence and war. The other is a precondition for the intimate and non-violent relations which, as the narrator of *Three Guineas* realises, must be formulated as poetry: "you have asked us how to prevent war. Let us then leave it to the poets to tell us what the dream [of peace] is" (*TG* 266).

Eight years before the outbreak of a second world war, Woolf imagined in *The Waves* a non-violent way of being with others, and her lyrical, introspective aesthetic weaves together her pacifist politics with an ethics of radical intimacy. In contrasting autonomous subjectivity, conformist thinking and aggressive, unreflected action to a fundamentally different mode of individuality which acknowledges passivity, vulnerability and extreme sensitivity, Woolf's poetics in this novel articulates key aspects of her pacifist stance in *Three Guineas*. One of

Bernard's musical metaphors, which aptly depicts the dramatic monologues of *The Waves*, will illustrate this point: "What a symphony with its concord and its discord, and its tunes on top and its complicated bass beneath, then grew up! Each played his own tune, fiddle, flute, trumpet, drum or whatever the instrument might be" (197).⁴⁵ *The Waves* stages such a symphony of distinct, yet interconnected melodies; the soliloquies resemble tunes which alternatively create dissonant contrasts and float into one another. By thus alerting us to separate perspectives which are contingent on others and subject to momentary dissolution, Woolf's most abstract novel sounds a strident alarm about the causal relationships between subjective autonomy and the prospect of perpetual war, but it also voices an intimate appeal to "think peace into existence" (*E* 6: 242).

Notes

Introduction

1. See Rachel Bowlby's astute reading of Woolf's trains and railway carriages as metaphors for the modernist-feminist writer's journey, staged in "Character in Fiction," from Edwardian conventions and the violence they inflict on the figure of Mrs Brown towards a new, more ethically viable aesthetic – one that must preserve the intimate carriage, where the novelist encounters her subject, as "a sign of strangeness" (5; see 3–15).
2. See, for instance, John Mepham's "Mourning and Modernism," Patricia Matson's "The Terror and the Ecstasy: The Textual Politics of Virginia Woolf's *Mrs Dalloway*," Kathy Mezei's "Who Is Speaking Here? Free Indirect Discourse, Gender and Authority in *Emma*, *Howards End*, and *Mrs Dalloway*" and Rachel Hollander's "Novel Ethics: Alterity and Form in *Jacob's Room*."
3. See "intimate, *adj.* and *n.*," def. A.3.a: "Close in acquaintance or association; closely connected by friendship or personal knowledge; characterized by familiarity (with a person or thing); very familiar. Said of persons, and personal relations or attributes. Also transf. of things, Pertaining to or dealing with such close personal relations"; and def. A.4: "Of knowledge or acquaintance: Involving or resulting from close familiarity; close."
4. Alongside landmark studies such as Mark Hussey's collection *Virginia Woolf and War: Fiction, Reality, and Myth* (1991) and Jane Marcus's ground-breaking 1970s and '80s accounts of a politically radical Virginia Woolf, Zwerdling's *Virginia Woolf and the Real World* (1986) contributed to a new turn in Woolf criticism by challenging the persistent idea of her fiction as detached from socio-political concerns.
5. To my knowledge, Zwerdling's distinction between Woolf's analysis of interiority and her socio-political, "real world" commitments (12) has remained generally unchallenged.
6. See Anna Snaith's book on the public-private problematic in Woolf's work, particularly Chapter 6 on Woolf's treatment of this problematic in the context of the Second World War.
7. See Marcus, "'No More Horses': Virginia Woolf on Art and Propaganda" (1976) and "Storming the Toolshed" (1988, 193–200).

8 See the chapter "Virginia Woolf and the Flight into Androgyny" in Showalter's 1977 study, *A Literature of Their Own: British Women Novelists from Brontë to Lessing* (263–97).
9 Significantly in terms of Moi's argument with Showalter, Woolf's narrator begins her story by saying, in parentheses: "call me Mary Beton, Mary Seton, Mary Carmichael or by any name you please – it is not a matter of importance" (*AROO* 5).
10 In *Virginia Woolf and Postmodernism: Literature in Quest and Question of Itself* (1991), a paradigmatic work representative of its time, Pamela Caughie notably argues that Woolf's writing resists "any attempt to *define* fiction by standards to which it conforms or from which it deviates" (4).
11 See also Christine Reynier's case for Woolf's short fiction as an ethico-political site which brings together "an openness to the other as human being . . . and an openness to the other as unfamiliar, innovative literary devices" (29). One precursor of this critical lineage is Michael Levenson, who reflects, in *Modernism and the Fate of Individuality: Character and Novelistic Form from Conrad to Woolf* (1991), that the twentieth century, arguably "the age of narcissism," is also the century in which "the ego suffered unprecedented attacks upon its great pretensions, to be self-transparent and self-authorized" (xi). Levenson traces this unsettling of subjective autonomy in the modernist vacillation between "the longing to recover some figure of the self, to preserve some vessel of subjectivity, and the willingness to let go, to release the knot of subjectivity."
12 See, for example, Ewa Ziarek's "Kristeva and Levinas: Mourning, Ethics, and the Feminine" and Monson's "A Trick of the Mind: Alterity, Ontology, and Representation in Virginia Woolf's *The Waves*."
13 My definition of intimacy overlaps to some extent with what Emily M. Hinnov has termed "choran community." Hinnov employs Kristeva's notion of the semiotic chora to argue that moments without subject-object distinction further anti-imperialist and anti-fascist modes of community in texts and pictures by modernist women writers and photographers.
14 See Scott's *Refiguring Modernism*, volume 2 (1995), Chapter 1, and Minow-Pinkey's "Virginia Woolf: 'Seen from a Foreign Land.'"
15 This assumption is developed in *Three Guineas*, where the narrator speaks of the need for women to form an "Outsiders' Society" (309).
16 Published in the same year as *Orlando*, Radclyffe Hall's realist novel *The Well of Loneliness* was condemned on moral grounds for its treatment of lesbian relations. In Parkes's account, Hall "provoked the British authorities into legal action by preaching an unacceptable sexual doctrine in an earnest tone," while *Orlando* resisted censorship by mocking and "destabilizing the very grounds on which sexological as well as legal conventions were founded" (434, 436). Cervetti observes similarly that "Humour is aggressive in its direct confrontation with dominant

forces, and that in *Orlando* Woolf laughs in the face of the law, the 'natural' body, codes of dress and behavior, and romantic love" (174–75).

17 While writing *Orlando*, Woolf noted that "Sapphism is to be suggested. Satire is to be the main note – satire & wildness" (*D* 3: 131). See Sherron E. Knopp on the playfully erotic letters exchanged between Woolf and Sackville-West around the composition of *Orlando*.

18 See Cramer, "Woolf and Theories of Sexuality," and Detloff, "Woolf and Lesbian Culture: Queering Woolf Queering," essays which offer helpful guides to the debates in which they partake. For landmark works representing lesbian and queer approaches to Woolf and Bloomsbury, see *Virginia Woolf: Lesbian Readings* (1997), edited by Eileen Barrett and Patricia Cramer, and *Queer Bloomsbury* (2016), edited by Brenda Helt and Madelyn Detloff.

19 See also Berman's 2011 book *Modernist Commitments* (40–62) and Hollander's reading of same-sex intimacy in *Jacob's Room* with Irigaray's ethics of eros (58–60). On feminist responses to Levinas's philosophy, including Irigaray's, see Tina Chanter's *Ethics of Eros* (1995), Section 5, and Chanter's edited collection *Feminist Interpretations of Emmanuel Levinas* (2001). For an illuminating account of the trajectory from ethics to politics in Irigaray's later work, see Penelope Deutscher.

20 This is not to say that the touch was not central in shaping social, ethical and political relations in early twentieth-century contexts of violence and war. Santanu Das's beautiful study *Touch and Intimacy in First World War Literature* (2005) has opened up a whole new field of inquiry into such connections.

21 Recall, for instance, Irigaray's critique, in the 1970s, of the supposedly universal masculine subject which claims to be "one"; Kristeva's notion of the ceaseless shattering of the symbolic subject by semiotic forces and Butler's observation that any assertion of a stable subject position, including that of the masculine 'I,' universalises and naturalises the culturally specific conditions of subject formation.

22 From the late 1990s, a dissatisfaction also emerged among Woolf scholars with the poststructuralist paradigm, a discontent visible in the many attempts to show that Woolf remodels rather than rejects the category of the individual subject. Jane Goldman, for one, argued in 1998 that Woolf counters a "solar model of [masculine] subjectivity" by developing a feminist, "interstellar model" which foregrounds intersubjectivity (*Feminist Aesthetics* 21). See also Roxanne J. Fand's *The Dialogic Self* (1999) and AnnKatrin Jonsson's *Relations: Ethics and the Modernist Subject* (2006) for readings which emphasise Woolf's reconfiguration of the subject as well as her focus on intersubjective relations.

23 While Irigaray took issue in the 1970s with Lacan's positing of the male 'I' as a universal model of subjectivity (see, for instance, "The Poverty of Psychoanalysis" [1977] and "The Power of Discourse and the Subordination of the Feminine" [1975]), Butler, as we have seen, criticised Kristeva in the 1990s for her theory of

the semiotic as the outside and beyond of culture. For recent accounts of productive intersections between Irigaray's philosophy and psychoanalysis, see Margaret Whitford and Catherine Peebles.

24 Butler argues in *Precarious Life* that a non-violent and more globally sustainable response to the attacks would have been not to deny but to acknowledge the state of national vulnerability, and to suspend the first-person perspective sustaining the American "fantasy of omnipotence" (9).

25 John Maynard Keynes warned in 1919 that the reparations imposed on Germany would leave an impoverished nation eager for revenge, and as Froula points out, Woolf emphasised Britain's complicity in the oppressive peace terms ("*Mrs. Dalloway's* Postwar Elegy" 139–44).

26 See Miller's *Modernism and the Crisis of Sovereignty* (2007), which explores modernist representations of a European crisis of political and personal modes of sovereignty following, among other events, the redrawing of the world map after the First World War and the rise of communism as a political force operating across national boundaries. See also Jane Marcus's "Britannia Rules *The Waves*," Kathy Phillips's *Virginia Woolf against Empire* (1994), Berman on *The Waves* and British fascism (*Modernist Fiction* 139–56), Merry M. Pawlowski's edited collection *Virginia Woolf and Fascism: Resisting the Dictators' Seduction* (2001), and Mia Spiro's *Anti-Nazi Modernism: The Challenges of Resistance in 1930s Fiction* (2012).

27 The most extensive study of Woolf and psychoanalysis remains Elizabeth Abel's *Virginia Woolf and the Fictions of Psychoanalysis* (1989).

28 Abel views Woolf's unwillingness to read Freud as a sign of "the anxiety provoked by the authoritative discourse on 'the dark places of psychology' to which she also staked a claim" (14).

29 Abel considers Freud's gendering of psychosocial development in relation to the conflicting psychoanalytic accounts, emerging in the 1920s, of the origins of the individual and society as either matricentric (Klein) or patricentric (Freud). She reads Woolf's 1920s fiction as aligned with Klein's foregrounding of maternal origins.

30 Froula stresses that Bloomsbury figures such as Virginia and Leonard Woolf and John Maynard Keynes did not simply hold an Enlightenment belief in the capacity of reason to produce such a civilisation. Rather, facing the "barbarities" within Britain and Europe, their cause was "not the grand one of 'saving' civilization, but the more modest one of fighting for its possibility" (*Bloomsbury Avant-Garde* 9). In 1938, however, Keynes remarked that the Bloomsbury thinkers had been "pre-Freudian" in their faith in "a continuing moral progress by virtue of which the human race already consists of reliable, rational, decent people" (qtd. in Zwerdling 295).

31 Klein delivered her 1925 lectures on child analysis, which made her a leading figure in British psychoanalysis, at the home of Woolf's brother and sister-in-law Adrian and Karin Stephen, both of whom were training to become analysts. See Abel

and Lyndsey Stonebridge for detailed accounts of the many connections between Bloomsbury and psychoanalysis throughout the 1920s and '30s.

32 See also "Thoughts for the Times" 61–76 and *Civilization* 298–307, 315–40.
33 See, for instance, "Thoughts for the Times" 68, 87–88; *Group Psychology* 130–31; *Civilization* 304, 313–14.
34 See Pamela Caughie, "Time's Exception," Jane Goldman, "Avant-Garde," and Derek Ryan 4–11.
35 For a survey of recent philosophical approaches to Woolf, see Derek Ryan 5–11. See also Bryony Randall's and Jane Goldman's collection *Virginia Woolf in Context* (2012); in their Preface, the editors argue for the centrality of theory to any successful attempt to contextualise Woolf's writing, and the first of two parts is devoted to "Theory and Critical Reception."
36 I concur here with Pamela Caughie's recent argument for the continuing relevance of poststructuralist approaches to Woolf ("Time's Exception"). On this point, I hope to complement Maud Ellmann's astute account of Woolf in light of early twentieth-century psychoanalysis. In *The Nets of Modernism: Henry James, Virginia Woolf, James Joyce, and Sigmund Freud* (2010), Ellmann focuses on the modernist disintegration of the self as an overwhelmingly corporeal phenomenon which links the subject to the public (economic, technological, linguistic) networks of modernity, at the same time as it "marks the primal wound of separation from the mother's body" – a wound by which the writer can only "memorializ[e] a pre-symbolic order" (5, 9).
37 Berman makes a similar claim in relation to Woolf's treatment of propaganda in the context of the Spanish Civil War (*Modernist Commitments* 62–76).
38 Jane Marcus, who traces Woolf's pacifism back to the legacy of her Quaker aunt Caroline Emilia Stephen, views it as "more moral than political" ("No More Horses" 120). While Marcus expresses reservations about pacifism as a political stance because it treats violence as an ethical problem, thereby preventing (necessarily violent) attacks on private property (108), other scholars have argued for the continuing political relevance of Woolf's pacifism. See especially the roundtable on "Woolf and Violence," held at the 2014 Annual International Conference on Virginia Woolf (Hussey et al., "Roundtable," 2–22), as well as the scholarship of two of its participants: Mills and Ashley Foster. See also Froula's and Cole's comprehensive accounts of Woolf as a deeply original theorist of violence and the conditions necessary for creating sustainable peace.

Chapter 1

1 While "Character in Fiction" stresses the Georgians' break with Edwardian realism, "How It Strikes a Contemporary" and "Poetry, Fiction and the Future"

(1927) posit a divide between Woolf's generation of writers and a past literary tradition stretching from Elizabethan drama to the novelists of the Victorian period. Woolf explains her distinction between Edwardian and Georgian writers in "Character in Fiction": "I will suggest that we range Edwardians and Georgians into two camps; Mr Wells, Mr Bennett, and Mr Galsworthy I will call the Edwardians; Mr Forster, Mr Lawrence, Mr Strachey, Mr Joyce, and Mr Eliot I will call the Georgians" (*E* 3: 421).

2 Pippin considers modernism as part of a broader Western high culture of "melancholy, profound scepticism and intense self-criticism," a culture entailing "a vast aesthetic expression of negativity, revolutionary dissatisfaction, the insistence on novelty, radical experimentation" (xi, xviii). John Mepham, too, relates the modernist break with the tenets of Enlightenment humanism, in which "literary forms were trusted because they were believed to have secure epistemological foundations" (146), to literary expressions of mourning.

3 See, for instance, Hollander's "Novel Ethics: Alterity and Form in *Jacob's Room*," Tammy Clewell's "Consolation Refused: Virginia Woolf, the Great War, and Modernist Mourning," John Mepham's "Mourning and Modernism" and Kathleen Wall's "Significant Form in *Jacob's Room*: Ekphrasis and Elegy."

4 "By naming her hero Jacob Flanders," Alex Zwerdling writes, "Woolf immediately predicts his fate. As her first readers in 1922 would certainly have known, Flanders was a synonym for death in battle" ("*Jacob's Room*: Woolf's Satiric Elegy" 896).

5 Mepham develops a similar argument, and Susan Stanford Friedman relies on the same poststructuralist notion of narrative control to argue that Woolf's "attack on the tyranny of plot" was a "rebellion against the authority of narrative to 'father' a meaning" (Stanford Friedman 163). Kate Flint views the experimental style of *Jacob's Room* as a response to the militaristic ideology of a society which at once privileges the voice of young men and sends them off to war (361–62).

6 This point is emphasised through the narrator's playfully ironic treatment of Betty Flanders's effusion, which complicates readings such as Flint's; Flint understands the novel's opening as expressing a particular kind of "woman's voice" which, she argues, Woolf developed in *Jacob's Room* (363): "Betty Flanders, on the beach, is composing a letter, a quintessentially private form of expression; one which, in this case, is redolent of emotion. The fluids of composition and sentiment seem interchangeable" (Flint 362).

7 In considering Woolf's Benjaminian storytellers to be mournful figures, I differ from Jessica Berman, who detects in Benjamin's essay a model for modernist reconfigurations of community in the direction of cosmopolitanism and translatability (*Modernist Fiction* 18–19). See also Angeliki Spiropoulou's book-length study of Woolf and Benjamin. Like Spiropoulou (172), I perceive in Woolf's late work an echo of Benjamin's concern with a loss of pre-modern orality in the modern novel.

8 For early examples of such scholarship, see Zwerdling, "Woolf's Satiric Elegy," and Mepham, "Mourning and Modernism."
9 Cf. Freud in "Mourning and Melancholia": "The complex of melancholia behaves like an open wound" (253). See also Kelly S. Walsh's reading of Rainer Maria Rilke's and Woolf's elegiac writings, which concurs with Clewell's notion of an anti-compensatory practice of writing-as-mourning, but emphasises these writers' "capacity to express a sensibility of loss that exceeds the power of language." For Walsh, both Woolf and Rilke "look longingly toward a new language, one that could actually reflect the unbearable openness of death, . . . and insist that art must continue to express the inexpressible" (17).
10 Handley emphasises Jacob's role as a victim in the objectifying discourses of "both narrative and political authorities" (113): "The unknown soldier is the most frightening victim of war, perhaps because he is faceless, and in this manner Jacob metonymically represents the millions" (130; see 116).
11 For an account of post-war mourning practices in Britain as normative and recuperative, see Ramazani. In his discussion of the twentieth-century elegy, Ramazani stresses a distinction between social and poetic mourning, where writers of modern elegies responded to a public "denial of mourning" exemplified in minimalist mourning rites, a growing popularity of cremation, a significant shortening of mourning periods, standardised and impersonal obituaries, and an increasingly common transposition of death and mourning to social spaces such as hospitals and memorial parks (15; see 10–23). See also Bahun's Chapter 1 for a discussion of the modern denial of death in light of two related conditions: the waning of traditional mourning rituals and a subsequent "inability to mourn." As Bahun notes (17), modern warfare contributed to all these conditions.
12 In her introduction to the essay collection *Modernism and Mourning* (2007), Patricia Rae voices similar reservations about a recent critical tendency to view literary/modernist expressions of melancholia as inherently progressive. She proposes, instead, the concept of "resistant mourning" as a productive term for ethically and politically progressive modernist responses to death, loss and recuperative mourning practices (22).
13 Similar claims have been made recently by Flatley, and by the contributors to Rae's volume.
14 I concur here with Bahun, who returns throughout her book to the relevance of Kristeva's *Black Sun* (1989) for modernist literary expressions of melancholia.
15 For a lucid survey of the relationship between the amorous and the melancholic in Kristeva's theory of art, see John Lechte, "Art, Love, and Melancholy in the Work of Julia Kristeva."
16 Woolf wrote in her diary when "making up" *To the Lighthouse*: "I have an idea that I will invent a new name for my books to supplant 'novel.' A new – by Virginia Woolf. But what? Elegy?" (*D* 3: 34).

17 Bahun argues that Freud's theory of melancholia should "be given the status of a modernist paradigm" (2; see 4): "the 'modernist' psychoanalytic descriptions of melancholia match the particular structure of affective experience that we associate with modernism – the synthesis of despair and revolt" (5). She emphasises Freud's re-conceptualisation of melancholia in *The Ego and the Id* (1923) as not (only) a pathological grief but also a psychic process central to individuation: the ego's identification with lost others/objects and introjection of the persisting affective bond to those others (28–29). Like Bahun, Flatley views Freud's later theory of melancholia as a compelling paradigm through which to understand modernist subjectivity (41–50). In her 1940 essay "Mourning and Its Relation to Manic-Depressive States," Melanie Klein accepts Freud's notion of melancholic introjection as intrinsic to ego-formation. Stressing the vital necessity of "overcoming the depressive position" (353; see 344–46, 369), Klein also speaks of the lost mother as "the one irreplaceable object" (352), and notes that "The pining for the lost loved object also implies dependence on it . . . of a kind which becomes an incentive to reparation and preservation of the object" (360).

18 Trudi Tate opens her landmark historical study of modernism and the First World War with a scene from *The Years* (1937), in which "Woolf remembers the First World War as a time of darkness and silence in which no one, including the combatants, knew what was going on or why they were involved. Whole nations found themselves bearing witness to events they did not understand and, by and large, could not see" (1). Regarding Grey's remark, he later recorded it in his memoirs (20), *Twenty-Five Years 1892–1916* (1937).

19 As elsewhere in *Jacob's Room*, the Acropolis episode evokes "the building of the British Empire . . . against the sharply drawn pillars of the Parthenon," a project which "enabled Britain to promote itself as the cultural, political, and . . . military apogee of western European civilisation" (Koulouris 124). See Vassiliki Kolocotroni, "Strange Cries and Ancient Songs: Woolf's Greek and the Politics of Intelligibility" for a survey of key scholarship on the novel's "transform[ation] [of] mourning into a political reflection on the deadly blindspots of a generation that presumed to possess . . . a unique licence to interpret the Greek spirit" (423; see 435).

20 See Jean Mills for an alternative account of a mode of primal intimacy (the Harrisonian thiasos) from which Jacob is severed when absorbed, like "a pawn in the larger machine of war," into the pre-war wave of classical hero-worship (92; see 92–100).

21 Focusing on the navel as a wound or "birth-scar," Ellmann argues that modernist writing exhibits a form of nostalgia for the object of primal loss; the navel "memorializes a pre-symbolic order" and "mark[s] an indelible debt to the lost mother" (4, 9; see 4–9).

22 Erotic instincts, in Freud's account, strive to "combine single human individuals, and after that families, then races, peoples and nations, into one great unity, the

unity of mankind" (*Civilization* 313). The idea that eros is the civilising force that builds communities pervades Freud's *Group Psychology and the Analysis of the Ego* (1921), which Woolf read alongside *Civilization and Its Discontents* while composing *Between the Acts*, nearly two decades after writing *Jacob's Room*.

23 Detloff observes that "Woolf seems especially aware of the consequences of triumphant or redemptive descriptions of public violence, overtly questioning the construction of believing, heroic, sacrificial, subjects willing to fight and die in order to belong to a larger collective" (*Persistence* 12).

24 Cf. "letter, *n.¹*," def. 2.a "An individual block of type.... Chiefly in plural"; def. 2.b "In singular. Such blocks of type collectively. Also: a set of these; a typeface, a font."

25 Cf. "letter, *v.*," def. 2.a "To inscribe, paint, or otherwise write out (a word, sentence, or passage); to write down."

26 On Woolf's exploration of intimacies through the print medium, see Jane Goldman, "Burning Feminism: Woolf's Laboratory of Intimacy."

27 In "Anon," Woolf describes how modern civilisation ended the sharing of emotion enabled by Anon's song, now seen as barbaric. Her historical chronology coincides with Teresa Brennan's ground-breaking work on affective transmission. The idea of affect as contained within the individual, Brennan says, is a residue of the Western notion of subjective autonomy; in all encounters there is a constant transmission of affect, a primary form of transfer which was taken for granted in pre-modern times but has been disavowed since the seventeenth century (*The Transmission of Affect* 2, 15–20).

28 See Kolocotroni on the political dimensions of the unintelligible, ancient cries reverberating throughout Woolf's writing.

29 Detloff, too, notes Woolf's ethically charged recognition that "When loss is figured metaphorically, the particularity of the referent is lost, becoming something else – insight, the consolation of philosophy ... the impetus for a beautiful elegy – anything but loss *as* loss" (*Persistence* 24).

30 During the process of composing *Jacob's Room*, Woolf multiplied strategies for limiting narrative omniscience. E. L. Bishop observes about her manuscript revisions that "where she described in her earlier novels, she now dramatizes – and the change occurs after the draft. Between the manuscript and the final text, she consistently reduces authorial comment and exposition, letting her scenes suggest" (122).

31 On the ethical implications of Jacob's radical alterity in view of Woolf's reinvention of literary mourning, see Clewell (206–09).

32 Considered through Butler's terminology, the realist narrator resembles a strictly autonomous individual. As John Mepham remarks about the Edwardian novel, "The narrator's authoritative pronouncements made things intelligible for the reader: the narrator summed up, defined, forced things to stand still in the clear light of his language" (138). Mepham's observation evokes a specific "realist vision" explored in Peter Brooks's thus titled book. Brooks likens realist fiction to a scale

model or "modèle réduit," which claims to be objectively "reproductive of the world" but actually seeks to master it (2).

33 In a different context, the narrator debunks the use of Japanese paper flowers at upper-middle-class parties: "It is surely a great discovery that leads to the union of hearts and the foundation of homes" (*JR* 70). More pervasively, however, she directs such satiric interrogation of "bonds and beings" towards the erotic and literary-cultural ties forming Jacob's Cambridge circle. In this, her melancholic lucidity might offer a key to the novel's complex tonality: as Zwerdling observes, *Jacob's Room* is alternatively satiric and elegiac ("Woolf's Satiric Elegy").

34 As a hyperlucid, modernist melancholic, Woolf's narrator refuses the realist narrator's role as mediator of the writer and reader's joint investment in a communal moral contract: "The [realist] narrator's lucid discourse is the one in which judgements are pronounced, explanations are provided, praise and blame are apportioned, moral worth is estimated" (Mepham 138).

35 See in particular Handley, Clewell and Hollander.

36 Pippin discusses and to some extent endorses a widely held notion of modernist art as "the deepest expression of the modern crisis, understood either as paradigmatically 'bourgeois art,' or ultimately as nihilistic, self-consuming" (41), and Halliwell similarly sets out to interrogate the view that in modernism "common moral values are abandoned either for a nihilistic realm without value or a solipsistic life in which the individual reinterprets moral action solely on his or her own terms" (19).

37 As Pippin puts it, "modernism has also been understood to propose . . . a great shift in European high culture, or at least an implicit insistence on a shift in authority, from philosophy primarily, but also from science and religion, to art as the leading or 'legislating' force in a genuinely modern culture" (29).

38 In his 1971 essay "The Philosophical Realism of Virginia Woolf" (reprinted in slightly altered form in *Aspects of Bloomsbury*), S. P. Rosenbaum argues that "Philosophically, G. E. Moore influenced Virginia Woolf more than anyone else," and that Woolf's first novel to fully engage Moore's philosophical realism was her "anti-novel" *Jacob's Room* (4, 10; see 9–14). See also Rosenbaum's extensive accounts of the deep connections between Moore's ethics and Bloomsbury in *Edwardian Bloomsbury* and *Aspects of Bloomsbury*.

39 In this, Comentale is following Raymond Williams's class-based approach to Bloomsbury. See Williams, "The Significance of 'Bloomsbury' as a Social and Cultural Group."

40 Several scholars have noted Woolf's critique, in *Jacob's Room*, of the sacrificial heroism pervading British pre-war propaganda, among them John Mepham (152–54), Handley (115–16), Koulouris (110, 124) and Mills (87, 92).

41 On Moore's theory of love and aesthetic beauty as intrinsic goods to be privileged over moral rules of conduct, and its influence on Bloomsbury, see Regan 17–18, 22–24, 27–28, 159, 163–67, 171, 239–40, 245–50.

42 On this problematic and the narrator's ambivalent, melancholic depiction of Jacob, see Zwerdling ("Woolf's Satiric Elegy") and Clewell (203–09). See also Hermione Lee on Woolf's alternative critique and idealisation of the classical culture which formed the "closed world of Cambridge Societies," but also her intellectual and affectionate relationship with Thoby (213; see 203–31 (chapters 11–12)). On Greek as Woolf's chosen language of mourning, in which she articulated her "poetics of loss," see Koulouris and Kolocotroni (423).

43 In taking the narrator's emotions towards Jacob to be primarily aggressive, Clewell accepts the early Freudian paradigm in which melancholia betrays a love-hate ambivalence towards the lost other/object ("Mourning and Melancholia" 250–52). This reading leaves unaddressed the ethical dimensions of the novel's more dominant affect: that of primal sadness.

44 In this, the novel's affective regime ranges beyond the Freudian deadlock where modern civilisation amounts to a ceaseless struggle between eros and death, and all human emotions can be reduced to the extremes of love and hate. In *Between the Acts*, Isa Oliver's reflection that "There were only two emotions: love; and hate" (82) recalls the "very simple and very exaggerated" feelings which, according to Freud's reading of Gustave Le Bon, characterise group psychology (*Group Psychology* 105). Freud's elaboration of Le Bon's theory, in which "intense emotional ties" and "lack of emotional restraint" within a group trigger unreflected action (148), found alarming validation, of course, in the rise of fascism with its capacity to orchestrate violent action by manipulating collective emotion.

Chapter 2

1 Jane Goldman has illuminated the multiple ways in which the image of unhinged doors "heralds the unhinging of the novel's own narrative portals" ("1925, London, New York, Paris" 68). In launching Clarissa's introspective "plunge" into the past and her ecstatic memory of kissing Sally Seton, this image also plunges the reader into Walt Whitman's democratic, self-pleasuring and homoerotic poetics in *Leaves of Grass* (1885) – "unscrew the locks from the doors!/ Unscrew the doors themselves from their jambs!" (Goldman 69–70) – and into a French Rumpelmayer's: the Parisian *salon de thé* in Rue de Rivoli where Woolf in 1923 met Hope Mirrlees, the lesbian companion of Woolf's mentor Jane Ellen Harrison (71).

2 Sedgwick holds that in its emphasis on reparation, Klein's theory of pleasure is more nuanced than Freud's, and more compelling than his claim that the reality principle (a paranoid imperative) must contain the irruptions of pleasure seeking (137).

3 When Zwerdling, in *Virginia Woolf and the Real World* (1986), sought to rescue Woolf's fiction from a persistent understanding of it as introspective and therefore disconnected from socio-political reality, he traced its complex relations between

the world of the mind and the world outside. Even so, he distinguishes sharply between Woolf's introspective impulse and what he terms "the real world." His observation that "Woolf had always been intensely interested in what her eye could see when she looked out rather than in" (12) indicates his indebtedness to a critical tradition of reading the modernist immersion in the thinking and perceiving mind as a sign of detachment from social, political and ethical concerns. My own book seeks to complicate these influential categories.

4 There is a moral dimension to this advice. About Woolf's physician George Savage Caramagno notes, among other things, his view of mental illness as "a 'defect' in 'moral character'"; Savage "should have had little difficulty in convincing Woolf that her excessive emotionalism fit the moral-weakness bill" (14).

5 Insofar as "emotional repression was an essential aspect of the British masculine ideal," Showalter observes, "The Great War was a crisis of masculinity" (196, 171). See also Jessica Meyer's account of shell shock as entailing not only a breakdown of the masculine-feminine binary but also a crisis encompassing the maturity men were supposed to reach by going to war. While femininity was defined by a lack of self-control, Meyer notes, men's loss of self-control in shell shock also "implied a return to childishness" (8; see 7–8).

6 Caramagno traces Savage's dismissal of his patients' experience of their illness back to an attitude typical among Victorian doctors: "either insanity was so biologically based that it was not intelligible at all (and so patients were warned not to think about their 'ill' experiences), or madness resulted from a weak character and immoral decisions voluntarily made" (15). Savage was an advocate of Silas Mitchell's rest cure, which was famously prescribed to Charlotte Perkins Gilman, but also repeatedly to Woolf throughout her life.

7 On Woolf's engagement with eugenics in *Mrs Dalloway* and *A Room of One's Own*, see Donald J. Childs, *Modernism and Eugenics* (2010), Chapter 2 and 3.

8 Unlike Quentin Bell's biography of Woolf, Lee's stresses the ways in which her fiction turns her experience of coercive medical practices into a textual politics: "There is no doubt that [Woolf's] development of her political position, her intellectual resistance to tyranny and conventionality, derived to a great extent from her experiences as a woman patient" (184).

9 In her Freudian reading of *Mrs Dalloway*, Froula addresses Woolf's insight that the nationalistic and totalitarian political orders beginning to form in the 1920s were linked in complex ways to "Britain's unacknowledged tyranny" ("Postwar Elegy" 144; see 128). For Froula, Doris Kilman thus represents "a defeated and still belligerent postwar Germany," whereas Clarissa Dalloway represents an England "heedless of the political consequences of the international . . . oppression instituted at Versailles"; "In facing these women off, *Mrs Dalloway* explores the competition, envy, hatred, and aggression between . . . nations that had already engulfed Europe in war and would slowly rise to a boil again in the 1920s and 1930s" (139).

10 For an account of Keynes, Freud, Virginia Woolf and Leonard Woolf as avant-garde thinkers aspiring to a peaceful international civilisation, see Froula, *Virginia Woolf and the Bloomsbury Avant-Garde*, Chapter 1.
11 Patricia Matson similarly explores the novel's concern with the "interconnected processes of writing, reading, meaning, and resistance" (164). In Matson's poststructuralist reading, representative of a critical tradition which appears exhausted a decade after Walkowitz's *Cosmopolitan Style* (2006), Woolf's writing amounts to a deconstructive poetics furthering "an antiauthoritarian politics" (166).
12 Rachel Blau DuPlessis, for one, has read Woolf's fictional narratives as exemplifying the "poetics of rupture and critique" which DuPlessis terms "writing beyond the ending" (32); a "metaphor for conventional narrative, for a regimen of resolutions," the notion of narrative ending is related, for DuPlessis, to Freud's theory of Oedipal resolution (21; see 35). Elizabeth Abel argues similarly that Woolf's writing of the 1920s responds to Freud's contemporaneous theory of the developmental process of acculturation, a theory "decisively split between a maternal prehistory and a paternal history" (8). Abel offers an extensive account of Woolf's experimental narratives as a critical revision both of the dominant role of the father in Freud's work and of the dominance of Freudian psychoanalysis as an institution.
13 For Minow-Pinkney, the novel's female characters exemplify the female subject's achievement of "a precarious balance" between the force of the repressed semiotic and masculine social structures (70). In order to achieve integration in the symbolic order of a patriarchal society, Minow-Pinkney concludes, Clarissa Dalloway "can only oscillate between these two positions" (81). Abel argues similarly that "Clarissa's recollected history proceeds from a female-centered natural world to the heterosexual and androcentric social world" and that "Woolf structures this progression as a binary opposition between past and present, nature and culture, feminine and masculine dispensations" (31).
14 According to Moi in her brief discussion of *Mrs Dalloway*, the novel depicts the symbolic as "a patriarchal order, ruled by the Law of the Father" and suggests that "any subject who tries to disrupt it, who lets unconscious forces slip through the symbolic repression, puts him or herself in a position of revolt against this regime" (12). Patricia Ondek Laurence, while critical of Kristeva's notion of the semiotic (69), nonetheless claims that Woolf's writing of women's inwardness and silence displaces Western logocentrism in a liberation of her female characters "from dependency on social facts and subjective imprisonment" (216).
15 Kristeva notes that the word "intimate" (as an adjective and a noun) "comes from the Latin *intimus*, the superlative of *interior*, thus 'the most interior'" (43).
16 *A Room of One's Own* is an extended version of the lectures on "Women and Fiction" given by Woolf in October 1928 at the two women's colleges at Cambridge.
17 See Mark S. Micale's collection *The Mind of Modernism* (2004) for illuminating accounts of the "massive 'turn inward'" (Micale, Introduction 2) which shaped the

emergence of psychology, psychiatry and psychoanalysis as well as the inward-looking strand of modernist literature in a time when disciplinary boundaries were less distinct than today. The last two essays by Jesse Matz and Martin Jay examine the competing, classical modernist "anti-psychologism," a reaction to the writing of interiority, or feminine subjectivity, through which, as Tamar Katz has argued, "modernist art [was] feminized" (Katz, *Impressionist Subjects* 174). See also Judith Ryan's study of the simultaneous and symbiotic development of modern psychology and literary modernism.

18 In its sensually vibrant, seductive mode of address, this passage exemplifies the woman speaker and writer's "rhetorical seduction" of her female audience and readership which Jane Marcus, in her brilliant reading of *A Room of One's Own*, terms "sapphistry" ("Sapphistry: Narration as Lesbian Seduction in *A Room of One's Own*").

19 See Keltner's lucid survey of the concept of intimacy as developed by Kristeva before and beyond *Intimate Revolt*, including her challenge to nationalist intimacy and interiority in Chapter 3 of *Strangers to Ourselves* (1991).

20 As Stonebridge points out, "Freud's image of a cultural super-ego which both represses aggression and demands it is one which rests at the core of Klein's work." She notes, further, that Klein's theory of aggression inspired notions of inter-war British society as "a culture that condones violence in the name of civilized values" (65, 12). While Stonebridge also engages Klein's focus on the therapeutic and reparative capacity of art, her emphasis on the centrality of aggression in Klein's writing is a critical response to Abel's reading of Woolf through Klein, in particular as regards Abel's focus on Klein's theory of reparation in the mother-infant relationship.

21 My notion of intimate focalisation both draws on and departs from earlier readings of Woolf's novel. As Walkowitz and Patricia Matson both observe, *Mrs Dalloway* resists narrative authority also through formal strategies such as a favouring of parataxis over subordination and conclusion (Walkowitz 93–95) and a "proliferation of phrases" in a "syntactically discordant manner" (Matson 169). For Walkowitz, Woolf's modernist aesthetic counters the values of nationalism through "evasions of syntax, plot and tone," deliberate "aimlessness" and "intellectual speculation" rather than a direct response to political events (82, 84, 85), thereby calling into question received definitions of political significance and response, and for Matson, Woolf's use of multiple perspectives and syntactic juxtaposition in *Mrs Dalloway* "forces us to make connections, and refuses to grant us a position of mastery over the text" (169).

22 In "The Psychologists," a section of her long essay "Phases of Fiction" (1929), Woolf writes about Proust's *La recherche*: "The common stuff of the book is made of this deep reservoir of perception. It is from these depths that his characters rise, like waves forming, then break and sink again into the moving sea of thought and comment and analysis which gave them birth" (*E* 5: 67). Woolf began reading

Proust in May 1922 and made continuous observations in her diary and letters about his writing. For an informative account of Proust's influence on Woolf's writings of the 1920s, see Pericles Lewis, "Proust, Woolf, and Modern Fiction."

23 See, for instance, Elizabeth Abel (36–38) and Tuzyline Jita Allan (108–09).
24 Caramagno writes about the manic phase in manic-depressive illness: "Accompanying the heightened mood are accelerated psychomotor activity and intensified sensory perceptions that provide further ammunition for the manic's belief that life is profoundly meaningful: objects simply look vivid and exciting" ("Manic-Depressive Psychosis" 14). See also Caramagno's convincing reading of Septimus's character as bipolar (210–43) in *The Flight of the Mind: Virginia Woolf's Art and Manic-Depressive Illness* (1992).
25 My reading of the aeroplane episode as a scene of ecstatic affects and sensual pleasures differs substantially from the "deconstructionist's vision of language" attributed to Woolf by poststructuralist critics such as Matson, for whom the aeroplane enacts a Derridean writing practice "dependent on the processes of deferral and displacement (différance)" (164, 65). It differs just as substantially from Sarah Cole's understanding of the episode as conveying "a kind of group shell shock that always registers the airplane as a potential weapon" (250). For Cole, the spectators exhibit a traumatised, "dawning awareness of the air as the site of warfare . . . whereby the city and its populace become targets for the lofty and dehumanized gaze of aerial bombers" (250).
26 The following reflection reads as a vivid description of Woolf's "vocal writing" in these lines, and indeed her poetic practice throughout *Mrs Dalloway*: in the text of bliss "Two edges are created: an obedient, conformist, plagiarizing edge [copying literary language as formed through centuries of 'good usage'], and *another edge* . . . the place where the death of language is glimpsed. . . . The subversive edge may seem privileged because it is the edge of violence; but it is not violence which affects pleasure, nor is it destruction which interests it; what pleasure wants is the site of a loss, the seam, the cut, the deflation, the *dissolve* which seizes the subject in the midst of bliss" (Barthes 6–7).
27 Septimus's deciphering of overwhelming "signals" and "messages" corresponds to a symptom of manic-depressive psychosis: "The strong emotions of mania skew perception, creating an obscure solipsistic symbolism. . . . Thus, a sudden vision of life's true meaning or the hearing of voices seems miraculously to 'explain' what the manic is feeling at the moment" (Caramagno, "Manic-Depressive Psychosis" 14).
28 On *Mrs Dalloway* and the treatment of war veterans in post-war Britain, see Karen L. Levenback, *Virginia Woolf and the Great War* (1999), Chapter 2. For substantial accounts of coercion, conformity and gender stereotypes in the treatment of shell shock after the First World War, see Showalter, *The Female Malady* (1985), Chapter 7, and Meyer, "Separating the Men from the Boys."

29 Minow-Pinkney's claim that "In this state Septimus enjoys colours, rhythms, sounds with extreme intensity as the thetic subject is dissolved into the semiotic *chora* it had formerly so severely repressed" (*Virginia Woolf and the Problem of the Subject* 79) is problematic in many ways. Septimus is psychotic and not "enjoying" a momentary dissolution of subjectivity in *jouissance*, and while the decomposition of the 'I' is only one phase in Woolf's critical poetics, Minow-Pinkney writes: "Woolf's texts disperse the transcendental unified subject that underpins male rationality and narrative. . . . Her writing subverts this positionality and tries to adumbrate the area anterior to the logical, judging, naming subjectivity" (60). This paradigmatic Kristevan reading tends to overlook Kristeva's (and Woolf's) emphasis on the centrality of the thetic in the poetic revolution or revolt.

30 In the first pages of her autobiographical essay "Sketch of the Past" (composed in 1939), Woolf describes moments of being in terms such as "exceptional," "shock" and "revelation" (83, 84, 85), and stresses the necessity of ordering these overwhelming experiences in writing. See *Moments of Being* (2002) 83–85.

31 Theoretically informed by Ricoeur's idea of a-linear time, Prudente's book touches only in passing on the influence of Bergson's thought on modernist configurations of temporality. For an account of Bergsonian intuition and involuntary memory in Woolf's fiction, see Gillies, Chapter 5. See also Shiv K. Kumar's chapter (4) on Woolf in *Bergson and the Stream of Consciousness Novel* (1962). Kumar's Bergsonian approach to Richardson, Woolf and Joyce is central to a critical tradition in which Gillies and Prudente partake, even if they would not go as far as claiming that for these novelists, "inner duration against chronological time [becomes] the only true mode of apprehending aesthetic experience" (Kumar 7).

32 See Caroline Levine, *Forms: Whole, Rhythm, Hierarchy, Network*, Chapter 3.

33 On the context and significance of the Freudian *Zeitlos* as developed by Kristeva in *Intimate Revolt*, see Keltner, Chapter 4.

34 On Woolf's pleasurable and socio-politically charged manipulations of the literary sentence, see Elsa Högberg and Amy Bromley (editors), *Sentencing* Orlando: *Virginia Woolf and the Morphology of the Modernist Sentence* (2018).

35 Jo Alyson Parker, too, observes that Woolf's consistent use of the past tense in *Mrs Dalloway* "blurs the boundary between past and present" in a "subversion of linear temporality" (101).

36 See Hägglund's development of his argument about a specifically modernist "chronolibido" in his Introduction and Chapter 2 on Woolf. Of the pleasurable sentence conveying Clarissa's ecstatic suspense above, Hägglund cites only the opening – "she fears 'time itself . . . how little the margin that remained was capable any longer of stretching'" (73) – as evidence for his claim that "the pathos of Woolf's *moments of living* stems from the fact that they are always already *moments of dying*" (78).

37 My understanding of Woolf's ideal of androgyny as a mode of intimacy is both indebted to and moves beyond the continental feminist tradition of theorised Woolf scholarship initiated by Toril Moi and pursued by critics such as Minow-Pinkney, Scott and Rachel Bowlby. For cogent accounts of, and incisive interventions into, critical debates on Woolf's literary treatment of androgyny, see Laura Marcus, "Woolf's feminism and feminism's Woolf," and Brenda S. Helt, "Passionate Debates on 'Odious Subjects': Bisexuality and Woolf's Opposition to Theories of Androgyny and Sexual Identity."

38 See, for instance, the section "Living in Each Other" in David Bradshaw's introduction to the Oxford University Press edition of the novel (*MD* xxxiv–xlii), which traces the many images, metaphors, character traits and experiences connecting Clarissa and Septimus's characters.

39 See Cesare Lombroso's *Criminal Man* (1876) and Max Nordau's *Degeneration* (1892) for two influential accounts of degeneration.

40 Fand advocates dialogism as a pragmatic alternative to deconstruction. Her reading of Woolf relies on the theoretical assumption that the subject is irrevocably split and incapable of self-grounding, but can assume a range of subject positions.

41 In *Why We Read Fiction: Theory of the Mind and the Novel* (2006), Lisa Zunshine draws on contemporary cognitive psychology to argue that reading and understanding fiction requires a mind-reading capacity, that is, the capacity to confer complex mental states on characters. As Zunshine observes, *Mrs Dalloway* places unusually high demands on the reader's mind-reading capacity, especially through Woolf's use of multiple levels of intentionality ("I know that you know that I know"). In terms of my discussion here, this strategy, like Woolf's free indirect discourse and focalising series, compels the reader to ask who is thinking here and, through this question, to apprehend the myriad psychologically complex perspectives which compose human relations.

Chapter 3

1 In "Ethical Folds," Berman traces Fry's and Bell's formalism back to Kant's separation of the reflective aesthetic judgement from the sensory experience of an aesthetic object. In this, she argues, Kant inspired their privileging of aesthetic form over sensory experience in life.

2 Critics exploring the relationship between Woolf's work and Fry's formalism tend to focus on Woolf's reception of Fry's distinction between art and life – especially in relation to questions involving the body – and on their respective concern with the different properties of the two media. See, for instance, Jane Goldman's *The Feminist Aesthetics of Virginia Woolf* (1998), Diane F. Gillespie's collection *The Multiple*

Muses of Virginia Woolf (1993), Marianna Torgovnick's *The Visual Arts, Pictorialism, and the Novel* (1985) and C. J. Mares's "Reading Proust: Woolf and the Painter's Perspective." For thorough accounts of the aesthetic ideas developed by the painters and writers of the Bloomsbury group, see S. P. Rosenbaum's *The Early Literary History of the Bloomsbury Group: Georgian Bloomsbury, 1910–1914* (2003) and David Dowling's *Bloomsbury Aesthetics and the Novels of Forster and Woolf* (1985).

3 On this point I diverge from feminist critics such as Berman, who maintains that arguing for Woolf's indebtedness to Fry means leaving "little room for any deep association between aesthetics and morality or ethics" (*Modernist Commitments* 49).

4 Goldman in *The Feminist Aesthetics of Virginia Woolf*, Laura Doyle, Randi Koppen and Louise Westling have all argued that while Woolf embraced central aspects of Fry's aesthetic theory, hers is an embodied formalism.

5 In *Vision and Design*, Fry distinguishes similarly between two senses of beauty: "sensuous charm" and "aesthetic approval" (22).

6 Desmond MacCarthy, who wrote the catalogue for the first Post-Impressionist Exhibition, shared Fry's view of Impressionist aesthetic practices. The Impressionists for MacCarthy "were interested in analysing the play of light and shadow into a multiplicity of distinct colours; they refined upon what was already illusive in nature" ("The Post-Impressionists," 175; see Goldman, *Feminist Aesthetics* 124–25). As Goldman observes, Post-Impressionism in MacCarthy's account is "at odds with the naturalistic project of the Impressionists" (Goldman 124).

7 Throughout "Some Questions in Esthetics," Fry emphasises the inevitable distinctness of the psychological and the aesthetic. He states repeatedly that, as an art critic, he has rarely been able "definitely to relate plastic with psychological considerations, or find any marked co-operation between the two experiences" (*T* 18).

8 In the chapter of *Aspects of the Novel* entitled "Pattern and Rhythm," Forster defines "pattern" in painterly terms. A novel's pattern, his text suggests, is similar to what Fry called form or design in a painting (151–70). For instance, Forster likens the "symmetry" of James's *The Ambassadors* to "the shape of an hour-glass" (155). The dominance of this abstract shape in the novel he calls "pattern triumphant" (154) and a "sacrifice" of "human life." As Woolf rightly responds in her review, Forster does not clearly define his notion of "life," nor does he explain why "most of human life has to disappear" in novels with a distinct pattern (161).

9 It should be noted that Woolf frequently expresses uneasiness about the view, held by both Forster and Fry, that literature is inherently closer to life than painting. In her review of Forster's book, she calls "the assumption that fiction is more intimately and humbly attached to the service of human beings than the other arts" (*E* 4: 461–62) an "unaesthetic attitude" which would be "Strange . . . in the critic of any other art" but "does not surprise us in the critic of fiction." "And perhaps," she writes in a tone of resignation, "the critics are right. In England, at any rate, the novel is not a work of art" (462–63).

10 Woolf made a similar statement in her opening address at the Roger Fry Memorial Exhibition at the Bristol Museum and Art Gallery (12 July 1935): "Here I come to a point in speaking of him where I doubt if he would let me go on. For I want to say that his understanding of art owed much to his understanding of life, and yet I know that he disliked the mingling and mixing of different things. He wanted art to be art; literature to be literature; and life to be life" (*E* 6: 61). As Torgovnick puts it, Woolf "saw Fry as never quite having divorced life and art as strongly as the rhetoric of *Vision and Design* implies that he wished to do; implicitly, Woolf believed that art derives strength from life experience" (65).

11 For a substantial account of the importance of mathematics and logic in Moore's and Russell's philosophies and a survey of the critique of idealism at Cambridge, which also marked Leslie Stephen's generation, see Banfield's Introduction.

12 On the context and detail of this exchange, see Banfield's Introduction.

13 Megan Quigley presents an alternative account. For Quigley, Woolf's "commitment to vagueness" exemplifies a modernist "revolt against positivism in the philosophy of language" ("Modern Novels and Vagueness" 103), whereby her aesthetic practice opposes the logic and precision privileged in realist writing and advocated by Russell. Michael Lackey argues more radically that Woolf sought to "deliver the deathblow to philosophy itself," and that her "scathing critique" of the "philosophical mindset" is representative of a pervasive "literary modernist assault on philosophy" (95).

14 In Fry's understanding, as Banfield observes, "Impressionism is pure empiricism" (274), and for Clive Bell, the Impressionists sought to "represent things as they are" and "paint what we see, not the intellectual superstructure that we build over our sensations" (Bell, *Art*, qtd. in Banfield 272). Bell's and Fry's conflation of Impressionism and literary realism is more polemical than it is nuanced. As Torgivnick emphasises, Impressionism may well have emerged as an "expansion of realism," but reality for the Impressionists resided less in the objects perceived in than in the subjective perceptions as such. Impressionism, that is, implied a transition of reality from object to subject (16).

15 For an elaboration of this argument in relation to Woolf's writing beyond and in *To the Lighthouse*, see Elsa Högberg, "Virginia Woolf's Object-Oriented Ecology."

16 For a survey of ecocritical approaches to Woolf, see Högberg, "Virginia Woolf's Object-Oriented Ecology."

17 Tammy Clewell considers Woolf's dismantling of the pathetic fallacy as an example of the ethical, anti-consolatory mourning practice she detects in "Time Passes" and the novel as a whole (210–13). See also David Sherman's Levinasian reading of "Time Passes." For Sherman, the narrator of this section "speaks with the ethically-inflected voice of selfhood bound to the other more than to its own being," thereby becoming a "voiceless exteriority" which "giv[es] what is other and alien a value that is not compatible with the internal economy of self" (160).

18 Critics tend to agree that Fry and Vanessa Bell, and to some extend Clive Bell, were the most influential on Woolf's engagement with the ideas and techniques of painting. Scholars from Dowling to Banfield have highlighted Fry's considerable influence on the three others. Goldman, however, follows Gillespie's *The Sisters' Art* in focusing on the primary importance of the sisters' relationship as artists. She thereby shares Gillespie's aim "to shift the emphasis in the ongoing discussion of Virginia Woolf and the visual arts from Roger Fry to Vanessa Bell; to shift the emphasis in the discussions of the sisters from the psychological to the professional and the aesthetic; and, in these contexts, to define and reveal more fully the pervasive role of the visual arts in Woolf's writing" (Gillespie, 2; see Goldman, *Feminist Aesthetics* 115). In her recent contribution to *The Edinburgh Companion to Virginia Woolf and the Arts* (2010), Gillespie stresses the sisters' independence from Fry (121–22), and offers a survey of as well as an intervention into the proliferating scholarship on their importance to one another as artists.

19 In "Walter Sickert: A Conversation," Woolf refers to "the silent kingdom of paint" as a world eluding the "impure medium" of words (*E* 6: 39). Torgovnick and Mares have both commented on the idea of painting as a medium to access the beyond of literary narratives. While Torgovnick discusses the common distinction between literature and painting in which the former is viewed as a temporal and the latter a static medium (30–36), Mares argues that the static, silent nature of painting was a crucial element in Woolf's attraction to formalism.

20 Christopher Reed and Panthea Reid Broughton have both pointed out that Fry frequently claimed literature to be representational in the strictest sense of the word and therefore outside the realm of art. However, as Reed observes, Fry's later aesthetic theories attempted to "reintegrate representation into the formalist paradigm without sacrificing an ideal of purely aesthetic experience" (15–16). Dowling argues similarly that Fry sought increasingly to "bridge the gap . . . between form and content, design and vision" (23).

21 Throughout her work, Woolf distinguishes between the enduring and the ephemeral, and she frequently employs images of material solidity and feathery evanescence to describe these alternative ways of perceiving reality. In contrast to the solid mantle of the night, the image of the thin net or veil serves in *To the Lighthouse* to describe subjective perceptions and impressions; Lily's mind is "an invisible elastic net" containing the impressions which "danc[e] up and down, like a company of gnats" (30), and Mrs Ramsay accuses her husband of "rend[ing] the thin veils of civilisation" with his "astonishing lack of consideration for other people's feelings" (37).

22 See Quigley on the idea of vagueness in modernist writing. While Quigley does not want to confuse vagueness with literary Impressionism (104), she uses Impressionist images such as the "luminous halo" of Woolf's "Modern Fiction" to

support her claim that "Rather than attempting to eliminate vagueness, modernist fiction probes vagueness as the best way to examine psychological depth" (105).

23 Fry's remarks about Impressionism's concern with life and sensory experience at the expense of form and design coincide with Matz's observation that Impressionism in both painting and literature implied "attention to evanescent effects, radical fidelity to perceptual experience. . . . Out were plot, schema, and other forms of rationalizing conceptual knowledge; freedom, informality, and emphasis on the experience of the senses enabled the artist to make art more perfectly reflect lived experience" (Matz 45). However, unlike Fry, Matz emphasises that the impression is "not merely a visual image or sensuous phenomenon," nor "an idea . . . a product of intellectualizing" (8, 7); rather, it lies in between the two (13). Yet, both remain aspects of the first-person perspective, of the subjective.

24 For Banfield, "Impressionism is where Woolf begins" (294), and Torgovnick argues about the painterly influences on Woolf's work that "the relevant movements are Impressionism, Post-Impressionism and abstract art, especially as viewed and interpreted by artists associated with Bloomsbury" (12).

25 Goldman claims that Woolf's fascination with Post-Impressionist colour expresses her sympathy with the suffrage movement, which made a similarly radical use of colour, and traces in Woolf's experimental texts "the possibility of an interventionist and feminist understanding of colour, more readily associated with aspects of Post-Impressionism than Impressionism" (*Feminist Aesthetics* 9). For an extensive account of politically radical modernist formalisms, see Goldman (*Modernism, 1910–1945* 33–76).

26 Fry considered architecture to inspire aesthetic emotions to a greater extent than both painting and sculpture. In "Some Questions in Esthetics," he delineates a clear hierarchy of art forms, in which the aesthetic mindset "may seem plausible enough with regard to our experience of certain peculiarly abstract musical constructions or even of certain kinds of architecture. It becomes far less plausible the moment representation of actual forms comes in, as in painting or sculpture, still less when, as in poetry, the novel or the drama, the very stuff of which these are constructed, namely words, calls up images and memories of things and emotions of actual life" (*T* 3).

27 For Auerbach, Woolf "does not seem to bear in mind that she is the author and hence ought to know how matters stand with her characters" (469). Critics like Christopher Reed have pointed out the problematic implications of Auerbach's realist bias. Reed observes that from a feminist point of view, Auerbach's assumption that Woolf withholds information about the "objects of her creative imagination" demonstrates "the critic's contest with an author who refuses him the conventional reader's (or viewer's) position of voyeuristic privilege" (Auerbach 472; Reed 22).

28 This "multipersonal representation of consciousness" exemplifies the "modern technique" Auerbach detected in his chapter "The Brown Stocking." Woolf's method, he notes, differs from "the unipersonal subjectivism which allows only a single . . . person to make himself heard and admits only that one person's way of looking at reality" (474).

29 My understanding of Woolf's fictional universe as a shared world draws inspiration from Goldman's notion of Woolf's "plural rather than singular model of the subject" (*Feminist Aesthetics* 50), an "interstellar" relational model in which "a contestive constellation of subjects addressing each other as well as the reader" displaces the solar, masculine Enlightenment subject (21, 22).

30 Elizabeth Abel relates this desire for oneness to "an infant longing both to fuse and to separate" with a mother figure (68–69), thus explaining Lily's aesthetic project in Kleinian terms; Lily, she writes, "finds in the 'language' of painting . . . a means of representing the boundary negotiations which characterize the mother-infant bond. . . . By conflating Lily's aesthetic and psychological tasks, Woolf engages issues Klein was exploring simultaneously" (69).

31 My reading of Fry here concurs with Randi Koppen's in her article "Embodied Form: Art and Life in Virginia Woolf's *To the Lighthouse*." Koppen points to a tension in Fry's work between, on the one hand, a strict separation of aesthetic emotion and sensory, bodily experience in life and, on the other, frequent indications that the latter is a precondition for the former. Ultimately, as Koppen observes, Fry and Woolf both interrogate "an oversimplified opposition between body/life and art," and both conceive of aesthetic form as "experientially grounded" (378).

32 In his essay "The Artist and Psycho-Analysis" (1924), Fry rejects Freud's notion of art as originating in sexual instincts and desires. Great art, Fry argues, originates in aesthetic emotion, which is "an emotion about form" detached from "the instinctive life." (6) See Lyndsey Stonebridge, who astutely argues that Fry was more ambivalent about the relationship between art and the body than his essay suggests (Chapter 2).

33 Stonebridge makes a similar observation in reading Fry between the lines. Despite his emphatic rejection of psychoanalysis, she notes, Fry suggested implicitly that art may be "the means by which we become *conscious* of the emotions and experiences which modernity consigns to the unconscious" (53).

34 Jack Stewart has observed a resemblance between the hazy colours of Woolf's first impressions in "A Sketch of the Past" and colours which, in her fiction, "overflow character boundaries." "Beyond optical *sensations*," he notes, "colour *interactions* reveal the psychological interrelation of beings" (27). Stewart does not, however, consider the ethical implications of these colour interactions.

35 The "combination of lines and colours" is Clive Bell's phrase for artworks which express "significant form" (20). "What quality," he asks, "is common to Sta. Sophia and the windows at Chartres, Mexican sculpture, a Persian bowl, Chinese carpets, Giotto's frescoes at Pauda, and the masterpieces of Poussin, Pierro della Francesca,

and Cézanne? Only one answer seems possible – significant form. In each, lines and colours combined in a particular way, certain forms and relations of forms, stir our aesthetic emotion" (17–18). Bell's significant form, then, is an ahistorical, succinctly defined equivalent of Fry's plastic colour; the term "include[s] combinations of lines and of colours. The distinction between form and colour is an unreal one; you cannot conceive a colourless line or a colourless space; neither can you conceive a formless relation of colours" (19).

36 Cam's mind similarly "wander[s] in imagination in that underworld of waters . . . where in the green light a change came over one's entire mind and one's body shone half-transparent enveloped in a green cloak"; then suddenly "The Lighthouse became immovable, and the line of the distant shore became fixed. The sun grew hotter and everybody seemed to come very close together and to feel each other's presence" (*TL* 198, 199).

Chapter 4

1 See Robin Majumdar and Allen McLaurin (editors), *Virginia Woolf: The Critical Heritage* (1997), 263–98, for a selection of early reviews. For substantial surveys of key criticism on *The Waves* across time, see Jane Goldman's *Virginia Woolf, To the Lighthouse, The Waves* (1997), and Eleanor McNees, *Virginia Woolf: Critical Assessments* (1994), 3–96.

2 Sykes's class-based dismissal of *The Waves* as an example of a "tea-room modernism" emerging "not in the midst of modern life, but far removed from it, in a hushed, luxurious library, surrounded by classics" (11) follows the lines of F. R. and Q. D. Leavis's persistent critique of Woolf's work. However, the view that Woolf's novels had nothing to do with the public world of politics was also held by members of her circle of friends and family such as E. M. Forster and Quentin Bell. "Improving the world," Forster writes, "she would not consider. . . . She has all the aesthete's characteristics . . . enforces patterns on her books; has no great cause at heart" (*Virginia Woolf* 8). See Jane Marcus's ground-breaking critique in *Art and Anger* (1988) of Bell's (and Forster's) representation of Woolf as apolitical.

3 Woolf noted about the novel she was composing that "The Waves is I think resolving itself . . . into a series of dramatic soliloquies" (*D* 3: 312).

4 See, for instance, Peter and Margaret Havard-Williams, whose close focus on Rhoda's character ultimately obscures their argument that *The Waves* problematises "the difficulties involved in the introspective mind's encounter with reality." The reader is left to wonder whether it is Rhoda or Woolf herself who finds "The very contact with reality . . . painful, unbearable" (13), and is ultimately "an artist *manqué*" (21).

5 See Patrick McGee, Cathy J. Phillips and Jessica Berman's *Modernist Fiction, Cosmopolitanism and the Politics of Community* (2001). Tamar Katz argues

convincingly that while *The Waves* delineates two versions of modernist subjectivity, subjectivity as abstracted from versus implicated in historical reality, the novel ultimately resists formalist abstraction ("Modernism, Subjectivity").

6 "Professions for Women" was Woolf's first working title for *Three Guineas*; it is also the title of the posthumously published, shortened version of the speech she gave to the London/National Society for Women's Service on 21 January 1931. *Life as We Have Known It*, edited by Margaret Llewelyn Davies, was published by the Hogarth Press on 5 March 1931. As part of her work for the Women's Co-operative Guild, Woolf organised the meetings of the Richmond section from 1917 to 1920. On the pacifism of the WCG, and Woolf's support for their pacifist ambitions, see Naomi Black, "The Mothers' International: The Women's Co-operative Guild and Feminist Pacifism" and her 2004 study *Virginia Woolf as Feminist* (38–41).

7 See, however, Christine Froula's insightful analysis of the "scapegoat psychology" which, she argues, structures the psychology of collective violence, both of which are exposed and undermined in *Three Guineas* (*Bloomsbury Avant-Garde* 259–84).

8 Marcus in *Art and Anger*, Zwerdling (*Real World*), Rebecca Walkowitz and Andrew John Miller all emphasise the interconnection of public and private in *Three Guineas* and in Woolf's writing more generally. At the time of its publication, however, *Three Guineas* was criticised by her close friends precisely for equating resistance to fascism with resistance to patriarchal domination in the private sphere of the family. Quentin Bell writes in his biography of Woolf that "What really seemed wrong with the book . . . was the attempt to involve a discussion of women's rights with the far more agonising and immediate question of what we were to do in order to meet the ever-growing menace of Fascism and war" (205). This dubious argument about the untimeliness of Woolf's feminist claims has been contested since Marcus's 1970s and '80s work; see especially the last section of "Storming the Toolshed" (193–200).

9 Marcus challenges a persistent consensus in Woolf scholarship by claiming *The Waves* to be "Consistent with the socialist politics and antifascist ethics of *The Years* and *Three Guineas*" ("Britannia" 81). Similar claims have been made by Berman (*Modernist Fiction*, Chapter 4) and Phillips.

10 In "Character in Fiction," Woolf complains that "in order to complete [the novels of Arnold Bennett, H. G. Wells and John Galsworthy] it seems necessary to do something – to join a society, or, more desperately, to write a cheque. . . . They were interested in something outside" (*E* 3: 427–28), but a decade later, she adopted a similar method herself. From 1932 to 1937, while working on *The Years* and *Three Guineas*, Woolf collected cuttings from newspapers, letters, manifestos, biographies and other documents of social relevance in three scrapbooks. See Brenda Silver, *Virginia Woolf's Reading Notebooks* (1983).

11 Woolf's narrator imagines her correspondent's reply: "you have no time to think; you have your battles to fight" (*TG* 243). The word "battles" refers to the narrator's efforts

to acquire means for the foundation of a college for women, and to her struggle for women to join "the procession of the sons of educated men" (244). Central to these battles is the question: "how can we enter the professions and yet remain civilized human beings; human beings, that is, who wish to prevent war?" (262).

12 The idea of disinterested thought is part of the feminist agenda of *Three Guineas* as well as the narrator's famous claim that "as a woman, I have no country. As a woman I want no country. As a woman my country is the whole world" (313). See Berman (*Modernist Fiction*, Chapter 4) and Walkowitz (Chapter 3) for substantial accounts of a feminist, cosmopolitan politics in Woolf's writing. Woolf's uncompromising pacifism became increasingly hard to sustain as the threat of a German invasion became a fact. This in combination with what many considered to be a misplaced and untimely focus on feminist questions caused severe critique of *Three Guineas*. See Marcus, "Storming the Toolshed" (193–200), Lee (678–98) and Abel Travis for critical accounts of the claim, made by Quentin Bell and others, that Woolf's polemic furthers no cause apart from "a paranoid and passé feminism" (Abel Travis 167). See also Marina MacKay's questioning of the common notion that Woolf's absolute pacifism remained consistent across her work (22–43).

13 This redefinition of the terms "active" and "passive" is Woolf's response to H. G. Wells's claim that "There has been no perceptible woman's movement to resist the practical obliteration of their freedom by Fascists and Nazis" (H. G. Wells, *Experiment in Autobiography* [1934], qtd. in *TG* 214). See Merry M. Pawlowski's essay, and her anthology more broadly, on Woolf's critique of the fascists' reactionary gender politics.

14 On Woolf's resistance to nationalism, see Berman (*Modernist Fiction*, Chapter 4), Walkowitz (Chapter 3), Froula (*Bloomsbury Avant-Garde*) and Miller (Chapters 1 and 5).

15 For illuminating discussions of Woolf's emphasis on Britain's complicity in the rise of fascism in Italy and Germany, see Lee (678–98), Berman (*Modernist Fiction*, 114–56), Froula (*Bloomsbury Avant-Garde* 1–32) and Abel Travis.

16 Zwerdling is quoting from a later typescript of *Three Guineas* held in the Berg Collection.

17 Walkowitz makes a related point when claiming that Woolf opposes nationalism and unreflected action by privileging intellectual speculation and drifting, aimless thought (79–105).

18 See AnnKatrin Jonsson and Tamlyn Monson for Levinasian accounts of the novel's many passages in which the presence and gaze of another subject unsettle the stability of the autonomous 'I.'

19 While Berman complicates this claim by pointing to the nurse's formative role in Bernard's narrative, she considers his frequent returns in memory to his friends "an attempt to regain, control, and draw strength from their lives" (*Modernist Fiction* 154; see 153).

20 Jonsson points out that Bernard develops a "narrative identity," a sense of self which encompasses those relations that call the autonomous 'I' into question (129; see 129–45). See Monson and Makiko Minow-Pinkney (*Virginia Woolf and the Problem of the Subject* 152–86) for readings of Bernard's character through Kristeva's theory of the subject-in-process.

21 Woolf's writing of Bernard's soliloquy anticipates Kristeva's *Revolution in Poetic Language*, which stresses the precedence of the semiotic to the symbolic order of subjectivity and language. The point Kristeva is making there is that the autonomous 'I' needs to be considered not as the origin of the subject, but as part of the signifying process which continues to produce the subject. The thetic positing of the subject, Kristeva holds, is "*producible*"; it is produced by "semiotic conditions." It is in this sense that the semiotic is "pre-thetic" (*RPL* 36).

22 In *About Chinese Women*, Kristeva discusses the suicides of three women writers – Woolf, Maria Tsvetaieva and Sylvia Plath – to show that "For woman, the call of the mother is not only a call beyond time, beyond the socio-political battle.... It generates voices, 'madness,' hallucinations." According to Kristeva, women can only survive in the symbolic through "A constant alteration between time and its 'truth,' identity and its loss, history and the timeless, signless, extra-phenomenal things that produce it. An impossible dialectic" (39, 38). Chloë Taylor thus reads the female characters in *The Waves* as examples of the subject positions available to women according to Kristeva.

23 Readers of *The Waves* were quick to note its radical departure from realist methods. Bullet, for instance, observed in 1931 that in her effort to "record the psychological minutiae of experience," Woolf has "discarded one by one ... the various devices which most writers, and nearly all readers, have held to be not merely aids but obvious necessities of narrative" (8). In her diary entry from November 1928, where she sets out to "give the moment whole," Woolf contrasts realist narrative devices to poetic writing: "The idea has come to me that what I want now to do is saturate every atom.... Waste, deadness, come from the inclusion of things that dont (sic) belong to the moment; this appalling narrative business of the realist: getting on from lunch to dinner: it is false, unreal, merely conventional. Why admit anything to literature that is not poetry – by which I mean saturated?" (*D* 3: 209–10).

24 For Minow-Pinkney, the novel maintains "a precarious dialectic between identity and its loss" (*Virginia Woolf* 155). Taylor argues similarly that "Woolf's writing accomplishes the uneasy balance between ... signifying language and maternal music, between the symbolic and the semiotic" (75).

25 In Monson's reading, Woolf represents the encounter with an irreducible other as a moment of disruption in which the autonomy of the subject disintegrates along with the language that expresses this autonomy.

26 Freud concurs with theorists such as Gustave Le Bon that the civilised individual's psychosocial composition undergoes a regression when influenced by a group.

He ascribes to group psychology characteristics such as "the inclination to exceed every limit in the expression of emotion and to work it off completely in the form of action . . . a regression of mental activity to an earlier stage such as we are not surprised to find among savages and children" (*Group Psychology* 148).

27 As critics have often observed, *Three Guineas* offers a feminist counterpart to Freud's and Einstein's 1932 correspondence around the question: "Is there any way of delivering mankind from the menace of war?" (*Why War?* 345). Woolf's gendered analysis of violence stands in contrast not only to this correspondence but also to Freud's earlier *Group Psychology* and *Civilization and Its Discontents*, which largely evade the question of gender as it relates to aggression.

28 This claim met with sharp critique from Woolf's family and friends. Quentin Bell, for one, insisted on a weakness in Woolf's argument that "men, unlike women, positively rejoice in war" while "the male pacifist is a rarity" ("*A Room of One's Own* and *Three Guineas*" 15, 16).

29 Against fascist attempts to "hypnotize the human mind," Woolf writes, "it must be our aim not to submit ourselves to such hypnotism" (*TG* 322). Freud's earlier analysis, in *Group Psychology*, similarly describes the "contagion" of thoughts and feelings within a group as hypnotic. Here, too, he agrees with Le Bon that such contagion effaces the individual's critical faculty (103; see 102–04). Furthermore, he sees conformist thought as "part of the normal constitution of human society," where "every individual is ruled by [the] attitudes of the group mind" (149).

30 See Berman's account of *The Waves* as a response to Oswald Mosley's New Party, which became a part of the British Union of Fascists in 1931, and its rhetoric of action, determination and dynamic progress (*Modernist Fiction* 114–56).

31 Like Percival, Louis occupies a position of authority in the British Empire: "I roll the dark before me, spreading commerce where there was chaos in the far parts of the world. . . . The globe is strung with our lines. I am immensely respectable" (*W* 128, 153). Compare these passages to Woolf's claim, in *Three Guineas*, that a woman must "absent herself from military displays, tournaments . . . and all such ceremonies as encourage the desire to impose 'our' civilization or 'our' dominion upon other people" (125). Marcus ("Britannia") and Phillips both offer postcolonial readings of Louis's and Percival's characters. See also Phillips's historical account of the relations, in the first decades of the twentieth century, between British imperialism, fascism and war.

32 Freud opens his later *Civilization and Its Discontents* with a consideration of "oceanic feeling," another primary relational mode which continues to unsettle subject-object boundaries: "Our present ego-feeling is, therefore, only a shrunken residue of . . . a more intimate bond between the ego and the world about it" (252, 255; see 251–55). Later, however, he dismisses the view that the "universal love of mankind and the world" inspired by such oceanic feeling may be "the highest [ethical] standpoint which man can reach" (291).

33 As Kate Flint points out in her introduction to the Penguin edition of the novel, Woolf's exploration of identity formation "makes a striking parallel with the account of subjectivity developed by ... Jacques Lacan in the 1930s" (*W* xxxix).

34 See Taylor on the aggressive birds and defenceless snails as a Kristevan antagonism between the paternal symbolic and the abject, earth-bound maternal body (67–69).

35 I differ here from a feminist critical lineage which has tended to foreground Woolf's italicised interludes as the primary locus of her novel's non-violent politics. While Marcus viewed the interludes as a series of Hindu sun prayers surrounding the soliloquies' "(Western) narrative of the fall of British imperialism" ("Britannia" 76), Berman reads their cyclical, oceanic poetics as feminist, anti-fascist narrative (*Modernist Fiction* 141).

36 In Taylor's Kristevan reading, Bernard's poetic experiments are incomprehensible to Susan as an earth-bound woman and mother. It should also be said, however, that Woolf's own aesthetic practice affirms Bernard's as well as Susan's ways of relating to the world. Also, as Stonebridge points out, to uncritically accept Kristeva's *About Chinese Women* as a valid theoretical framework for reading Woolf is to rid her writing of critical and political agency (61–62).

37 In *A Room of One's Own*, the 'I', "hard as a nut" (130), is connected throughout with anger and possessiveness.

38 A striking example of the soliloquies' interdependence is the following beginning: "'How strange,' said Jinny, 'that people should sleep, that people should put out the lights and go upstairs.... I feel myself shining in the dark. Silk is on my knee.'" These lines read as a continuation of the previous soliloquy, which ends with Susan's words: "But evening comes and the lamps are lit.... I look at the quivering leaves in the dark garden and think 'They dance in London. Jinny kisses Louis'" (*W* 75).

39 Even Steven Putzel's wide-ranging book on the theatrical aspects of Woolf's textual experiments comments only briefly on her dramatic strategies in *The Waves*.

40 Winifred Holtby, for one, reads Woolf's soliloquies as "taking place in the subconscious ... minds of the six characters" (6), and Peter and Margaret Havard-Williams suggest that *The Waves* explores "*the work of the mind* ... as it reacts to the external world and, in a lesser degree, to other minds with which it comes into contact" (12). Likewise, for Zwerdling, the novel "record[s] the thoughts and impressions of its six main characters," whereas conversation and other "circumstantial reality ... have been virtually eliminated" (*Real World* 10).

41 While "The phantasm of the *subject* is a fictitious entity generated by philosophy," Cavarero writes (171), singularity unmasks the categories of "Man," "subject" and "individual" (26).

42 Woolf's politicised notion of the dramatic chorus in *The Waves* needs critical attention. Putzel observes about her use of choruses more generally that they stimulate audience response, "give voice to unspoken emotion" and allow her to

build a "'narrow bridge of art' connecting music, theater, poetry and fiction" (30). He also notes the capacity of the chorus in Woolf's writing to "transform a solitary 'reader' into part of a collective 'audience'" (116). In *The Waves*, however, the chorus does not have the democratic potential Woolf ascribes to the collective sharing of emotions in her unfinished essay "Anon"; rather, it anticipates her Freudian account, in *Three Guineas*, of societies as inherently prone to aggression.

43 Cavarero traces poetry back to "the centrality of the acoustic sphere in the bard's performance." She relies on Kristeva's theory of poetic writing to explore these links between the vocal and the textual, and notes that modernist writing is particularly effective in its vocal-textual subversion of language and autonomous subjectivity (10; see 132, 168). Like Kristeva, though, Cavarero nonetheless stresses that "In the signifying process, there is no symbolic without the semiotic. . . . the semiotic vocalic is therefore – at the same time – the precondition of the semantic function and its uncontrollable excess" (138).

44 Observing that the Latin *vox* is related etymologically to *vocare*, which means "to call" or "invoke," Cavarero defines the voice as "an invocation that is addressed to the other." This is the scene of the infant's first cry: the baby appeals to an ear as well as "to another voice which responds" (169).

45 See Elicia Clements's perceptive reading of *The Waves* in relation to Beethoven's String Quartet in B-flat Major, Opus 130, to which Woolf was listening while composing the novel. For Clements, Woolf's appropriation of musical devices highlights the ways in which music "facilitates [an] intermingling of 'form,' subjectivity, and cultural critique" (162). See also Emma Sutton on Woolf's political uses of Wagner's work in *The Waves* (Chapter 6). Sutton contrasts Bernard's last soliloquy and Wagner's emphasis on a "single, authoritative story" to the novel's celebration of "pluralist narratives" (140).

Bibliography

Abel, Elizabeth. *Virginia Woolf and the Fictions of Psychoanalysis*. U of Chicago P, 1989.

Abel Travis, Molly. "Eternal Fascism and Its 'Home Haunts' in the Leavises' Attacks on Bloomsbury and Woolf." Pawlowski, *Virginia Woolf and Fascism*, pp. 165–77.

"affect, *v.2*." *OED Online*, Oxford UP, Dec. 2018.

Allan, Tuzyline Jita. "The Death of Sex and the Soul in Mrs. Dalloway and Nella Larsen's Passing." Barrett and Cramer, pp. 95–114.

Allen, Judith. *Virginia Woolf and the Politics of Language*. Edinburgh UP, 2010.

Auerbach, Erich. *Mimesis: The Representation of Reality in Western Literature*. 1946. Doubleday, 1954.

Bahun, Sanja. *Modernism and Melancholia: Writing as Countermourning*. Oxford UP, 2014.

Banfield, Ann. *The Phantom Table: Woolf, Fry, Russell and the Epistemology of Modernism*. Cambridge UP, 2000.

Barrett, Eileen, and Patricia Cramer, editors. *Virginia Woolf: Lesbian Readings*. NYU Press, 1997.

Barthes, Roland. *The Pleasure of the Text*. Translated by Richard Miller, Hill and Wang, 1975.

Beer, Gillian. *Virginia Woolf: The Common Ground: Essays by Gillian Beer*. Edinburgh UP, 1996.

Bell, Clive. *Art*. 1914. Capricorn, 1958.

Bell, Quentin. "*A Room of One's Own* and *Three Guineas*." Pawlowski, *Virginia Woolf and Fascism*, pp. 13–20.

Bell, Quentin. *Virginia Woolf: A Biography. Vol. 2: Mrs Woolf, 1912–1941*. Hogarth, 1973.

Benjamin, Walter. "The Storyteller: Reflections on the Works of Nikolai Leskov." 1936. Translated by Harry Zohn. *The Novel: An Anthology of Criticism and Theory 1900–2000*, edited by Dorothy Hale, Blackwell, 2006, pp. 361–78.

Berlant, Lauren, editor. *Intimacy*. U of Chicago P, 2000.

Berlant, Lauren. "Intuitionists: History and the Affective Event." *American Literary History*, vol. 20, no. 4, Winter 2008, pp. 845–60.

Berman, Jessica. "Ethical Folds: Ethics, Aesthetics, Woolf." *MFS: Modern Fiction Studies*, vol. 50, no. 1, Spring 2004, pp. 151–72.

Berman, Jessica. *Modernist Commitments: Ethics, Politics, and Transnational Modernism*. Columbia UP, 2011.

Berman, Jessica. *Modernist Fiction, Cosmopolitanism and the Politics of Community*. Cambridge UP, 2001.

Bersani, Leo, and Adam Phillips. *Intimacies*. U of Chicago P, 2008.
Black, Naomi. "The Mothers' International: The Women's Co-operative Guild and Pacifist Feminism." *Women's Studies Int. Forum*, vol. 12, no. 6, 1984. pp. 467–76.
Black, Naomi. *Virginia Woolf as Feminist*. Cornell UP, 2004.
Bishop, E. L. "The Shaping of *Jacob's Room*: Woolf's Manuscript Revisions." *Twentieth Century Literature*, vol. 32, no. 1, Spring 1986, pp. 115–35.
Brennan, Theresa. *The Transmission of Affect*. Cornell UP, 2004.
Brooks, Peter. *Realist Vision*. Yale UP, 2005.
Bowlby, Rachel. *Feminist Destinations and Further Essays on Virginia Woolf*. Edinburgh UP, 1997.
Broughton, Panthea Reid. "The Blasphemy of Art: Fry's Aesthetics and Woolf's Non-'Literary' Stories." Gillespie, *The Multiple Muses of Virginia Woolf*, pp. 36–57.
Bullet, Gerald. "Virginia Woolf Soliloquises." 1931. McNees, pp. 8–9.
Butler, Judith. "The Body Politics of Julia Kristeva." Oliver, pp. 164–78.
Butler, Judith. "The Desire to Live: Spinoza's *Ethics* under Pressure." *Senses of the Subject*, Fordham University, 2015, pp. 63–79.
Butler, Judith. *Frames of War: When Is Life Grievable?* Verso, 2010.
Butler, Judith. *Gender Trouble: Feminism and the Subversion of Identity*. Routledge, 1990.
Butler, Judith. *Giving an Account of Oneself*. Fordham UP, 2005.
Butler, Judith. *Precarious Life: The Powers of Mourning and Violence*. Verso, 2004.
Caramagno, Thomas C. "Manic-Depressive Psychosis and Critical Approaches to Virginia Woolf's Life and Work." *PMLA*, vol. 103, no. 1, Jan. 1988, pp. 10–23.
Caramagno, Thomas C. *The Flight of the Mind: Virginia Woolf's Art and Manic-Depressive Illness*. U of California P, 1992.
Caughie, Pamela L. "Time's Exception: Response to Hilary Thompson." Ross, pp. 99–111.
Caughie, Pamela L. *Virginia Woolf and Postmodernism: Literature in Quest and Question of Itself*. U of Illinois P, 1991.
Caughie, Pamela L., and Diana L. Swanson, editors. *Virginia Woolf Writing the World: Selected Papers from the Twenty-Fourth Annual International Conference on Virginia Woolf*. Clemson UP, 2015.
Cavarero, Adriana. *For More than One Voice: Toward a Philosophy of Vocal Expression*. Translated by Paul A. Kottman, Stanford UP, 2005.
Cervetti, Nancy. "In the Breeches, Petticoats, and Pleasures of 'Orlando.'" *Journal of Modern Literature*, vol. 20, no. 2, Winter 1996, pp. 165–75.
Chanter, Tina. *Ethics of Eros: Irigaray's Rewriting of the Philosophers*. Routledge, 1995.
Chanter, Tina, editor. *Feminist Interpretations of Emmanuel Levinas*. The Pennsylvania State UP, 2001.
Childs, Donald J. *Modernism and Eugenics: Woolf, Eliot, Yeats, and the Culture of Degeneration*. Cambridge UP, 2001.
Cimitile, Maria C., and Elaine P. Miller, editors. *Returning to Irigaray: Feminist Philosophy, Politics, and the Question of Unity*. State U of New York P, 2007.

Clements, Elicia. "Transforming Musical Sounds into Words: Narrative Method in Virginia Woolf's *The Waves*." *Narrative*, vol. 13 no. 2, May 2005, pp. 160–81.

Clewell, Tammy. "Consolation Refused: Virginia Woolf, the Great War, and Modernist Mourning." *Modern Fiction Studies*, vol. 50, no.1, Spring 2004, pp. 197–223.

Cole, Sarah. *At the Violet Hour: Modernism and Violence in England and Ireland*. Oxford UP, 2012.

Comentale, Edward B. *Modernism, Cultural Production, and the British Avant-Garde*. Cambridge UP, 2004.

Cramer, Patricia Morgne. "Woolf and Theories of Sexuality." Randall and Goldman, pp. 129–48.

Cuddy-Keane, Melba. "Ethics." Ross, pp. 208–18.

Das, Santanu. *Touch and Intimacy in First World War Literature*. Cambridge UP, 2005.

Davies, Margaret Llewelyn, editor. 1931. *Life as We Have Known It*. Norton, 1975.

Derrida, Jacques. "By Force of Mourning." Translated by Pascale-Anne Brault and Michael Naas. *Critical Inquiry*, vol. 22, no. 2, Winter 1996, pp. 171–92.

Detloff, Madelyn. *The Persistence of Modernism: Loss and Mourning in the Twentieth Century*. Cambridge UP, 2009.

Detloff, Madelyn. "'Tis Not My Nature to Join in Hating, But in Loving': Toward Survivable Public Mourning." Rae, pp. 50–68.

Detloff, Madelyn. "Woolf and Lesbian Culture: Queering Woolf Queering." Randall and Goldman, pp. 342–52.

Deutscher, Penelope. *A Politics of Impossible Difference: The Later Work of Luce Irigaray*. Cornell UP, 2002.

Dickson, Albert, editor. *The Pelican Freud Library*. Vol. 12: *Civilization, Society and Religion:* Group Psychology, Civilization and Its Discontents *and Other Works*. Translated by James Strachey, Penguin, 1985.

Dowling, David. *Bloomsbury Aesthetics and the Novels of Forster and Woolf*. Macmillan, 1985.

Doyle, Laura. "'These Emotions of the Body': Intercorporeal Narrative in *To the Lighthouse*." *Twentieth Century Literature*, vol. 40, no. 1, Spring 1994, pp. 42–71.

DuPlessis, Rachel Blau. *Writing Beyond the Ending: Narrative Strategies of Twentieth-Century Women Writers*. Indiana UP, 1985.

Eliot, T. S. "Tradition and the Individual Talent." 1919. *The Norton Anthology of English Literature*, general editor Stephen Greenblatt, vol. 2, 9th edition, W. W. Norton & Company, 2012, pp. 2554–59.

Ellmann, Maud. *The Nets of Modernism: Henry James, Virginia Woolf, James Joyce, and Sigmund Freud*. Cambridge UP, 2010.

Fand, Roxanne J. *The Dialogic Self: Reconstructing Subjectivity in Woolf, Lessing, and Atwood*. Susquehanna UP, 1999.

Fisher, Jane. "'Silent as the Grave': Painting, Narrative, and the Reader in *Night and Day* and *To the Lighthouse*." Gillespie, *The Multiple Muses of Virginia Woolf*, pp. 90–109.

Flatley, Jonathan. *Affective Mapping: Melancholia and the Politics of Modernism*. Harvard UP, 2008.

Flint, Kate. "Revising *Jacob's Room*: Virginia Woolf, Women, and Language." *The Review of English Studies*, vol. 42, no. 167, 1991, pp. 361–79.
Forster, E. M. *Aspects of the Novel*. 1927. Penguin, 1970.
Forster, E. M. *Virginia Woolf*. Cambridge UP, 1942.
Freud, Sigmund. *Beyond the Pleasure Principle*. 1920. Edited and translated by James Strachey, Norton, 1989.
Freud, Sigmund. *Civilization and Its Discontents*. 1930. Dickson, pp. 243–340.
Freud, Sigmund. *Group Psychology and the Analysis of the Ego*. 1921. Dickson, pp. 91–166.
Freud, Sigmund. "Mourning and Melancholia." 1917. *The Standard Edition of the Complete Psychological Works of Sigmund Freud. Vol. XIV* (1914–1916): On the History of the Psycho-Analytic Movement; Papers on Metapsychology *and Other Works*, edited and translated by James Strachey, Hogarth, 1978, pp. 237–58.
Freud, Sigmund. "Thoughts for the Times on War and Death." 1915. Dickson, pp. 57–89.
Freud, Sigmund. *Why War?* Dickson, pp. 341–62.
Frost, Laura. "Stories of O: Modernism and Female Pleasure." in Högberg, *Modernist Intimacies* (forthcoming, EUP).
Froula, Christine. "*Mrs. Dalloway*'s Postwar Elegy: Women, War, and the Art of Mourning." *Modernism/Modernity*, vol. 9, no. 1, 2002, pp. 125–63.
Froula, Christine. *Virginia Woolf and the Bloomsbury Avant-Garde: War, Civilization, Modernity*. Columbia UP, 2004.
Fry, Roger. *Cézanne: A Study of His Development*. Hogarth, 1952.
Fry, Roger. "The Artist and Psycho-Analysis." 1924. *Psicoart*, vol. 1, no. 1, 2010, 1–23. Web. 16 July 2012.
Fry, Roger. *Transformations: Critical and Speculative Essays on Art*. Chatto & Windus, 1926.
Fry, Roger. *Vision and Design*. 1920. Edited by J. B. Bullen, Dover, 1998.
Gillespie, Diane F., editor. *The Multiple Muses of Virginia Woolf*. U of Missouri P, 1993.
Gillespie, Diane F. *The Sisters' Art: The Writing and Painting of Virginia Woolf and Vanessa Bell*. Syracuse UP, 1991.
Gillespie, Diane F. "Virginia Woolf, Vanessa Bell and Painting." *The Edinburgh Companion to Virginia Woolf and the Arts*, edited by Maggie Humm, Edinburgh UP, 2010.
Gillies, Mary Ann. *Henri Bergson and British Modernism*. McGill-Queen's UP, 1996.
Goldman, Jane. "Avant-Garde." Ross, pp. 225–36.
Goldman, Jane. "Burning Feminism: Woolf's Laboratory of Intimacy." Högberg, *Modernist Intimacies* (forthcoming).
Goldman, Jane. *Modernism, 1910–1945: Image to Apocalypse*. Palgrave, 2004.
Goldman, Jane. "1925, London, New York, Paris: Metropolitan Modernisms – Parallax and Palimpsest." *The Edinburgh Companion to Twentieth-Century Literatures in English*, edited by B. McHale and R. Stevenson, Edinburgh UP, 2006.
Goldman, Jane. *The Feminist Aesthetics of Virginia Woolf: Modernism, Post-Impressionism and the Politics of the Visual*. Cambridge UP, 1998.

Goldman, Jane, editor. *Virginia Woolf: To the Lighthouse, The Waves*. Columbia UP, 1998.

Gorsky, Susan. "'The Central Shadow': Characterization in *The Waves*." 1972. McNees, pp. 40–55.

Grey, Edward. *Twenty-Five Years 1892–1916*. Vol. 2, Frederick A. Stokes Co., 1937.

Halliwell, Martin. *Modernism and Morality: Ethical Devices in European and American Fiction*. Palgrave, 2001.

Hammond, Meghan Marie. *Empathy and the Psychology of Literary Modernism*. Edinburgh UP, 2010.

Handley, William R. "War and the Politics of Narration in *Jacob's Room*." Hussey, *Virginia Woolf and War*, pp. 110–33.

Havard-Williams, Margaret, and Peter Havard-Williams. "Mystical Experience in Virginia Woolf's *The Waves*." 1954. McNees, pp. 12–22.

Helt, Brenda, "Passionate Debates on 'Odious Subjects': Bisexuality and Woolf's Opposition to Theories of Androgyny and Sexual Identity." Helt and Madelyn Detloff, pp. 114–32.

Helt, Brenda, and Madelyn Detloff, editors. *Queer Bloomsbury*. Edinburgh UP, 2016.

Hinnov, Emily M. *Encountering Choran Community: Literary Modernism, Visual Culture, and Political Aesthetics in the Interwar Years*. Susquehanna UP, 2009.

Hollander, Rachel. "Novel Ethics: Alterity and Form in *Jacob's Room*." *Twentieth Century Literature: A Scholarly and Critical Journal*, vol. 53, no. 1, 2007, pp. 40–66.

Holtby, Winifred. "An Explorer's Record." 1931. McNees, pp. 5–7.

Hussey, Mark. "Introduction." Hussey, *Virginia Woolf and War*, pp. 110–33.

Hussey, Mark, editor. *Virginia Woolf and War: Fiction, Reality, and Myth*. Syracuse UP, 1991.

Hussey, Mark, et al. "Roundtable: Woolf and Violence." *Virginia Woolf Writing the World: Selected Papers from the Twenty-Fourth Annual International Conference on Virginia Woolf*, edited by Pamela L. Caughie and Diana L. Swanson, Clemson UP, 2015, pp. 2–22.

Hägglund, Martin. *Dying for Time: Proust, Woolf, Nabokov*. Harvard UP, 2012.

Högberg, Elsa. "The Melancholic Translations of Anon." *Trans-Woolf*, edited by Claire Davison-Pégon and Anne-Marie Smith-Di Biasio, Morlacchi Editore Perugia, 2017, pp. 45–63.

Högberg, Elsa, editor. *Modernist Intimacies*. Edinburgh UP, forthcoming.

Högberg, Elsa. "Virginia Woolf's Object-Oriented Ecology." Caughie and Swanson, pp. 148–53.

Högberg, Elsa, and Amy Bromley, editors. *Sentencing* Orlando: *Virginia Woolf and the Morphology of the Modernist Sentence*. Edinburgh UP, 2018.

Illouz, Eva. *Cold Intimacies: The Making of Emotional Capitalism*. Polity Press, 2007.

"intimate, *adj.* and *n.*" *OED Online*, Oxford UP, Dec. 2018.

Irigaray, Luce. *An Ethics of Sexual Difference*. 1984. Translated by Carolyn Burke and Gillian C. Gill, Athlone, 1993.

Irigaray, Luce. "The Poverty of Psychoanalysis." 1977. Translated by David Macey and Margaret Whitford, Whitford, pp. 79–104.

Irigaray, Luce. "The Power of Discourse and the Subordination of the Feminine." 1975. Translated by Catherine Porter and Carolyn Burke, Whitford, pp. 118–32.

Irigaray, Luce. *Sharing the World*. Continuum, 2008.

Irigaray, Luce. *The Way of Love*. Translated by Heidi Bostic and Stephen Pluháček, Continuum, 2002.

Jay, Martin. "Modernism and the Specter of Psychologism." Micale, pp. 352–65.

Jonsson, AnnKatrin. *Relations: Ethics and the Modernist Subject in James Joyce's* Ulysses, *Virginia Woolf's* The Waves *and Djuna Barnes's* Nightwood. Peter Lang, 2006.

Katz, Tamar. *Impressionist Subjects: Gender, Interiority, and Modernist Fiction in England*, U of Illinois P, 2000.

Katz, Tamar. "Modernism, Subjectivity, and Narrative Form: Abstraction in *The Waves*." *Narrative*, vol. 3, no. 3, Oct. 1995, pp. 232–51.

Keltner, S. K. *Kristeva: Thresholds*. Polity Press, 2011.

Klein, Melanie. "Mourning and Its Relation to Manic-Depressive States." *Love, Guilt and Reparation and Other Works 1921–1945*. Introduction by R. E. Money-Kyrle, Hogarth, 1975. *The International Psycho-Analytical Library*, edited by M. Masud R. Khan, no. 103, pp. 344–69.

Kolocotroni, Vassiliki. "Strange Cries and Ancient Songs: Woolf's Greek and the Politics of Intelligibility." Randall and Goldman, pp. 423–38.

Koppen, Randi. "Embodied Form: Art and Life in Virginia Woolf's *To the Lighthouse*." *New Literary History*, vol. 32, no. 2, Spring 2001, pp. 375–89.

Koulouris, Theodore. *Hellenism and Loss in the Works of Virginia Woolf*. Ashgate, 2010.

Knopp, Sherron E. "'If I Saw You Would You Kiss Me?': Sapphism and the Subversiveness of Virginia Woolf's *Orlando*." *PMLA*, vol. 103, no. 1, Jan. 1988, pp. 24–34.

Kristeva, Julia. *About Chinese Women*. 1974. Translated by Anita Barrows, Marion Boyars, 1986.

Kristeva, Julia. *Black Sun: Depression and Melancholia*. 1987. Translated by Leon S. Roudiez, Columbia UP, 1989.

Kristeva, Julia. *Intimate Revolt*. The Powers and Limits of Psychoanalysis. 1997. Translated by Jeanine Herman, Columbia UP, 2002.

Kristeva, Julia. "Oscillation between Power and Denial." 1974. Translated by Marilyn A. August. *New French Feminisms*, edited by Isabelle de Courtivron and Elaine Marks, Harvester, 1981, pp. 165–67.

Kristeva, Julia. *Revolution in Poetic Language*. 1974. Translated by Margaret Waller, Columbia UP, 1984.

Kristeva, Julia. *The Sense and Non-Sense of Revolt*. The Powers and Limits of Psychoanalysis. 1996. Translated by Jeanine Herman, Columbia UP, 2000.

Kristeva, Julia. *Strangers to Ourselves*. 1988. Translated by Leon S. Roudiez, Columbia UP, 1991.

Kumar, Shiv K. *Bergson and the Stream of Consciousness Novel*. Blackie & Son, 1962.

Lackey, Michael. "Modernist Anti-Philosophicalism and Virginia Woolf's Critique of Philosophy." *Journal of Modern Literature*, vol. 29, no. 4, Summer 2006, pp. 76–98.

Laurence, Patricia Ondek. *The Reading of Silence: Virginia Woolf in the English Tradition*. Stanford UP, 1991.

Lechte, John. "Art, Love, and Melancholy in the Work of Julia Kristeva." *Abjection, Melancholia, and Love: The Work of Julia Kristeva*, edited by Andrew Benjamin and John Fletcher, Routledge, 1990, pp. 24–41.

Lee, Hermione. *Virginia Woolf*. Vintage, 1997.

"letter, *n.1*." *OED Online*, Oxford UP, Dec. 2018.

Levenback, Karen. *Virginia Woolf and the Great War*. Syracuse UP, 1999.

Levenson, Michael H. *Modernism and the Fate of Individuality: Character and Novelistic Form from Conrad to Woolf*. Cambridge UP, 2004.

Levine, Caroline. *Forms: Whole, Rhythm, Hierarchy, Network*. Princeton UP, 2015.

Lewis, Pericles. "Proust, Woolf, and Modern Fiction." *The Romanic Review*, vol. 99, no. 1–2, 2008, pp. 77–86.

Lombroso, Cesare. *Criminal Man*. 1876. Introduction and translated by Mary Gibson and Nicole Hahn Rafter, Duke UP, 2006.

Love, Heather. *Feeling Backward: Loss and the Politics of Queer History*. Harvard UP, 2007.

MacCarthy, Desmond, "The Post-Impressionists." 1910. *Modernism: An Anthology of Sources and Documents*, edited by V. Kolocotroni, et al., U of Chicago P, 1998, pp. 174–78.

MacKay, Marina. *Modernism and World War II*. Cambridge UP, 2007.

Majumdar, Robin, and Allen McLaurin, editors. *Virginia Woolf: The Critical Heritage*. Routledge and Kegan Paul, 1975.

Marcus, Jane. *Art and Anger: Reading Like a Woman*. Ohio State UP, 1988.

Marcus, Jane. "Britannia Rules *The Waves*." 1991. McNees, pp. 75–96.

Marcus, Jane. "'No More Horses': Virginia Woolf on Art and Propaganda." Jane Marcus, *Art and Anger*, pp. 101–21.

Marcus, Jane. "Sapphistry: Narration as Lesbian Seduction in *A Room of One's Own*." Jane Marcus, Indiana UP, 1987. *Virginia Woolf and the Languages of Patriarchy*, pp. 163–87.

Marcus, Jane. "Storming the Toolshed." Jane Marcus, *Art and Anger*, pp. 182–200.

Marcus, Laura. "Woolf's Feminism and Feminism's Woolf." *The Cambridge Companion to Virginia Woolf*, edited by Susan Sellers, Cambridge UP, 2010, pp. 142–79.

Mares, C. J. "Reading Proust: Woolf and the Painter's Perspective." *Comparative Literature*, vol. 41, no. 4, Autumn 1989, pp. 327–59.

Matro, Thomas G. "Only Relations: Vision and Achievement in *To the Lighthouse*." *PMLA*, vol. 99, no. 2, 1984, pp. 212–24.

Matson, Patricia. "The Terror and the Ecstasy: The Textual Politics of Virginia Woolf's *Mrs Dalloway*." Mezei, *Ambiguous Discourse*, pp. 162–86.

Matz, Jesse. *Literary Impressionism and Modernist Aesthetics*. Cambridge UP, 2001.

Matz, Jesse. "T. E. Hulme, Henri Bergson, and the Cultural Politics of Psychologism." Micale, pp. 339–51.

McGee, Patrick. "The Politics of Modernist Form; or, Who Rules *The* Waves?" *Modern Fiction Studies*, vol. 38, no. 3, Autumn 1992, pp. 631–50.

McNees, Eleanor, editor. *Virginia Woolf: Critical Assessments. Critical Responses to the Novels* The Waves, The Years *and* Between the Acts; *Essays; Critical Evaluations; Comparative Studies*. Vol. 4, Helm Information, 1994.

Mepham, John. "Mourning and Modernism." *Virginia Woolf: New Critical Essays*, edited by Patricia Clements and Isobel Grundy, Barnes & Noble, 1983, pp. 137–56.

Meyer, Jessica. "Separating the Men from the Boys: Masculinity and Maturity in Understandings of Shell Shock in Britain." *Twentieth Century British History*, vol. 20, no. 1, 2009, pp. 1–22.

Mezei, Kathy, editor. *Ambiguous Discourse: Feminist Narratology & British Women Writers*. U of North Carolina P, 1996.

Mezei, Kathy. "Who Is Speaking Here? Free Indirect Discourse, Gender, and Authority in *Emma, Howards End*, and *Mrs. Dalloway*." Mezei, *Ambiguous Discourse*, pp. 66–92.

Micale, Mark S. "Introduction." Micale, pp. 1–19.

Micale, Mark S., editor. *The Mind of Modernism: Medicine, Psychology, and the Cultural Arts in Europe and America, 1880–1940*. Stanford UP, 2004.

Miller, Andrew John. *Modernism and the Crisis of Sovereignty*. Routledge, 2007.

Mills, Jean. *Virginia Woolf, Jane Ellen Harrison, and the Spirit of Modernist Classicism*. Ohio State UP, 2014.

Minow-Pinkney, Makiko. *Virginia Woolf and the Problem of the Subject: Feminine Writing in the Major Novels*. Rutgers UP, 1987.

Minow-Pinkney, Makiko. "Virginia Woolf 'Seen from a Foreign Land.'" *Abjection, Melancholia, and Love: The Work of Julia Kristeva*, edited by Andrew Benjamin and John Fletcher, Routledge, 1990, pp. 157–77.

Moi, Toril. *Sexual/Textual Politics: Feminist Literary Theory*. 1985. Routledge, 2002.

Monson, Tamlyn. "A Trick of the Mind: Alterity, Ontology, and Representation in Virginia Woolf's *The Waves*." *Modern Fiction Studies*, vol. 50, no. 1, Spring 2004, pp. 173–96.

Moore, G. E. *Principia Ethica*. Cambridge UP, 1903.

Nieland, Justus. *Feeling Modern: The Eccentricities of Public Life*. U of Illinois P, 2008.

Nordau, Max. *Degeneration*. 1892. Introduction by George L. Mosse, U of Nebraska P, 1993.

Nussbaum, Martha C. "The Window: Knowledge of Other Minds in Virginia Woolf's *To the Lighthouse*." *New Literary History*, vol. 26, no. 4, 1995, pp. 731–53.

Oliver, Kelly, editor. *Ethics, Politics, and Difference in Julia Kristeva's Writing*. Routledge, 1993.

Oser, Lee. *The Ethics of Modernism: Moral Ideas in Yeats, Eliot, Joyce, Woolf, and Beckett*. Cambridge UP, 2007.

Parker, Jo Alyson. *Narrative Form and Chaos Theory in Sterne, Proust, Woolf, and Faulkner*. Palgrave, 2007.

Parkes, Adam. "Lesbianism, History, and Censorship: *The Well of Loneliness* and the Suppressed Randiness of Virginia Woolf's *Orlando*." *Twentieth Century Literature*, vol. 40, no. 4, Winter 1994, pp. 434–60.

"passion, *n*." *OED Online*, Oxford UP, Dec. 2018.

Pawlowski, Merry M. "Towards a Feminist Theory of the State: Virginia Woolf and Wyndham Lewis on Art, Gender, and Politics." Pawlowski, *Virginia Woolf and Fascism*, pp. 39–55.

Pawlowski, Merry M., editor. *Virginia Woolf and Fascism: Resisting the Dictators' Seduction*. Palgrave, 2001.

Peebles, Catherine. "Knowing the Other: Ethics and the Future of Psychoanalysis." Cimitile and Miller, pp. 223–42.

Phillips, Kathy J. *Virginia Woolf against Empire*. U of Tennessee P, 1994.

Pippin, Robert B. *Modernism as a Philosophical Problem: On the Dissatisfactions of European High Culture*. Blackwell, 1999.

Prudente, Teresa. *A Specially Tender Piece of Eternity: Virginia Woolf and the Experience of Time*. Lexington, 2009.

Putzel, Steven. *Virginia Woolf and the Theater*. Fairleigh Dickinson UP, 2012.

Quigley, Megan. "Modern Novels and Vagueness." *Modernism/modernity*, vol. 15, no. 1, 2008, pp. 101–29.

Rabaté, Jean-Michel. *The Pathos of Distance: Affects of the Moderns*. Bloomsbury Academic, 2016.

Rae, Patricia, editor. *Modernism and Mourning*. Bucknell UP, 2007.

Ramazani, Jahan. *Poetry of Mourning: The Modern Elegy from Hardy to Heaney*. U of Chicago P, 1994.

Randall, Bryony, and Jane Goldman, editors. *Virginia Woolf in Context*. Cambridge UP, 2012.

Reed, Christopher. "Virginia Woolf's Relation to Bloomsbury Aesthetics." Gillespie, *The Multiple Muses of Virginia Woolf*, pp. 11–35.

Regan, Tom. *Bloomsbury's Prophet: G. E. Moore and the Development of His Moral Philosophy*. Temple UP, 1986.

Reynier, Christine. *Virginia Woolf's Ethics of the Short Story*. Palgrave Macmillan, 2009.

Rosenbaum, S. P. *Aspects of Bloomsbury: Studies in Modern English Literary and Intellectual History*. Macmillan, 1998.

Rosenbaum, S. P. *The Early Literary History of the Bloomsbury Group: Edwardian Bloomsbury*. Vol. 2, Macmillan, 1994.

Rosenbaum, S. P. *The Early Literary History of the Bloomsbury Group: Georgian Bloomsbury*, 1910–1914. Vol. 3, Palgrave Macmillan, 2003.

Rosenbaum, S. P. "The Philosophical Realism of Virginia Woolf." Rosenbaum, *Aspects of Bloomsbury*, pp. 1–36.

Ross, Stephen, editor. *Modernism and Theory: A Critical Debate*. Routledge, 2009.

Ryan, Derek. *Virginia Woolf and the Materiality of Theory: Sex, Animal, Life*. Edinburgh UP, 2015.

Ryan, Judith. *The Vanishing Subject: Early Psychology and Literary Modernism*. U of Chicago P, 1991.
Sanger, Tam, and Yvette Taylor, editors. *Mapping Intimacies: Relations, Exchanges, Affects*. Palgrave Macmillan, 2013.
Scott, Bonnie Kime. *Refiguring Modernism: Postmodern Feminist Readings of Woolf, West, and Barnes*. Vol. 2, Indiana UP, 1995.
"sensation, *n.*" *OED Online*, Oxford UP, Dec. 2018.
Sedgwick, Eve Kosofsky. *Touching Feeling: Affect, Pedagogy, Performativity*. Duke UP, 2003.
Seymour, Julie, and Paul Bagguley, editors. *Relating Intimacies: Power and Resistance*. Macmillan, 1999.
Shackleton, Edith. "Review." 1931. McNees, pp. 3–4.
Sherman, David. "A Plot Unraveling into Ethics: Woolf, Levinas, and 'Time Passes.'" *Woolf Studies Annual*, vol. 13, 2007, pp. 159–79.
Sherry, Vincent. *The Great War and the Language of Modernism*. Oxford UP, 2003.
Showalter, Elaine. *A Literature of Their Own: British Women Novelists from Brontë to Lessing*. Princeton UP, 1977.
Showalter, Elaine. *The Female Malady: Women, Madness, and English Culture, 1830–1980*. Virago, 1985.
Silver, Brenda. *Virginia Woolf's Reading Notebooks*. Princeton UP, 1983.
Snaith, Anna. *Virginia Woolf: Public and Private Negotiations*. Palgrave Macmillan, 2003.
Sontag, Susan. *Regarding the Pain of Others*. Penguin, 2004.
Spiro, Mia. *Anti-Nazi Modernism: The Challenges of Resistance in 1930s Fiction*. Northwestern UP, 2013.
Spiropoulou, Angeliki. *Virginia Woolf, Modernity and History: Constellations with Walter Benjamin*. Palgrave Macmillan, 2010.
Stanford Friedman, Susan. "Lyric Subversion of Narrative in Women's Writing: Virginia Woolf and the Tyranny of Plot." *Reading Narrative: Form, Ethics, Ideology*, edited by James Phelan, Ohio State UP, 1989, pp. 162–85.
Stewart, Jack. *Colour, Space, and Creativity: Art and Ontology in Five British Writers*. Farleigh Dickinson UP, 2008.
Stonebridge, Lyndsey. *The Destructive Element: British Psychoanalysis and Modernism*. Palgrave, 1998.
Sutton, Emma. *Virginia Woolf and Classical Music: Politics, Aesthetics, Form*. Edinburgh UP, 2013.
Sykes, Gerald. "Modernism." 1931. McNees, pp. 10–11.
Tate, Trudi. *Modernism, History and the First World War*. Manchester UP, 1998.
Taylor, Chloë. "Kristevan Themes in Virginia Woolf's *The Waves*." *Journal of Modern Literature*, vol. 29, no. 3, Spring 2006, pp. 57–77.
Taylor, Julie. *Modernism and Affect*. Edinburgh UP, 2015.
Torgovnick, Marianna. *The Visual Arts, Pictorialism, and the Novel: James, Lawrence and Woolf*. Princeton UP, 1985.

Walkowitz, Rebecca L. *Cosmopolitan Style: Modernism Beyond the Nation.* Columbia UP, 2006.

Wall, Kathleen. "Significant Form in *Jacob's Room*: Ekphrasis and Elegy." *Texas Studies in Literature and Language*, vol. 44, no. 3, Autumn 2002, pp. 302–23.

Walsh, Kelly S. "The Unbearable Openness of Death: Elegies of Rilke and Woolf." *Journal of Modern Literature*, vol. 32, no. 4, Summer 2009, pp. 1–21.

Westling, Louise. "Virginia Woolf and the Flesh of the World." *New Literary History*, vol. 30, no. 4, 1999, pp. 855–75.

Whitford, Margaret. "Irigaray and the Culture of Narcissism." Cimitile and Miller, pp. 205–22.

Whitford, Margaret, editor. *The Irigaray Reader*, Blackwell, 1991.

Williams, Raymond. "The Significance of 'Bloomsbury' as a Social and Cultural Group." *Keynes and the Bloomsbury Group*, edited by D. Crabtree et al., pp. 40–67.

Wolfe, Jesse. *Bloomsbury, Modernism, and the Reinvention of Intimacy.* Cambridge UP, 2011.

Woolf, Virginia. *Between the Acts.* 1941. Edited and Introduction by Frank Kermode, Oxford UP, 2008.

Woolf, Virginia. *The Complete Shorter Fiction of Virginia Woolf.* Edited by Susan Dick, Harcourt, 1989.

Woolf, Virginia. *The Diary of Virginia Woolf.* Edited by Anne Olivier Bell and Andrew McNeillie, Penguin, 1979–85. 5 vols.

Woolf, Virginia. *The Essays of Virginia Woolf.* Edited by Andrew McNeillie (vols 1–4) and Stuart N. Clarke (vols. 5–6), Hogarth, 1986–2011. 6 vols.

Woolf, Virginia. *Jacob's Room.* 1922. Edited and Introduction by Sue Roe, Penguin, 1992.

Woolf, Virginia. *The Letters of Virginia Woolf.* Edited by Nigel Nicolson and Joanne Trautmann, Hogarth, 1975–80. 6 vols.

Woolf, Virginia. *Moments of Being: Autobiographical Writings.* 1976. Edited by Jeanne Schulkind and Introduction by Hermione Lee, Pimlico, 2002.

Woolf, Virginia. *Mrs Dalloway.* 1925. Edited and Introduction by David Bradshaw, Oxford UP, 2009.

Woolf, Virginia. *Orlando: A Biography.* 1928. Edited by Brenda Lyons, Introduction and Notes by Sandra M. Gilbert, Penguin, 1993.

Woolf, Virginia. *Roger Fry: A Biography.* 1940. Introduction by Frances Spalding, Hogarth, 1991.

Woolf, Virginia. *A Room of One's Own.* 1929. A Room of One's Own *and* Three Guineas, edited and Introduction by Morag Shiach, Oxford UP, 2008.

Woolf, Virginia. *Three Guineas.* 1938. A Room of One's Own *and* Three Guineas, edited and Introduction by Morag Shiach, Oxford UP, 2008.

Woolf, Virginia. *To the Lighthouse.* 1927. Edited by Stella McNichol, Introduction and Notes by Hermione Lee, Penguin, 1992.

Woolf, Virginia. *The Waves.* 1931. Edited and Introduction by Kate Flint, Penguin, 2006.

Woolf, Virginia. *The Years*. 1937. Edited and Introduction by Anna Snaith, Cambridge UP, 2013.

Ziarek, Ewa. "Kristeva and Levinas: Mourning, Ethics, and the Feminine." Oliver, pp. 62–78.

Zunshine, Lisa. *Why We Read Fiction: Theory of the Mind and the Novel*. Ohio State UP, 2006.

Zwerdling, Alex. "*Jacob's Room*: Woolf's Satiric Elegy." *ELH*, vol. 48, no. 4, Winter 1981, pp. 894–913.

Zwerdling, Alex. "*Mrs. Dalloway* and the Social System." *PMLA*, vol. 92, no. 1, Jan. 1977, pp. 69–82.

Zwerdling, Alex. *Virginia Woolf and the Real World*. U of California P, 1986.

Index

Abel, Elizabeth 18, 19, 89, 190 nn.27–9, 199 n.13, 200 n.20, 200 n.30
affect 44, 52, 59, 66, 70, 73–4, 76, 194 n.17, 197 nn.43–4, 201 n.25. *See also* intimacy, and interiority; intimacy, via *jouissance;* reparative reading; textual melancholia
  affective economy of modern letters 39, 46, 50, 57, 67, 68, 74
  affective mapping 71, 72, 73
  detachment 25, 38, 60–74, 95–8, 101, 119, 144 (*see also* formalism)
    ethical value of 25–6, 39–40, 60–74
    from ethics 60, 62
    from intense emotion 37, 53, 56–7, 67, 68, 70, 72, 101, 197 n.44
    as loss 25, 38, 59, 63
  and empathy 24
  and ethics 12, 23, 24
  joy 26, 76, 78, 83, 95–6
  oceanic feeling 20, 56, 171, 180, 213 n.32
  primal sadness 26, 44, 52, 53, 51–60, 72, 73–4, 76, 79, 197 n.43
  repression of 27, 80, 82, 83
  "reuniting with affect" (Kristeva) 15, 27, 76, 80, 85, 86, 95–106 (*see also* intimacy, intimate revolt [Kristeva])
  sharing of 24, 37, 39, 67, 68, 195 n.27
  studies 5, 6, 22, 23, 66, 78, 96
  as a verb 2, 4, 37, 50
Allen, Judith 22
androgyny 11, 106, 188 n.8, 203 n.37
Auerbach, Erich 135, 139, 207 n.27, 208 n.28

Bagguley, Paul 6
Bahun, Sanja 42, 43, 45, 67, 193 n.11, 193 n.14, 194 n.17

Bakhtin, Mikhail 112
Banfield, Ann 22, 125–7, 129, 130, 147, 205 nn.11–12, 205 n.14, 206 n.18, 207 n.24
Barrett, Eileen 189 n.18
Barthes, Roland 96, 100, 105, 201 n.26
Beer, Gillian 52
Bell, Anne Olivier 199 n.16
Bell, Clive 116, 130, 203 n.1, 205 n.14, 206 n.18, 208 n.35
Bell, Quentin 198 n.8, 209 n.2, 210 n.8, 211 n.12, 213 n.28
Bell, Vanessa 130, 206 n.18
Benjamin, Walter 31–2, 32–3, 37, 38, 50, 71, 192 n.7
  "The Storyteller: Reflections on the Works of Nikolai Leskov" 31
Bennett, Arnold 2–3, 28, 92, 192 n.1, 210 n.10
Bergson, Henri 101, 102, 202 n.31
Berlant, Lauren 6, 66
Berman, Jessica 9, 12, 116, 163, 171, 180, 203 n.1, 204 n.3, 211 n.19, 213 n.30, 214 n.35
Bersani, Leo 6
Bishop, E. L. 195 n.30
Black, Naomi 210 n.6
Blake, William 15
Bloomsbury group 12–13, 18–19, 34, 126, 145, 168, 189 n.18, 190 nn.30–1, 196 nn.38–9, 199 n.10, 203 n.2. *See also* Bell, Clive; Bell, Vanessa; Fry, Roger; Moore, G. E.; Post-Impressionism; Russell, Bertrand
Bon, Gustave Le 197 n.44, 212 n.26, 213 n.29
Bowlby, Rachel 145, 188 n.1, 203 n.37
Bradshaw, David 203 n.38
Brecht, Bertoldt 71
Brennan, Theresa 195 n.27

Bromley, Amy   202 n.34
Brooks, Peter   195 n.32
Broughton, Panthea Reid   206 n.20
Bullet, Gerard   151, 212 n.23
Butler, Judith   8–9, 13–15, 18, 21, 25, 26, 27, 28, 171, 189 n.21, 189 n.23, 195 n.32
  Frames of War: When Is Life Grievable?   91, 158–9, 174, 180
  Gender Trouble: Feminism and the Subversion of Identity   11–12
  Giving an Account of Oneself   14–15, 83, 86, 106–7, 110, 160, 161, 162, 163–4, 176
  Precarious Life: The Powers of Mourning and Violence   16–17, 55, 56, 83, 158–9, 163, 163–4, 173, 174, 178, 180, 181, 190 n.24

Caramagno, Thomas C.   80, 81, 198 n.4, 198 n.6, 201 n.24, 201 n.27
Caughie, Pamela   188 n.10, 191 n.36
Cavarero, Adriana   28, 181–3, 184–5, 214 n.41, 215 n.43, 215 n.44
Cervetti, Nancy   11, 188 n.16
Cézanne, Paul   130, 147
Chanter, Tina   189 n.19
Childs, Donald J.   198 n.7
Clements, Elicia   215 n.45
Clewell, Tammy   41–2, 46, 72, 193 n.9, 195 n.31, 197 nn.42–3, 205 n.17
Cole, Sarah   6, 191 n.38, 201 n.25
Comentale, Edward P.   63, 66, 196 n.39
Cramer, Patricia Morgne   12, 189 n.18
Cuddy-Keane, Melba   60–1

Das, Santanu   189 n.20
Davies, Margaret Llewelyn   153, 201 n.6
Derrida, Jacques   46
Detloff, Madelyn   12, 24, 42, 174, 189 n.18, 195 n.23,195 n.29
Deutscher, Penelope   189 n.19
Dowling, David   204 n.2, 206 n.18, 206 n.20
Doyle, Laura   204 n.4
DuPlessis, Rachel Blau   7, 86–7, 199 n.12

Einstein, Albert   19, 213 n.27
Eliot, T. S.   23, 192 n.1
Ellmann, Maud   48–9, 191 n.36, 194 n.21

eros. *See* ethics, of eros (Irigaray); intimacy, erotic
ethics. *See also* affect, detachment; Butler, Judith; formalism; Irigaray, Luce; Levinas, Emmanuel; Moore, G. E.
  accountability (Butler)   14–17, 86–7, 106–13, 121, 159–64
  of eros (Irigaray)   12, 51–2, 116, 189 n.19
  Post-Impressionist   4, 27, 64, 115–50
  post-Levinasian   8–9, 12–13, 16–17, 21–2, 45, 53–4, 73–4, 115–16, 158, 166–7, 179
  war as crisis for   20–1, 23–5, 32–6, 41–2, 46, 60–1, 67–70, 73–4

Fand, Roxanne J.   112, 189 n.22, 203 n.40
feminist criticism and theory   6–7, 9–12, 84, 152, 189 n.19, 203 n.37, 204 n.3, 210 n.6, 210 n.8, 211 n.12, 213 n.27, 214 n.35
Fisher, Jane   122
Flatley, Jonathan   71, 74, 194 n.17
Flint, Kate   192 nn.5–6, 214 n.33
formalism   26–7, 60–74, 116–17, 118–25, 134, 137–8, 143–4, 153, 203 nn.1–2, 204 n.4. *See also* affect, detachment; Bell, Clive; Fry, Roger; Post-Impressionism; textual melancholia
Forster, E. M.   120, 192 n.1, 204 nn.8–9, 209 n.2
Foucault, Michel   78, 81
Freud, Sigmund   17–21, 89, 102–3, 190 n.29, 199 n.10, 199 n.12, 200 n.20, 202 n.33, 208 n.32, 215 n.42
  Beyond the Pleasure Principle   19, 90
  Civilization and Its Discontents   18, 20–1, 49, 90, 90–1, 191 n.32, 191 n.33, 194 n.22, 213 n.27, 213 n.32
  The Ego and the Id   194 n.17
  Group Psychology and the Analysis of the Ego   20, 168, 171, 191 n.33, 195 n.22, 197 n.44, 212 n.26, 213 n.27, 213 n.29
  "Mourning and Melancholia"   35, 37, 72–3, 193 n.9, 197 n.43

"Thoughts for the Times on War and Death" 18, 20, 21, 42, 90, 191 nn.32–3
Why War? 19, 49, 213 n.27
Frost, Laura 97, 98
Froula, Christine 6, 18–19, 34, 81–2, 101, 168, 190 n.25, 190 n.30, 198 n.9, 199 n.10, 210 n.7, 211 n.15
Fry, Roger 19, 63–72, 116–23, 125–7, 131–3, 203 nn.1–2, 204 nn.3–4, 204 n.9, 205 n.14, 206 n.18, 206 n.20, 207 n.23, 208 n.31, 208 n.33
  "The Artist and Psycho-Analysis" 208 n.32
  "An Essay in Aesthetics" 60, 61–2, 68–9, 70, 71, 72, 118, 119–20, 144
  "The French Post-Impressionists" 64, 143
  "Retrospect" 118, 144
  "Some Questions in Esthetics" 118–19, 204 n.7, 207 n.26
  Transformations 118–19, 130, 132–3, 134, 146, 147, 204 n.7, 207 n.26
  Vision and Design 64, 143–5, 146, 147–8, 204 n.5, 205 n.10

Galsworthy, John 192 n.1, 210 n.10
Gillespie, Diane F. 203 n.2, 206 n.18
Gillies, Mary Ann 101–2, 202 n.31
Goldman, Jane 48, 132, 189 n.22, 195 n.26, 197 n.1, 203 n.2, 204 n.6, 206 n.18, 207 n.25, 208 n.29
Gorsky, Susan 151
Grey, (Sir) Edward, British Foreign Secretary (1905–16) 46, 194 n.18

Hall, Radclyffe 188 n.16
Halliwell, Martin 60, 196 n.36
Hammond, Meghan Marie 24
Handley, William R. 7, 36, 42, 56, 193 n.10, 196 n.40
Havard-Williams, Peter and Margaret 209 n.4, 214 n.40
Helt, Brenda 189 n.18, 203 n.37
Hinnov, Emily M. 106, 188 n.13

Hollander, Rachel 7–8, 50, 51–2, 54, 60, 189 n.19
Holtby, Winifred 151, 214 n.40
Hussey, Mark 16, 187 n.4
Hägglund, Martin 105, 202 n.36
Högberg, Elsa 202 n.34, 205 nn.15–16

Illouz, Eva 6
intimacy. *See also* affect, affective economy of modern letters; affect, and empathy; affect, oceanic feeling; affect, "reuniting with affect" (Kristeva); affect, sharing of; affect, as a verb; Berman, Jessica; Butler, Judith; Cavarero, Adriana; ethics; Freud, Sigmund; Irigaray, Luce; Klein, Melanie; Kristeva, Julia; Post-Impressionism; psychoanalysis, identification; psychoanalysis, *jouissance*; soliloquy; voice
  beyond emotional, erotic and physical attachment 4–6, 12–13, 20–1, 40, 52, 69, 108, 139–40, 145, 158
  as emotional and physical attachment 1, 4–6, 12–13, 21, 116, 145
  erotic 11–12, 40, 45–6, 48–9, 51–2, 68, 70, 74, 96–8, 116, 189 n.17, 189 n.19, 194 n.22, 197 n.1
  and interiority 2, 23, 89
    conveyed 2, 3, 13, 94
    shared 2, 4, 20, 75, 93, 112, 115–16, 143–6, 165
  intimate revolt (Kristeva) 15–16, 26, 28, 76, 83, 85–6, 94, 95–106, 159, 164–7, 181
  via introspection 2, 13–14, 16–17, 23, 76, 79–80, 83, 87, 158, 182, 75–113, 151–86 *passim* (*see also* intimacy, intimate revolt [Kristeva])
  via *jouissance* 26, 76, 95–106, 146 (*see also* psychoanalysis, *jouissance*)
  as knowledge and familiarity 2, 4, 5–6, 140
  via letters 26, 37–40, 49–51, 72, 74, 168, 192 n.6

literary intimacy, post-war crisis
  of   25, 32, 33, 37, 38, 54–5,
  66
non-heteronormative   11–12, 97–8
pre-modern and archaic   25–6, 38,
  40–1, 41–51, 55, 62–3, 67–8, 79
and print technology   50–2, 67, 74,
  195 n.26
as private-public nexus   6, 9
as return to the pre-subjective   9,
  14–15, 20, 27, 95, 103, 106–13,
  141, 159–64, 172, 178
as shared perception   3, 4, 139–50,
  115–50 *passim,* 163, 172–3
and unfamiliarity   4, 89, 106–13,
  140–1
as unity and oneness   1–2, 13, 24–5,
  40, 115–16, 139–50, 157–8, 163
Irigaray, Luce   8–9, 12, 13–15, 18, 21,
  119, 123–4, 189 n.19, 189 n.21,
  189 n.23
  Sharing the World   27, 115–17, 123–4,
  125, 129, 134–5, 135–6, 138–9,
  140–2, 145–6
  The Way of Love   115, 123, 141

James, Henry   204 n.8
Jameson, Fredric   71
Jay, Martin   200 n.17
Jonsson, AnnKatrin   7, 8, 166, 189 n.22,
  211 n.18, 212 n.20, 212
jouissance. See under intimacy;
  psychoanalysis
Joyce, James   192 n.1

Kant, Immanuel   203 n.1
Katz, Tamar   200 n.17, 209 n.5
Keltner, S. K.   89, 200 n.19, 202 n.33
Keynes, John Maynard   19, 82, 190 n.25,
  190 n.30, 199 n.10
Klein, Melanie   19, 78–9, 90–1, 190 n.29,
  190 n.31, 194 n.17, 197 n.2,
  200 n.20, 208 n.30
Knopp, Sherron E.   189 n.17
Kolocotroni, Vassiliki   194 n.19, 195 n.28,
  197 n.42
Koppen, Randi   204 n.4, 208 n.31
Koulouris, Theodore   47, 68, 194 n.19,
  196 n.40, 197 n.42

Kristeva, Julia   8–11, 13–17, 21, 43–6,
  83–7, 166–7, 188 n.13, 189 n.21,
  202 n.29, 214 n.34, 215 n.43
  About Chinese Women   165, 212 n.22,
  214 n.36
  *Black Sun: Depression and
    Melancholia*   43, 47, 52, 53, 55,
    56, 57–8, 59, 74, 76, 79
  Intimate Revolt   14, 15, 85, 94, 95–6,
    100, 102–3, 104, 106, 159,
    164
  Revolution in Poetic Language   10,
    83–5, 87, 165, 212 n.21
  *The Sense and Non-Sense of
    Revolt*   85, 95, 99, 102–3, 159,
    164–5
Kumar, Shiv K.   202 n.31

Lacan, Jacques   189 n.23, 214 n.33
Lackey, Michael   63, 205 n.13
Laurence, Patricia Ondek   199 n.14
Lawrence, D. H.   192 n.1
Leavis, F. R. and Q. D.   209 n.2
Lechte, John   193 n.15
Lee, Hermione   80, 81, 197 n.42, 198 n.8,
  211 n.12
Leroy, Louis   132
Levenback, Karen L.   6, 201 n.28
Levenson, Michael   188 n.11
Levinas, Emmanuel   7–9, 12, 54,
  158, 167, 179, 182, 189 n.19,
  205 n.17, 211 n.18
Levine, Caroline   102, 153, 170
Lewis, Pericles   201 n.22
LGBTQ studies. *See* queer theory
Lombroso, Cesare   203 n.39
Love, Heather   35

MacCarthy, Desmond   204 n.6
MacKay, Marina   211 n.12
Marcus, Jane   6, 152–3, 187 n.4, 191 n.38,
  200 n.18, 209 n.2, 210 nn.8–9,
  213 n.31, 214 n.35
Marcus, Laura   203 n.37
Mares, C. J.   117, 203 n.2, 206 n.19
Matro, Thomas G.   122
Matson, Patricia   199 n.11, 200 n.21,
  201 n.25
Matz, Jesse   132, 200 n.17, 207 n.23

melancholia. *See under* psychoanalysis; textual melancholia
Mepham, John   192 n.2, 192 n.5, 195 n.32, 196 n.34, 196 n.40
Meyer, Jessica   198 n.5, 201 n.28
Mezei, Kathy   112
Micale, Mark S.   88, 199 n.17
Miller, Andrew John   6, 156, 169, 190 n.26
Mills, Jean   25, 194 n.20, 196 n.40
Minow-Pinkney, Makiko   7, 9–10, 84–5, 165, 167, 199 n.13, 202 n.29, 203 n.37, 212 n.20, 212 n.24
Mitchell, Silas   198 n.6
Moi, Toril   6–7, 81, 84–5, 188 n.9, 199 n.14, 203 n.37
Monson, Tamlyn   7–8, 166–7, 179, 211 n.18, 212 n.20, 212 n.25
Moore, G. E.   63–4, 66, 69, 145, 196 n.41, 205 n.11
Mosley, Oswald   213 n.30
mourning   34–8, 40–1, 41–51, 79, 192 nn.2–3, 192 n.7, 193 n.8, 193 nn.11–12, 193 n.31, 197 n.42. *See also* psychoanalysis, melancholia; textual melancholia
 compensatory   41–2, 195 n.29
 as consolation refused   41–6, 53–4, 57–8, 205 n.17
 consolatory (*see* mourning, compensatory)
 countermourning (Bahun)   42–3
 non-lethal mourning (Butler)   55–6

Nerval, Gérard de   55
Nieland, Justus   23
Nordau, Max   203 n.39
Nussbaum, Martha C.   140

Oser, Lee   62, 63–4, 66
Owen, Wilfred   69

pacifism   6, 15–16, 27–8, 152–9, 165, 171, 185, 151–86 *passim*, 191 n.38, 210 n.6, 211 n.12
Parker, Jo Alyson   202 n.35
Parkes, Adam   11, 188 n.16
Pawlowski, Merry M.   211 n.13

Peebles, Catherine   190 n.23
Phillips, Adam   6
Phillips, Kathy   210 n.9, 213 n.31
Pippin, Robert B.   33–4, 35, 49, 192 n.2, 196 nn.36–7
Plath, Sylvia   212 n.22
Post-Impressionism   4, 27, 61, 64–5, 115–20, 204 n.6, 207 nn.24–5. *See also* Bell, Clive; Bell, Vanessa; Fry, Roger
Proust, Marcel   67, 95–6, 99, 200 n.22
Prudente, Teresa   102, 202 n.31
psychoanalysis   14–15, 17–19, 24, 89–91, 159, 189 n.23, 190 n.29, 190 n.31, 191 n.36, 208 n.33. *See also* Freud, Sigmund; Klein, Melanie; Kristeva, Julia
 aggression   17–21, 82, 89–91
 and ethics   14–15, 19–21, 74, 90–1, 107, 110, 159, 171
 identification   20, 72–3, 171, 194 n.17
 jouissance   10, 15, 23, 26, 76–7, 95–106, 146, 202 n.29 (*see also* intimacy, via *jouissance*)
 matricide (Kristeva)   41–51, 55, 57, 72–3, 79
 melancholia   26, 35, 41–4, 45–7, 52–3, 55–60, 72–4
 repression   9–10, 19–20, 42, 76, 82, 84, 90–2, 96–8, 198 n.5, 200 n.20
Putzel, Steven   214 n.39, 214 n.42

queer theory   11–12, 97–8
Quigley, Megan   205 n.13, 206 n.22

Rae, Patricia   193 n.12
Ramazani, Jahan   41, 45, 58, 193 n.11
Randall, Bryony   191 n.35
Reed, Christopher   206 n.20, 207 n.27
Regan, Tom   63, 66, 69, 145, 196 n.41
reparative reading   26–7, 78–9, 82, 85, 94, 105, 112–13, 125, 167, 197 n.2, 200 n.20
Reynier, Christine   188 n.11
rhythm   102, 104, 122, 128, 164–71, 182
Ricoeur, Paul   78, 102, 202 n.31
Rilke, Rainer Maria   193 n.9
Rosenbaum, S. P.   196 n.38, 204 n.2
Ross, Stephen   21

Russell, Bertrand   125–7, 129, 205 n.11, 205 n.13
Ryan, Derek   22, 191 n.35
Ryan, Judith   200 n.17

Sackville-West, Vita   12, 51, 189 n.17
Sanger, Tam   6
Sassoon, Siegfried   69
Savage, George   81, 198 n.4, 198 n.6
Scott, Bonnie Kime   9–10, 97–8, 203 n.37
Sedgwick, Eve Kosofsky   78–9, 82, 96, 197 n.2
Seymour, Julie   6
Shackleton, Edith   151
Sherman, David   7–8, 205 n.17
Sherry, Vincent   6, 34
Showalter, Elaine   6–7, 80, 188 n.9, 198 n.5, 201 n.28
Silver, Brenda   210 n.10
Snaith, Anna   187 n.6
soliloquy   27–8, 151–86, 214 n.38. *See also* intimacy, and interiority; intimacy, as return to the pre-subjective; intimacy, as shared perception; intimacy, as unity and oneness; intimacy, intimate revolt (Kristeva); intimacy, via introspection; voice
Sontag, Susan   24
Sophocles   67
Spiropoulou, Angeliki   22, 47, 67, 72, 192 n.7
Stanford Friedman, Susan   7, 192 n.5
Stephen, Leslie   125–6, 127, 205 n.11
Stewart, Jack   208 n.34
Stonebridge, Lyndsey   19, 90, 170, 190 n.31, 200 n.20, 208 n.31, 208 n.33, 214 n.36
Strachey, Lytton   192 n.1
Sutton, Emma   215 n.45
Sykes, Gerald   152, 209 n.2

Tate, Trudi   194 n.18
Taylor, Chloë   167, 212 n.22, 214 n.34, 214 n.36
Taylor, Julie   22–3, 23, 212 n.24
Taylor, Yvette   6

textual melancholia   23, 25–6, 31–74, 79, 194 n.17, 196 nn.33–4. *See also* formalism; mourning; psychoanalysis, melancholia
Tolstoy, Leo   144
Torgovnick, Marianna   203 n.2, 205 n.10, 205 n.14, 206 n.19, 207 n.24
Travis, Abel   211 n.12, 211 n.15
Tsvetaieva, Maria   212 n.22

voice   36, 37, 38, 51, 53, 75, 100, 112–13, 124, 152, 165–6, 181–6, 215 n.44
vulnerability   28, 158–9, 162, 174–5, 176, 178, 180, 185, 151–86 *passim*, 190 n.24

Walkowitz, Rebecca   6, 82, 92, 199 n.11, 200 n.21, 211 n.14, 211 n.17
Wall, Kathleen   58
Walsh, Kelly S.   193 n.9
Wells, H. G.   2–3, 28, 92, 192 n.1, 210 n.10, 211 n.13
Westling, Louise   204 n.4
Whitford, Margaret   190 n.23
Whitman, Walt   197 n.1
Williams, Raymond   196 n.39
Wolfe, Jesse   12–13
Woolf, Leonard   19, 127, 129, 190 n.30, 199 n.10
Woolf, Virginia, writings
  "Anon"   32, 38, 39, 43, 51, 52, 62–3, 67, 195 n.27, 215 n.42
  Between the Acts   39, 170, 195 n.22, 197 n.44
  "Character in Fiction"   2, 3, 6, 31, 32, 33, 40, 92, 191 n.1, 210 n.10
  The Diary of Virginia Woolf
    vol. 1   8, 54
    vol. 2   11, 26, 75, 77, 78, 92, 98–9, 101
    vol. 3   128, 155, 167, 181, 182, 189 n.17, 193 n.16, 199 n.16, 209 n.3, 212 n.23
    vol. 5   18
  "Freudian Fiction"   18, 89
  "How It Strikes a Contemporary"   32, 191 n.1
  "Is Fiction an Art?"   120

Jacob's Room 2, 7, 25–6, 35–67, 69–74, 192 n.6, 193 n.10, 194 nn.19–20, 195 n.30, 196 nn.33–4, 197 n.43
"The Leaning Tower" 33
The Letters of Virginia Woolf 51, 96, 166
"Life and the Novelist" 65
"The Mark on the Wall" 92
"Modern Fiction" 2, 65, 79, 206 n.22
Moments of Being 202 n.30
Mrs Dalloway 18, 26–7, 51–2, 75–113, 197 n.1, 198 n.9, 199 nn.13–14, 200 n.21, 201 nn.24–8, 202 n.29, 202 nn.35–6, 203 n.41
"On Not Knowing Greek" 63, 66, 73–4
Orlando: A Biography 11–12, 188 n.16, 189 n.17
"Phases of Fiction" 200 n.22
"Pictures" 120
"Poetry, Fiction and the Future" 33, 191 n.1
"Professions for Women" 88, 153, 210 n.6
"The Reader" 38, 52, 62–3
Roger Fry: A Biography 120–2, 125, 128, 143
A Room of One's Own 3, 6–7, 10, 11, 62, 76–7, 86–8, 177–8, 198 n.7
"A Sketch of the Past" 202 n.30, 208 n.34

Speech to the London and National Society for Women's Service 88
"The Sun and the Fish" 48
"Thoughts on Peace in an Air Raid" 15, 25, 66, 155
Three Guineas 16, 19–25, 28, 153–9, 161, 163, 164, 168–71, 183, 210 nn.9–11, 211 n.12, 213 n.27, 213 n.29, 213 n.31
  Typescript from Berg collection 156–7
To the Lighthouse 1–2, 4, 15, 27, 40, 50, 115–17, 119–25, 127–50, 172, 205 n.17, 206 n.21, 209 n.36
"An Unwritten Novel" 2
"Walter Sickert: A Conversation" 206 n.19
The Waves 15–16, 27–8, 151–5, 158–86, 209 nn.4–5, 211 nn.18–19, 212 nn.20–5, 213 nn.30–1, 214 nn.33–4, 214 n.36, 214 nn.38–40, 214 n.42, 215 n.45
"Why Art To-Day Follows Politics" 65–6
The Years 152, 194 n.18, 210 nn.9–10

Ziarek, Ewa 45, 57
Zunshine, Lisa 203 n.41
Zwerdling, Alex 72, 80, 81–2, 90, 152, 187 nn.4–5, 192 n.4, 197 n.42, 197 n.3, 214 n.40